Constitutional Design

Mayer Emerson

Printed in the United States of America
ISBN: Softcover 979-8-89518-218-5
eBook 979-8-89518-219-2
Republished by: WP Lighthouse
Publication Date: 03/15/2024

To order copies of this book, contact:
WP Lighthouse
Phone: (888) 668-2459
support@wplighthouse.com
www.wplighthouse.com

CONTENTS

PART 3 | THE FRAMEWORK: AN ACTIVE SYSTEM BEGINS

The Preamble

Our Constitution has a Framework. There is an inherent and deliberate system that includes a geometric configuration with integrated concepts. Each aspect of the Constitution is connected to all the others in terms of geometry and meaning. The concepts and ideas are then organized within the system. This book is a practical and historical compilation of components and anecdotal stories intended to incorporate the Framework as a vital part of our interpretation and application of the Constitution. Patterns emerge and stories give insight.

In 1987, I was invited to Mayor Tom Bradley's office to introduce an organizing system based on the Tree of Life (a rabbinical Jewish concept explained later in this work). I suddenly recognized "The Framework of the Constitution has the same format." It was then apparent that no one considered our Framework as the mathematical diagram of an open, stable system with ancient origins. The idea was not recognized or even considered. That flash of insight led to the long discovery process of this book. Every aspect of this paradigm fits that context.

It is mandatory to know the Paradigm for the Framework in order to recognize it. Once you are aware of the patterns, it is readily cognizable. The stories and the reasons it was kept secret are obvious. In this book there is an observable pattern once you understand that there were three Freemason Grand Masters, who put the plan in place without a debate about the system. The bulk of this book from Chapter 16 until near the end and Chapter "Bonds of our Fathers" is specifically devoted to explanations of the system. The purpose of this book is to bring forth knowledge. There is a positive, purposeful ancient system that is the organizing structure and how to use it. Hopefully, it can now be revitalized to include knowledge of the system in operation. Our Founding Fathers had no experience within a system. It had been theoretical. They did not know that past presidents could have a useful dynamic. Their concern for having literate voters dissolved once communication developed in so many readily forms was available. They did not foresee voters rights as a target by the inscrutable people. This book contains suggestions from the system itself.

There is also lack of understanding of timeliness. There was no problem with evangelical mindset since The Second Awakening did not begin until after 1789. Our founding Fathers would not have foreseen the dynamic that followed with an evangelical basis and priority.

The definitions of some words have changed significantly since the Eighteenth Century. Thus, definitions found in Noah Webster's Dictionary of 1828 are inserted frequently in this book. Understanding the context and the meanings the Founders would have had is critical to modern comprehension. While it is centuries later, his definitions show the meaning within the constitution and society in the early years.

Virtually all studies and applications of our constitution have started with the records of James Madison and the Federalist Papers. Madison was actually dismissive of The Committee of Detail and it is rarely considered with any depth. It seems Madison considered them to be acting as clerks bringing some order to the discussions in the convention. He was busy simultaneously tidying his own notes. That committee, however, was central to the entire convention. John Rutledge, leader of the Committee of Detail, carefully edited the drafts to affect the Framework itself. This document was the culmination of a strategic plan initiated by Benjamin Franklin ten years earlier. The primary influences were the Freemasonry, including the Jewish Freemasons, and the Iroquois. Franklin and others were specifically against European politics and religions.

PART ONE | ESTABLISHING THE FRAMEWORK

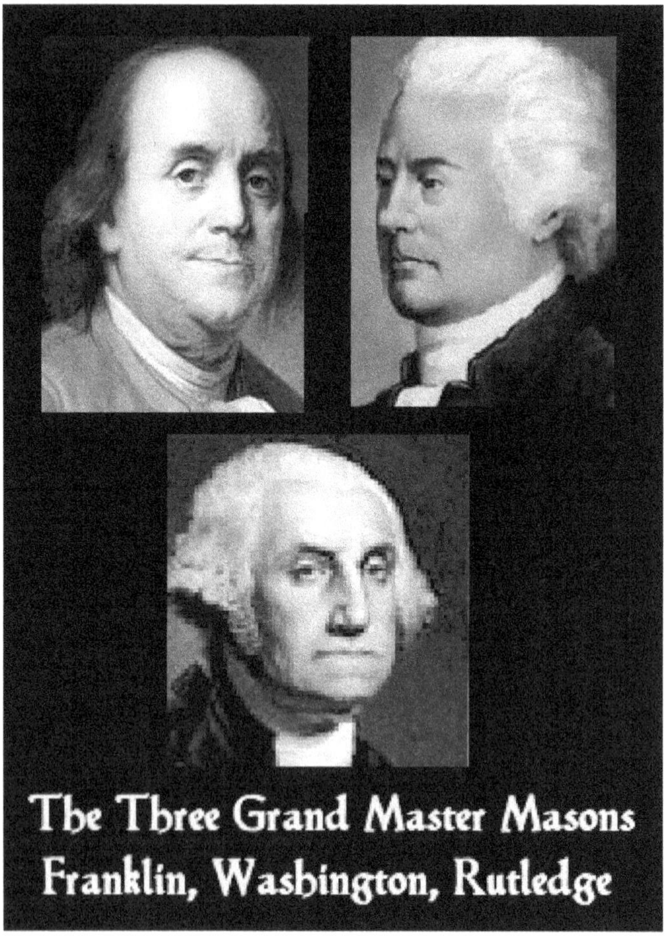

These three men established the Soul of our Constitution: The Framework

CHAPTER 1|
The Declaration of Independence

IN CONGRESS. JULY 4, 1776.

The unanimous Declaration [illegible] States of America.

We hold these truths to be self-evident, that all men are created equal, that they are endowed by their Creator with certain unalienable Rights, that among these are Life, Liberty and the pursuit of Happiness.–That to secure these rights, Governments are instituted among Men, deriving their just powers from the consent of the governed, –That whenever any Form of Government becomes destructive of these ends, it is the Right of the People to alter or to abolish it, and to institute ***new Government, laying its foundation on such principles and organizing its powers in such form***, as to them shall seem most likely to affect their Safety and Happiness.

Above is the beginning of the second paragraph, elucidating key concepts. While the document as a whole was written by the enlightened Thomas Jefferson, it was edited by Benjamin Franklin and John Adams. This statement may well have been suggested by Franklin: "New Government, laying its foundation on such principles and organizing its powers in such form," It can be seen as a connection to the Framework, which Franklin would be introducing later.

Virtually all patriots were passionately connected to the philosophical theories of the time, considered to be "The Enlightenment." The Enlightenment applied scientific reasoning to politics, science, and religion. It promoted religious tolerance and restored literature, arts, and music as important disciplines worthy of study in colleges. It became the philosophical foundation of all the colleges in the colonies at the time. It was a movement rather than a structured belief system.

While it is dated July 4, 1776, the new Continental Congress actually voted for The Declaration of Independence on July 2, 1776. It was not signed until August 2, beginning with John Hancock, President of the Continental Congress, making his famous bold signature. How would such a paradox come to be? Hancock and others could have spent July 3rd making sure the document was in order. Note there is no date on this draft.

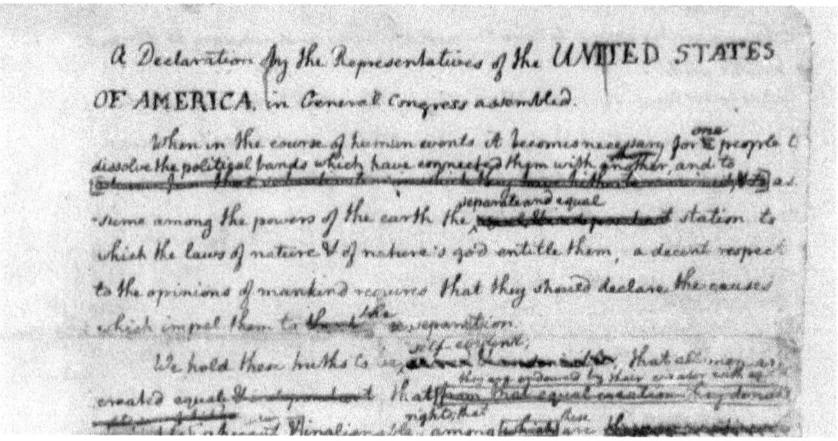

A Declaration by the Representatives of the UNITED STATES OF AMERICA, in General Congress assembled.

When in the course of human events it becomes necessary for one people to dissolve the political bands which have connected them with another, and to

-sume among the powers of the earth the separate and equal station to which the laws of nature & of nature's god entitle them, a decent respect to the opinions of mankind requires that they should declare the causes which impel them to the separation.

We hold these truths to be self-evident, that all men are created equal

Facsimile of Draft

On July 4th Hancock would have presented the approved draft to a Penman, an expert in the fine art of Penmanship. It took weeks to finish and the Penman used the date it was given to him. Then Hancock would have made a grand event for the signing. He staged the event to correspond with his bold signature in the center of the document.

Chapter 2 | Continental Congress & The Great Seal

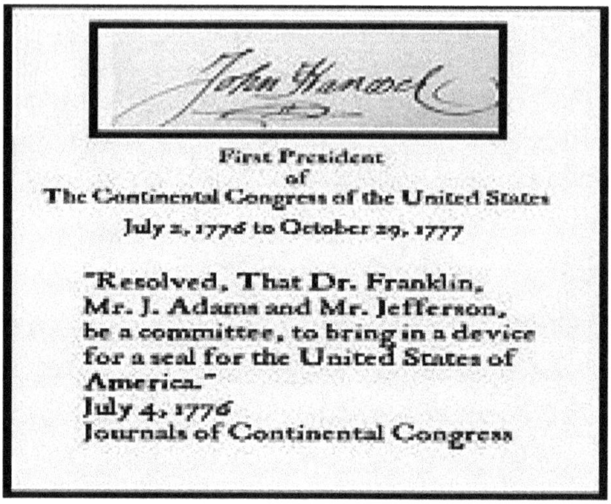
First President
of
The Continental Congress of the United States
July 2, 1776 to October 29, 1777
"Resolved, That Dr. Franklin, Mr. J. Adams and Mr. Jefferson, be a committee, to bring in a device for a seal for the United States of America."
July 4, 1776
Journals of Continental Congress

The significant event on July 4, 1776 was Hancock's appointment of the same three men to design our Great Seal. "Resolved, That Dr. Franklin, Mr. J. Adams, and Mr. Jefferson, be a committee, to bring in a device for a seal for the United States of America." – July 4, 1776, (Journals of Continental Congress.)

The July 4th event to initiate our Great Seal resulted in the designs on our one-dollar bill. This was significant but in a far different way. Rather than voting for or signing the Declaration, July 4, was actually the first step toward our identity and our constitution.

The Hallowed Trio: Franklin, Adams and Jefferson

Franklin, Adams and Jefferson formed the committee that drafted our Declaration of Independence They were all advocates of the Enlightenment movement. The Declaration of Independence was ratified on July 2, 1776. On July 4 the document was sent to be printed. Also that day, this committee continued their work to design the Great Seal. The designs they initiated at this time provide considerable insight into the symbology our Founders envisioned. Ultimately, their sacred concepts for the left side of our dollar were obliterated.

Benjamin Franklin was the Founder of the Founders. He was critical in our revolution as well as the founding of our republic. He was the only signer of the Declaration of Independence, a designer of our Great Seal and thus the framework of our Constitution as well as our constitution. During the years of the Confederation, Adams and Jefferson were on diplomatic missions to Europe.

Thus, the three men who had drafted the Declaration of Independence were brought together in the first act of our new nation as the Continental Congress:

The Great Seal.

SEAL, *NOUN* [L. *sigillum*]

A piece of metal or other hard substance, usually round or oval, on which is engraved some image or device, and sometimes a legend or inscription. This is used by individuals, corporate bodies, and states, for making impressions on wax upon instruments of writing, as evidence of their authenticity. (Webster, 1828)

A Great Seal has two sides, the Obverse or the upper side and the Reverse or the lower side. The Obverse side represents the practical or earthly realm. Whereas the Reverse or backside is the spiritual or enlightened realm. In ordinary usage, it is top and bottom. However, in the parlance of enlightened thinking, there is significant meaning.

The Term "As Above, So Below"

"**As above, so below, as within, so without, as the universe, so the soul...**" is attributed to Hermes Trismegistus. In his Biographia Antiqua, Francis Barrett says of Hermes:

> "* * * if God ever appeared in man, he appeared in him, as is evident both from his books and his Pymander; in which works he has communicated the sum of the Abyss, and the divine knowledge to all posterity; by which he has demonstrated himself to have been not only an inspired divine, but also a deep philosopher, obtaining his wisdom from God and heavenly things, and not from man."

His transcendent learning caused Hermes to be identified with many of the early sages and prophets

"'*That which is above is the same as that which is below."The present issues from the past, and the future from the present. Everything is made one by this continuity. Time is like a circle, where all the points are so linked that one cannot say where it begins or ends, for all points precede and follow one another forever."*
The excellence of the soul is understanding; for the man who understands is conscious, devoted, and already godlike." (Hermetic Philosophy)

To Franklin, The All-Seeing Eye was the highest consciousness or intelligence that exists in the universe. It is far beyond the comprehension of any human being. It would be the highest possibility. There is nothing beyond the All-Seeing Eye. The All-Seeing Eye, The Eye of Illumination and The Eye of Providence are interchangeable. In this book they are all used so that all are familiar to the reader and understood as interchangeable.

This concept of "As Above, So Below" is stated in The Lord's Prayer in Matthew 6:10. "Thy kingdom come, thy will be done, on earth as it is in heaven."

Benjamin Franklin was responsible for including the Eye of Providence on the seal, commonly considered to denote God or a divine entity. This would be the design to depict the heavenly realm on the Reverse side of the Seal AS ABOVE.

Franklin offered two design concepts for the Great Seal. In the pattern relating to the aspect of "As Above," he conceived of 13 attributes or steps of human behavior leading up to the Eye of Providence, the light of illumination. He was thinking of steps to godliness. The following designs show Franklin's design and the Final Design.

Franklin's Design

DEO FAVENTE
With (God's) Favor
PERENNIS
Everlasting

THE EYE OF ILLUMINATION
An omniscient & just Supreme Being.

Thomson's Design

ANNUIT COEPTIS
(God) Favors our Beginnings.
NUVUS ORDO SECLORTUM
New Order for the Ages

BOUNDED EYE
Trinitarian God

Franklin's 13 steps were not connected to a pyramid. They were steps leading to a higher level of conscious behavior. Ultimately, this would be Universal Consciousness. Any concepts of a pyramid are mathematical. Obliterating the top of a pyramid is not part of sacred geometry. Sacred Geometry has been defined as "the synchronicity of the universe is determined by certain mathematical constants which express themselves in the form of 'patterns' and 'cycles' in nature. (Whitaker)

ALL-SEEING EYE, whom the SUN, MOON, and STARS obey, and under whose watchful care even COMETS perform their stupendous revolutions, pervades the inmost recesses of the human HEART, and will reward us according to our merits. (Sacred-Texts)

As a Freemason, Franklin would have been acutely disturbed regarding the huge change in the meaning of the Eye of Illumination becoming enclosed as well as the 13 Steps to the Eye being changed to a pyramid. Instead of a pure universal intelligence & glory, it became something staring at us through a keyhole.

The Eye of Providence is the idea that some divine force is watching over us all, sees our deeds and actions, and judges accordingly. In Noah Webster's Dictionary, this is the definition of Providence as applies to the use in our Great Seal.

PROV''IDENCE, noun:
In theology, the care and superintendence which God exercises over his creatures. He that acknowledges a creation and denies providence involves himself in a palpable contradiction; for the same power which caused a thing to exist is necessary to continue its existence. Some persons admit a general providence but deny a particular providence not considering that a general providence consists of particulars. A belief in divine providence is a source of great consolation to good men. "By divine providence" is often understood as "God Himself."
(Webster, 1828)

There are three names that appear in Masonic imagery during the 18th century: The Eye of Illumination, The Eye of Providence, and the All-Seeing Eye. All refer to the same image of an unrestricted presence of a divine Universal being. Today, these could be described as attributes of God. Arguably, we are each implying our own vision of God. Three hundred years ago, these terms were used to depict a Universal Intelligence.

Shawn Eyer is a fine researcher at Harvard. His research interests are strongly focused upon the development of Freemasonry in the seventeenth and eighteenth centuries. Regarding the All-Seeing Eye, he writes;

"This is a symbol with strong traditional foundations, belonging to the common symbolic vocabulary of Western culture. It evokes a powerful monotheistic God, aware of and involved with his creation, probing the conscience of every man. The effulgence of the single radiant eye suggests a pervasive, divine consciousness that recognizes us even as it is recognized by us, that contemplates us even as we contemplate it as the ultimate source of all. "

"In 1766, Bro. Isaac Head gave a Charge in the Scilly Isles of England, in which he asked that the brethren remain "ever mindful that the Eye which pervades the immeasurable Regions of Space, and sees through the thickest Darkness, is ever-present with us...Perhaps it is ironic that today, it is looked upon primarily as a Masonic emblem—even by those outside of our Fraternity. For, in truth, the All-Seeing Eye is a profound symbol that belongs to everyone who perceives the reality of an omniscient and just Supreme Being. The Eye of Providence is the idea that some divine force is watching over us all, sees our deeds and actions, and judges accordingly. "(Eyer)

The thirteen steps and the Eye of Providence are discussed more thoroughly in "Chapter 11: The Great Seal" and "Chapter 12: Definitions." The image on our dollar, is in reality, botched history. After 249 years the bounded eye is here to stay on our Great Seal. The bounded eye and the pyramid itself now have their own mythology. it is also significant as a marker in Botched History since the intent was totally misconstrued.

Franklin's design for the Great Seal depicting Jews after they left Egypt

The second design by Franklin is shown above. It represents a totally different concept from his design for the 13 steps to Illumination. Franklin described his depiction as "Moses standing on the Shore, and extending his Hand over the Sea, thereby causing the same to overwhelm the Pharaoh who is sitting in an open Chariot, a Crown on his Head and a Sword in his hand. Rays from a Pillar of Fire in the Clouds reaching to Moses, to express that he acts by Command of the Deity. This represents the Jews after they left Egypt.

This illustration conveys freedom from oppression, the Jews fleeing the domination by the Pharaoh and the Egyptians. His Motto "Rebellion to Tyrants is Obedience to God" is the quintessential statement.

TYR'ANNY, noun 1. Arbitrary or despotic exercise of power; the exercise of power over subjects and others with a rigor not authorized by law or justice, or not requisite for the purposes of government. Hence tyranny is often synonymous with cruelty and oppression. (Webster, 1828)

REBEL'LION, noun [Latin rebellio. among the Romans, rebellion was originally a revolt or open resistance to their government by nations that had been subdued in war. It was a renewed war] . An open and avowed renunciation of the authority of the government to which one owes allegiance; or the taking of arms traitorously to resist the authority of lawful government; revolt. rebellion differs from insurrection and from mutiny. Insurrection may be arising in opposition to a particular act or law, without a design to renounce wholly all subjection to the government. Insurrection may be, but is not necessarily, rebellion Mutiny is an insurrection of soldiers or seamen against the authority of their officers.(Webster, 1828)

Franklin's insight was to connect and elucidate our American story to the biblical story of the Jews fleeing the oppressors, Pharaoh, and the Egyptians. In other words, our Revolutionary War was the American Exodus. Following the Pillars of clouds, they would be following the heavenly spirit. These were actions and thus represent the right side, the action. AS BELOW

Thomas Jefferson's design for the Great Seal

Jefferson's design represents the Jews after they left Egypt. It is notable that of all the stories and legends that Jefferson could have chosen for the first Great Seal of a democracy was also of the Jews fleeing Egypt under the guidance of God. Their common theme images would have been significant and astonishing when they were presented in their committee, to each other and to Adams. They were both ideal depictions of the biblical concept.

It is noteworthy that Jefferson took Franklin's motto for his personal seal. Had he been privy to Franklin's design in advance, he would have used it in his own design.

Jefferson's design Franklin's design

Franklin's depiction of the Jews's fleeing Egypt fit the earthly realm as context. This would illustrate "SO BELOW." The people took action in alignment with the practical sphere .

Jefferson, interestingly, chose this concept fitting AS ABOVE. As Jews left the Egyptian oppressors, they followed the clouds as guidance from God to be in the desert for 40 years. That could be analogous to the time in our country from signing the Declaration of Independence until Washington was inaugurated. Importantly, this happened during the Age of Enlightenment. The practice at that time would be to dedicate to concepts of higher consciousness on the left side.

Whereas, the Front or Right side was depicted in a practical, fundamental context. In other words, the left side depicts AS ABOVE and the right side, SO BELOW, In Franklin's design the Jews are taking an active role against tyranny while being guided by signs of illumination. Jefferson's design represents the Promised Land. Our Colonists were in the Promised Land but had to eliminate the oppressor, England.

Franklin and Jefferson both chose inspiration from the Jews leaving the oppression in Egypt. One analysis of the Reverse side is that Franklin's vision escaping FROM oppression, whereas Jefferson's depiction is of the Divine Inspiration FORWARD.

Franklin's 13 steps to Enlightenment topped by the All-Seeing Eye of Providence or Illumination was their other main principle. Adam's design was intellectual rather than inspirational.

Together, the two images form an ideal depiction of the ancient enlightened concept, "As Above, So Below. This is the same placement for the two final images in our Great Seal. On our one-dollar bill, the Pyramid represents As Above (poorly) and the Eagle represents So Below (well). The point of this topic is that these were the images that were significant to our Founding Fathers, who fought for our freedom from England. They considered England as analogous to the Egyptians. The two later committees eliminated the sacred concepts totally.

This is the clear reason that Washington, Franklin, and Rutledge kept the Framework a secret. All the Colonists who fought for independence were united against tyranny, against taxation without representation. They fought for self-determination. The conflict for the foundation of our government, for the Framework, began right here. Masonic leaders were dominant in the revolution. The next challenge, also led by Masons, was to establish a constitution with the same principles. There were plenty of Colonists who did not think past the establishment of another monarchy. Most were oblivious that there was a Framework, much less one based on ancient sacred geometry.

Consider these two images

THESE ARE PAIRS, NOT OPPOSITES

THE REVERSE	THE OBVERSE
THE ENLIGHTENED	THE PRACTICAL
AS ABOVE	SO BELOW
ESOTERIC	REALISTIC

On our Great Seal
The Pyramid is obscuring
The actual heavenly realm

Consider this definition

Syncretism (/ˈsɪŋkrətɪzəm/) is the combining of different beliefs, while blending practices of various schools of thought. Syncretism involves the merging or assimilation of several originally discrete traditions, especially in the theology and mythology of religion, thus asserting an underlying unity and allowing for an inclusive approach to other faiths. Syncretism also occurs commonly in expressions of arts and culture (known as eclecticism) as well as politics (syncretic politics). Hermetic writings are allegorical expositions of great philosophic and mystic truths, and its hidden meaning may be comprehended only by those who have been "raised" into the presence of the True Mind.

Hermes' concepts are aligned to Benjamin Franklin as a Mason and to Thomas Jefferson considered aligned to the Age of Enlightenment and would have been considered Intellectually Elite.

John Adams' design for the Great Seal

John Adams' design was based on Greek mythology as The Choice of Hercules. Hercules decides which path to walk in life by deliberating with the female personifications of Pleasure and Virtue. As Adams explains:: "The Hero resting on his Clubb. Virtue pointing to her rugged Mountain, on one Hand, and persuading him to ascend. Sloth, glancing at her flowery Paths of Pleasure, wantonly reclining on the Ground, displaying the Charms both of her Eloquence and Person, to seduce him into Vice."

These designs more than anything depict the clear differences between Franklin and Jefferson with Adams that continued throughout their public careers. The theme of Freedom from Tyranny by the people is in a totally different realm from the conflict for the individual between Virtue and Vice. These two themes clearly show the strong differences between the Freemasons and the Intellectually Elite, such as Jefferson, as differentiated from the Puritans. Freemasons were positioned exactly between Church and State, with no alignment with either. Puritans, however, were focused on biblical judgments, particularly good versus evil.

During the process in the first committee, Franklin, Jefferson, and Adams requested the help of the artist Pierre Eugene du Simitiere because of his expertise in heraldry. The unintended, but perhaps inevitable consequence, is that the left side of the seal was radically altered. European monarchical precepts entered the design process and the schism began.

du Simitiere used Franklin's design concept but altered the image and consequently the meaning. The steps became a pyramid and the EYE bounded. It is contradictory to think of a limited, restricted, contained dynamic in connection to any higher consciousness and light. Hence, all the designers of our Seal proceeded with elements of the very European Monarchs and heraldry that our Founding Fathers were absolutely against. The bounded Eye of Providence would have compelled Franklin to pursue his quest to create a democratic constitution in secrecy.

In a letter to his wife on August 14, 1776, John Adams wrote: "This Mr. du Simitière is a very curious Man. He has begun a Collection of Materials for a History of this Revolution. He begins with the first "Advices of the Tea Ships". He cuts out of the Newspapers, every Scrap of Intelligence, and Every Piece of Speculation, and pastes it upon clean Paper, arranging them under the Head of the State to which they belong and intends to bind them up in Volumes. He has a List of every Speculation and Pamphlet concerning Independence, and another of those concerning forms of government." (Founders Online: John Adams to Abigail Adams)

Du Simitière's sketch follows along with the image on the right, a later version. It dates the inclusion of the bounded EYE for the first time.

Adams' letter to his wife shows the problems Franklin and others had with the heraldists. European Monarchies formed the context for their expertise. It was a bad fit for our new nation, which was specifically dedicated to distinct governance, a democracy of the people, by the people, and for the people. Symbols of monarchies were abhorrent to these leaders.

It is also important to note that John Adams placed no value on Freemasonry. His son, President John Quincy Adams, was an adamant Anti-Mason. Having been a delegate to Prussia during the Constitutional Convention, he would have witnessed the intense dedication of the Monarchies and the Catholic Church first hand. There does not appear to have the same level of intense reaction to Masonry during these years in America.

du Simitière submitted the first diagram that was heraldic. It contained a shield for each of the six primary ancestral European Monarchies for the colonists.

Most importantly, by introducing the Bounded Eye, du Simitière put the Eye of Illumination in confinement. It was and is disrespectful. Franklin, in particular, would have thought it disparaging. In his customary non-confrontational matter, he would have been working to divert the seal from European and unenlightened concepts. The roots of his secrecy began right then. Secrecy is a significant aspect of Free-Masonry.

This change of the image to a pyramid reflected totally different and competing values of some delegates to those of Washington, Franklin, and Rutledge. Franklin's steps to enlightenment were aligned to ancient wisdom, patterns, and symbols. For the heraldists to shift symbols of a monarchy, this to a bounded Eye and a pyramid was the antithesis to their original value depicting the Jews fleeing their Egyptian oppressors. This and other issues are discussed in "Chapter 9| The Great Seal."

A formal depiction of the design by du Simitiere

Franklin and Jefferson and possibly Adams were aghast. The Eye of Providence was confined in a triangular box. There were six emblems in the center representing the monarchies from which most colonists had come. Each new state had a symbol of its own, signifying self-identity rather than unity.

The three patriots deferred voting on this theme. Their participation ended. Soon the images were combined and the steps to enlightenment became a pyramid, the symbol of oppression. The Eye was bounded and a new set of meanings evolved. Future renditions evolved from the picture itself rather than from enlightened concepts. Just after the end of a war that had drained everyone, it was clearly impossible for them to get past the steps to enlightenment becoming the symbol of oppression.

The fine analysis for our seal from conventional sources comes from The AishDas Society. There is a religious subtext to all this.

Jefferson called upon the citizens of the new nation to follow God through the desert. G-d provides direction and protection for his people.

Franklin expects more autonomy. While he shows God drowning the Egyptians, he adds a motto to tell us this as an example for us to follow "Rebellion to Tyrants is Obedience to God". Man is expected to redeem himself.

But the design that actually emerged from all this is neither Jefferson's "God saving man image" nor Franklin's "man partnering with God to redeem himself image," The God of the final design is that of a Deist. It depicts a well-designed but incomplete world, represented by the pyramid. God is depicted as an eye, watching from above, but not acting. It is man's job to complete the pyramid on his own.

This account speaks well for the interpretation of the pyramid in our seal but not knowing the backstory. It was designed by the Monarchy Heraldists and approved by the Continental Congress. It is important to understand that this pyramid was a far cry from Franklin's intentions and the fact that it is on the spiritual or mystical side of the Great Seal.

Yet another aspect is significant. John Rutledge was a member of the third committee on the Great Seal. He left immediately. Undoubtedly, he realized the vision of the three Grand Masons was hopeless. The story behind this realization is the Seal for the State of South Carolina in 1777, where he was a participant.

The right and left oval are opposite to the customary Obverse and Reverse significance. That is an error by subsequent people, who did not understand the significance in the sides. However, the left oval was in the front to the great seal when it was two-sided.

The motto, "Animis Opibusque Parati," is Latin for "Prepared in Mind and Resources." This precisely fits the practical aspect. The picture of a palmetto tree represents a battle victory against the British at present-day Fort Moultrie during the Revolutionary War.

The right oval was originally the reverse side of the seal. This is the spiritual or illumination aspect. "Dum Spiro Spero," is Latin for "While I Breathe, I Hope." It depicts the Roman goddess Spes, who was the goddess of hope. (South Carolina Seal)

It is easily seen as the image Rutledge favored. He and Franklin would have found the pyramid totally unacceptable.

The design for the Great Seal was dormant for six years.

Chapter 3 | Opinions Galore

In honor of the 200th anniversary of the Declaration of Independence, our State Department published an exhaustive study of our Great Seal. Titled THE EAGLE AND THE SHIELD: A History of the Great Seal of the United States. It was written by Richard S. Patterson and Richardson Dougall. It can be found on our Reading List as the National Archives.

Near the end is a chapter called "Questions and Answers." The query was "Did Freemasonry Influence the Great Seal Design? However, the significant question should be "Why were Freemasonry concepts and symbols NOT included in the Great Seal Design?" They weren't. Any that were included were there by happenstance. The Masons did not argue. They left. The design was the work of Monarchy Heraldists.

"Did Freemasonry Influence the Great Seal Design?

The question arises from time tot time, What influence, if any, did Freemasonry have on the design of the Great Seal? Because membership records for the Revolutionary period are scattered and imperfect, it is not possible to ascertain with certainty which persons among the fourteen who participated in the designing of the Great Seal were Masons and which were not.

Conrad Hahn, Executive Secretary of the Masonic Service Association of the United States, Silver Spring, Maryland, who has checked into the matter, has furnished the following information:

1. Definitely a Mason: Benjamin Franklin.
2. Definitely not Masons: John Adams and Charles Thomson.
3. No firm evidence of a Masonic connection, although allegations of such a connection have been noted: Thomas Jefferson, James Lovell, Francis Hopkinson, Arthur Middleton, and John Rutledge.
4. No record at all, so presumably not Masons: Pierre Eugene DuSimitiere, John Morin Scott, William Churchill Houston, Arthur Lee, Elias Boudinot, and William Barton (although he has at times been confused with another William Barton who was a Mason).

Although George Washington was a Mason, he played no role in designing the Great Seal. And although Franklin, a Mason, was a member of the first seal committee, his proposal had no influence on the final designs for the seal, and he was in France when those designs were drawn up. The only individual listed above who contributed something definite to the final seal design who has been said to be a Mason (although with no firm evidence) is Francis Hopkinson, whose pyramid design for the Continental currency's $50 bill clearly influenced the final reverse of the Great Seal. The pyramid, the eye above it, and the radiant triangle enclosing the eye have often been considered to be of Masonic origin. Writers who are Masons have also seen Masonic symbolism in the eagle, in the number of feathers on the eagle's wings, in the number of the eagle's tail feathers, in the ground cover near the pyramid (which some of them assume—without known authority—to be acacia), in the number of words as specified in the blazon, the glories on each face of the seal, and in possible combinations of numbers, considered cabalistically or " by gematria."

It should perhaps be noted that some of the details studied and interpreted by these writers are those of comparatively recent realizations of the Great Seal blazon—details which are not stated in the blazon itself and are not to be found in the Great Seal die of 1782. Without questioning the fact that elements of the Great Seal design are also to in the mottoes, in the number of points of the stars and in the pattern of the entire constellation, the colo be found as Masonic symbols, one may question whether the designers of the seal intended the seal blazon to be given a specifically Masonic interpretation. Since there is no evidence that either Charles Thomson or the Philadelphia William Barton was a Mason, and as they were the two individuals responsible for the final design, the presumption would be that they did not intend their work to be given a Masonic interpretation. And even if Francis Hopkinson intended his pyramid as a Masonic symbol (which is by no means certain), his design was filtered through the non-Masonic eyes and pens of Barton and Thomson.

Were there sources other than Freemasonry from which symbols such as the all-seeing eye and the unfinished pyramid could have been taken? The answer is yes. Use of the eye in art forms, including medallic art, as a symbol for an omniscient and ubiquitous Deity, was a well-established artistic convention quite apart from Masonic symbolism, and Du Simitiere, an artist, would have been aware of this. As to the pyramid, there was widespread interest in Egypt and things Egyptian in the eighteenth century, and in the Library Company of Philadelphia, there was a detailed work entitled "Pyramidographia" which would have been available to both Hopkinson and Barton. This work included a drawing of the "First Pyramid", which was stepped, did not come to a complete point and had an entrance in the center on the ground level—a detail found also in Hopkinson's design. While these points are not conclusive, it seems likely that the designers of the Great Seal and the Masons took their symbols from parallel sources, and unlikely that the seal designers consciously copied Masonic symbols with the intention of incorporating Masonic symbolism into the national coat of arms." (Patterson & Dougall)

Imagine the tremendous horror Franklin, Jefferson, and Rutledge, and, probably, Adams felt when the design devolved to a pyramid? In fact, the pyramid is the icon of tyranny and thus, of England. The Eye of Illumination was confined and limited. It was the opposite of Enlightenment.

Patterson and Dougall proudly proved how the ancient sacred aspects from Freemasonry were not included. In fact, the original concept for our Great Seal were obliterated.

Later writers pay attention to John Adams. His was an intellectual approach, which did not connect to the ancient symbology. He was oblivious to the others and to Masonic concepts. He would have been politely ignored by the Freemasons.

There are no records of Franklin confronting anyone directly. He always withdrew and found another approach. Look at his thirteen rules.

Consider this:

"The Great Seal of the United States"

"An Overview by John D. MacArthur

On July 4, 1776, the same day America's thirteen separate states united to declare themselves an independent nation, the Continental Congress took the next step necessary to demonstrate this Independence. They began to create their national emblem, the Great Seal of the United States.

During the next six years of the Revolution, three different committees submitted ideas for this graphic image of America, but none were acceptable. On June 13, 1782, Congress turned the task over to their trusted Secretary, Charles Thomson.

Using symbolic elements from all three committees, plus imagery and mottoes of his own, Thomson created a bold and elegant design. A week later, he presented the written description of this two-sided design to Congress, and Congress approved it that same day. The Great Seal of the United States was officially adopted on June 20, 1782. Ever since its design has remained unchanged."

These are the only preliminary drawings of the final design for the Great Seal: After these were drawn, a few revisions were made.

- The Eagle's shield was given vertical red & white stripes.
- New Latin mottos were chosen for the pyramid side.
- A triangle was placed around the eye of providence.
- MDCCLXXVI (1776) was placed beneath the pyramid. (MacArthur, J. D)

No new drawings were made to illustrate the seals. Only the descriptions were submitted. The official Great Seal was adopted on June 20, 1782,

"The Trusted Secretary" Charles Thomson had designed the final choice. He was also in charge of the approval of the Seal. He had served under many Masons, who were Presidents of the Confederation. He had never served under Franklin, Washington or Adams. We do not know his personal viewpoint about Freemasonry. We do know his decision.

Future renditions evolved from the picture itself rather than from enlightened concepts. Just after the end of a war that had drained everyone, it was clearly impossible for them to get past the steps to enlightenment becoming the symbol of oppression.

This account speaks well for the interpretation of the pyramid in our seal. It was designed by the Monarchy Heraldists and approved by the Continental Congress. It is important to understand that this pyramid was a far cry from Franklin's intentions and the fact that it is on the spiritual or mystical side of the Great Seal.

It is the assertion of this book that George Washington, Benjamin Franklin, and John Rutledge took it upon themselves to create our Constitution in alignment with their highest level of understanding. It is probable that Benjamin Franklin, the elder of this group, was also the initiator and leader. It is unlikely that Washington would have come out of retirement for anyone other than Franklin. He was then instrumental, not only in designing and leading the constitutional convention but also in putting the government into action. Rutledge was a protégé of Franklin and clearly performed in that relationship.

Franklin had great savvy. His judgments were careful and shrewd. He was dedicated to having a constitutional republic, but he learned his lessons in the design of the Great Seal. He chose Washington and Rutledge astutely without fanfare. He served in that first meeting for the seal with Adams and Jefferson. Adams had an intellectual concept of Hercules, which Franklin would have been against. Thomas Jefferson did not have the same spiritual bent. Franklin made his plan for the convention when Jefferson was the American Minister to France and Adams was in London as the American Minister to the Court of St James. It seems highly likely that part of Franklin's timing is that their participation would have solely by letter.

Through their participation in the process of designing a seal, they learned that they did not want a debate on the sacred symbols. Ideas could and would be debated always. However, they wanted the ideal preserved. They announced the fact by calling the Constitution "The Framework" and the delegates the "Framers." They did not communicate more; they just did it.

No one asked.

Chapter 4 | The 2nd and 3rd Committees

Final images for our Great Seal are imprinted on our one-dollar bill.
These images totally diverge from the concepts of our Committee.

The Second Committee met in 1782

John Hanson was the first president after the Articles of the Continental were passed. He instigated the new effort to design a Great Seal. Charles Thomson was put in charge of this committee. Thomson was the Secretary to all 15 Presidents in the Continental Congress so he had unparalleled power and responsibility during that whole period. While he hired two heraldists, he was the decision-maker.

Frances Hopkinson, a heraldist, was hired by the committee. He had designed the flag sewn by Betsy Ross. In the Seal, he contributed some elements, such as a constellation of 13 stars. He also included two figures (a Native American and a woman or a soldier and a woman), a shield of thirteen stripes, an olive branch, and arrows. This design was not even put to a vote.

The Third Committee met in 1783.

John Rutledge served on the Third Committee, which met in 1782. Evidently, there was no path to creating a Great Seal using the ancient symbols that matched the vision of the Three Grand Framers. Rutledge left the committee without voting, but he gave William Barton the drawing by Franklin. Rutledge would have told Barton their objections to the bounded eye and to the pyramid, Barton submitted the designs acceptable to Franklin and said nothing.

It turns out that he was also a member of a fraternal society, The Society of Cincinnati. This was a fraternal society formed by people who served in the Revolutionary War. Therefore, there was understanding of the objections. Twenty-three of the framers were members of this society. More participated. Their members included Washington, Hamilton, and Franklin. (Hume, Edgar)

Elias Boudioent, the President for this term, was a Huguenot. Therefore, he would have had no particular interest in symbology. He, thus, continued the work on the seal to conclusion without any input of his own.

The decision for an altered pyramid and the bound eye was by all considerations made by Charles Thomson, the administrator for all fifteen years of the Continental Congress. He was against the ancient traditions. Nowadays, his depiction is considered sacred, even by Masons. Washington, Franklin and Rutledge would have been outraged. Thomson gave Washington his oath of office, at the onset of our government. Washington did not appointment Thomson to any federal office. Washington made his disapprovals clearly recognized without ever saying a word.

In this version, the motto "ANNUIT COEPTIS" (meaning: He (God) has approved our undertakings.) is at the top and the eye is bound. This begins the shift to depict the steps as a pyramid with a separate top. The eye is bounded.

A second motto was chosen for this side of the seal. Novus ordo seclorum (meaning new order of the ages) originates from lines by the Roman poet Virgil. Note that this motto has 26 letters, which can be reduced to 13. The two mottos together have 39 letters, which can be reduced to 13.

Negativists misinterpret this motto as indicating domination and conspiracy. Nothing could be further from the truth. Their conviction was that our democracy would be the first of many.

The Roman numeral at the base of the Pyramid is 1776. Coincidentally, it reduces to the number 3, corresponding to the three pillars of our Constitution.

Now that we understand how upset Franklin, Washington, and Rutledge were, should we change the symbol? Absolutely not! Now it is a long-established tradition. We know the contrived explanations. The distortions have a tradition of their own. We should all know the story, however. Most of all, it explains their decision to keep the sacred aspects secret.

It is a long-established symbol of the forces our revolution overturned and has contrived meanings. The biblical story of Jews fleeing slavery in Egypt is an ancient story of oppression. The pyramid is the symbol of Pharaoh. It represents hierarchy, with the masses at the bottom and no connection to the eye of illumination, which is contained. Thus the eye is not only limited but unavailable. The following quotes by these presidents strive to make this symbol positive and meaningful. The symbol so disliked by Franklin, Washington and Rutledge is now part of our National lore.

Thus the original meaning has changed through the times to embody thoughts of our leaders. We have made the symbol valid in our terms. Thus it should not be changed. However, it shall always be a symbol Franklin and Rutledge and, probably, Washington opposed strongly as a symbol of

European Monarchists. It shows the context of our Seal. The meaning has evolved as a living system.

Charles Thomson, Administrator of the Continental Congress by Pierre Eugene du Simitiere

Then, when the story seems complete, a new significant aspect emerges. Charles Thomson was the Secretary of the Continental Congress during all fifteen Presidents. Each had a one year term. He was the Administrator for the entire period. He had the leadership position for the Declaration of Independence, for the three committees to design the Great Seal, for the Constitutional Convention

He was the designer of the final sides of our Great Seal. He gave the Oath of Office to George Washington. Washington did not appoint him to a position in our new government. When asked, Washington wrote a glowing letter of recommendation several months later. As we shall see, Washington was decisive when making his appointments as president. His displeasure over the Great Seal may have contributed to Thomson not going forth into our first administration.

Chapter 5 | The Secret

The process of the Constitutional Convention in 1787 proceeded in keeping the Framework a secret.

As history goes, the Great Seal, the first order by John Hancock, the first President of the Continental Confederation, shows the significance of Benjamin Franklin as leader of the Founding Fathers and his penchant for secrecy. It also indicates the reasons Franklin carefully timed the Continental Convention to occur when Jefferson and Adams were both in Europe as envoys. His careful and conscious choice of Washington and Rutledge as his partners in calling the convention and leading the process was evident. With Washington being the front-man, he was able to gather sufficient well-qualified delegates. The stated purpose of the convention was to amend the Articles of Confederation. Whereas the true purpose was to establish a Federal Government with a Constitution based on a format aligned to ancient teachings and wisdom.

With Rutledge leaving the committee dominated by the heraldists, Franklin stepped back and proceeded with his plan for a federal government. It was based on Masonic Principles structured on the ancient system of the Two Trees in the Garden of Eden: The Tree of Knowledge and The Tree of Life.

The three Grand Masons, Benjamin Franklin, George Washington, and John Rutledge went behind the scenes to establish a new constitution, Their model for their system became the Framework. The debacle with symbols of monarchies becoming The Great Seal was a game-changer. They did not give a clue regarding their purpose or for having a spiritual foundation for the new government. One might call them the three masterminds.

Consider these two images

THESE ARE PAIRS, NOT OPPOSITES

THE REVERSE	THE OBVERSE
THE ENLIGHTENED	THE PRACTICAL
AS ABOVE	SO BELOW
ESOTERIC	REALISTIC

On our Great Seal
The Pyramid is obscuring
The actual heavenly realm

These were the images that were approved for the Great Seal. The words for the description had been approved before Rutledge spoke on behalf of Franklin and other

Masons against the broken Pyramid. William Barton, the heraldist, included Franklin's ideological concept as an image.

It is apparent that Charles Thomson, who was not remotely interested in the esoteric foundation of our government and constitution, include the words from his design. The only way to consider the broken pyramid is that it commenced with our Great Seal.

The depiction on our Great Seal where in the All-Seeing Eye is bounded and limited with no indication of the highest realm possible was put in place by men who had no spiritual cognizance. In the most bizarre outcome, this design has become "spiritual." There are no known depictions of this bounded eye in prior history. Yet, the image on our Great Seal is cited in all references to the "Eye of Illumination" or related names. The interpretation that it is an unfinished pyramid is standard.

The Framework was kept a secret as Franklin, Washington and Rutledge went forward in establishing our Federal Constitutional Republic.

It is also significant that there were masonic concepts and principles that were never written, but were known only to Grand Masters.

To repeat the words of Shawn Eyer: "The Framework evokes a powerful monotheistic God, aware of and involved with his creation, probing the conscience of every man. The effulgence of the single radiant eye suggests a pervasive, divine consciousness that recognizes us even as it is recognized by us, that contemplates us even as we contemplate it as the ultimate source of all."(Eyer)

Chapter 6 | The Tree of Knowledge as an integrated system

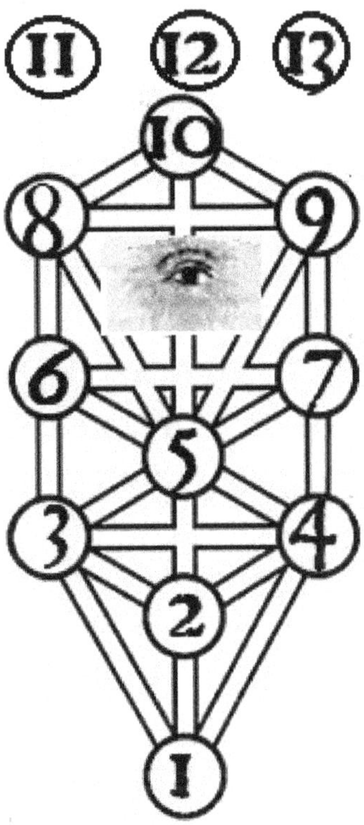

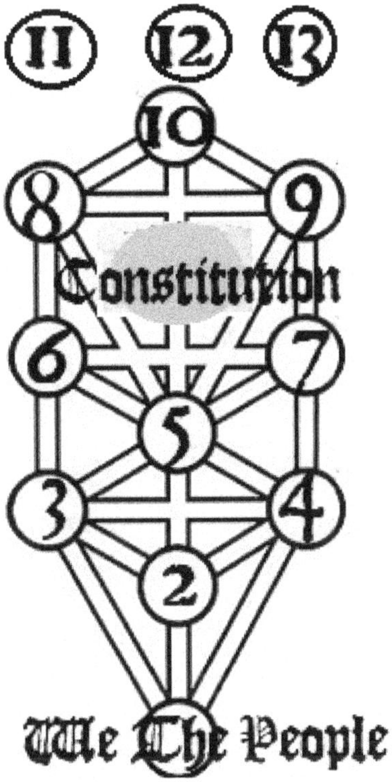

These two configurations show the basic diagrams of the Tree of Knowledge and the Constitution as conceptualized from knowledge from King Solomon by both Jews and Learned Gentiles. The Biblical basis are the two trees in the Garden of Eden as well as Hermes. From Jacob's Ladder we know the flow can go up or down according to the context or use.

The entire system of the Two Trees is explained in Chapters 11 and 12. The diagrams showing the All-Seeing Eye as positioned within the diagram is an imperative in understanding that our Framework was intended to follow the sacred patterns. Franklin and his 13 Steps to Enlightenment were the most significant aspects of our new country.

The All-Seeing, All-Knowing Eye is located in the spiritual side and is considered to illuminate the entire system.

This configuration is universal. It can be defined as a framework, a pattern, a system, a structure, an organizing system.

Virtually any purpose or any set of data, any content, can be organized on this pattern. It is sacred, only if the data is sacred. If the format is used for secular topics and information, it is certainly not sacred.

It is not binary. It begins with sets, with patterns of three. The sets have relatedness within each pattern and within the whole. Each element has a definition. All definitions can be changed as sets. The terms can be numbers and/or attributes. The frames can be combined. The spheres can be a set and the pathways, other sets. For instance, the number 12 can be depicted on the diagonal lines. The Tree of Knowledge begins at the base, with the individual. The number 7 is clearly a set, whereas sets streaming down have more oblique relationships.

Chapter 7 | The Architecture

Solomon's Temple: The First Temple

Then he called for Solomon his son, and charged him to build a house for the LORD, the God of Israel. David said to Solomon,

"My son, I had it in my heart to build a house to the name of the LORD my God. But the word of the LORD came to me, saying, You have shed much blood and have waged great wars; you shall not build a house to my name, because you have shed so much blood before me upon the earth. Behold, a son shall be born to you; he shall be a man of peace. I will give him peace from all his enemies round about; for his name shall be Solomon, and I will give peace and quiet to Israel in his days. He shall build a house for my name. (TheTempleofSolomon)

The Temple was dedicated by King Solomon in 953 BC. In all the celebrations, prayers, and joy, the most important aspect was that this Temple had no idols.

There are two significant components related to the Temple of Solomon. The spiritual traditions are very clear. Torah, the first five books of the bible, are the primary sacred source. The remaining sacred texts complete the Tanakh, the Prophets and Writings. These are essentially the Old Testament for Christians. Torah, itself, is written with a mathematical format. Particularly important are the Psalms that were written by King David and the three books.

According to Jewish tradition, King Solomon wrote three books of the Bible:

- *Mishlei* (Book of Proverbs), a collection of fables and wisdom of life

- *Kohelet* (Ecclesiastes), a book of contemplation and his self-reflection.

- *Shir ha-Shirim* (Song of Songs), an unusual collection of poetry interspersed with verse, whose interpretation is either literal (i.e., a romantic and sexual relationship between a man and a woman) or metaphorical (a relationship between God and his people)

Judaism and Kabbalah, in particular, follow this tradition.

Sacred geometry

The other distinct tradition is derived from King Solomon's Temple, the actual structures. The architecture was based on all the ancient sacred geometry. These included The Flower of Life. Within this formation is the Tree. Both the Tree of Knowledge and the Tree of Life are represented in this format, since the only distinction is the direction from the onset of the flow.

The ten spheres represent the ten archetypal numbers of the Pythagorean system. There are 32 paths on the Tree. The first 10 are the Sefirot or spheres (not including Daat, the 11th sphere, the sphere without form). The remaining 22 correspond to the lines or channels of energy that join the Sefiroth together. Each of these, in turn, corresponds to one of the 22 letters of the Hebrew alphabet. These comprise the 32 degrees of Freemasonry.

This Tree shows the 33rd degree of Freemasonry, It is called the Sphere without Form or the Da'at. It represents the connection to higher consciousness when ascending the flow beyond the first seven spheres. God or The Great Architect or Identifier of Supreme Intelligence supersedes the entire tree.

The following tree indicates the dynamics for the Star of David.

Pythagoras studied many spiritual traditions, particularly from Hermes, as well as Rabbis. He had many significant students, such as Euclid, who followed his teachings and extended them notably in geometry, He even studied sacred sounds. This diagram also shows the concept of Ein soph, above the tree itself . 000.

Ayin (Nothing; אין)

00. Ein Sof (Limitlessness; אין סוף)

0. Ohr Ein Sof (Endless Light; אור אין סוף)

These aspects exist before the actual emanations of energy exist.

Many centuries later stone masons, who built the great cathedrals, learned his geometric patterns. In the process, they also learned his spiritual teachings. Thus, their lives were focused on both traditions through Pythagoras.

About the year 1000, steel was produced. Thus the steel rim and the front of the plow were developed and people could produce more than they could sell locally, Jews became the traders since they could speak Hebrew or Yiddish without limitation of boundaries.

Thus, both groups could have interacted and interconnected.

In the seventeenth century, intellectuals became interested in the wisdom of the Stone Masons in Europe. They formed a non-operative (not builders) society, namely, the Freemasons. Not surprisingly, Jews and Christians alike became involved with the Society. It appears that Jewish freemasons moved to New York and other cities. In 1732, Benjamin Franklin published "The Constitutions of the Free-Masons." This topic is addressed further in Chapter 9 "Freemasonry."

It is entirely probable that Franklin had the sight to use the patterns as the foundation for our Constitution. Easily, he could have created the term "Framework." With the debacle of the design of the Great Seal by Charles Thomson, Franklin, Washington and Rutledge kept the Framework a secret. It was there all the time had anyone asked.

Interestingly, at the same time that Freemasonry was being launched in America in the early 1800s, the Baal Shem Tov was launching Kabbalah. They were not connected in any way whatsoever.

Chapter 8 | The Framework

The terms Framework and Framers were used in our Constitutional Convention and have remained in common usage. Yet most today remain unaware of the dedicated organizational structure of the Constitution. The content of our founding document has been studied and interpreted, but the substantive and distinctive mindsets of the Framers have remained unexamined. Franklin, Washington, and Rutledge, the three major contributors to the framing of the Constitution, were dedicated to an ancient system based on knowledge and wisdom. They kept the structure secret, so the content could be debated and defined by the delegates, and even adjusted later by amendment, while the structure itself remained intact. Though hidden, the primary structure remains.

Noah Webster's 1828 dictionary:

FRAME, verb transitive [Latin armus, Eng. arm.

3. To make; to compose; as, to frame a law.

4. To regulate; to adjust; to shape; to conform; as, to frame our lives according to the rules of the gospel.

5. To form and digest by thought; as, to frame ideas in the mind. How many excellent reasonings are framed in the mind of a man of wisdom and study in a length of years!

6. To contrive; to plan; to devise; as, to frame a project or design.

7. Order; regularity; adjusted series or composition of parts. We say, a person is out of frame; the mind is not in a good frame. Your steady soul preserves her frame

8. Form; scheme; structure; constitution; system; as a frame of government.

FRA'MER, noun One who frames; a maker; a contriver.

FRA'MEWORK, noun Work done in a frame.

This above list of definitions shows the use of important terms in the proper timeline. The terms were known in the convention, but not explained. The terms ``Framework" and "Framer" were used in the government, but obviously not in society at large. In the last definition of "frame," it slides in, almost as an afterthought. Noah Webster was a Wordsmith par excellence, but the usage within government was not significant. It is, however, a remarkably fine set of words to introduce the new constitution and the process. It was a new government with a new vocabulary.

Again, one has to look to Franklin. Number 5 on this list could be used to describe Franklin himself. "How many excellent reasonings are framed in the mind of a man of wisdom and study in a length of years!"

In referring to the delegates to the Constitutional Convention as Framers, we must note that this is the intended use of frame from that time period. Though the term has other possible meanings and its use is sometimes sloppy, the original use is precise. If the content was the only thing of significance, then "authors" would have been a sufficient term. That "Framers" was chosen invites us to look beyond the content itself and discover the underlying scheme. It can be identified as a form, structure, and system of our founding document. Again, there is an infrastructure, a configuration. It is organized and deliberate. Unlike architectural blueprints, our Framework has an entire system of integrated relationships and meanings. This distinction is integral in distinguishing the cohesive, highest level system that defined the organization and stability of our government.

The Framework of our Constitution is different from other systems of management. The Constitution is an open, stable, unified, and integrated system. It clearly defines the three parallel and co-equal branches. In contrast, most management systems are pyramidal and hierarchical. Much harm can result from assuming that our Constitution gives us a hierarchical structure.

Our Constitution has numerous factors that have set a standard; the power rests in the people, not by heredity, by birth, or battle. There is no pre-eminent position. Our president represents all the people, not only those who vote for him or her. The president does not have power over the other two branches or their leaders. There is no element for a religion or dedicated power group or political party.

The genesis of this book began with the recognition that this Framework, the actual organizing system of the Constitution, was clearly patterned on ancient systems. More specifically, the Framework parallels the Tree of Life, a pattern developed within the Jewish mystical movement Kabbalah. Both are sourced by patterns in the Book of Genesis. The content is not similar, but the organizational structure matches precisely. In other words, the Tree of Life expresses the relationship between Creator and Creation, whereas the Tree of Knowledge defines the organization of government. The content is different. But the manner in which the content is organized is the same. The system in the Tree of Life, and/or its reverse, The Tree of Knowledge, can be used for any set of data or an organization. It is a comprehensive organizational system in which the components are interconnected in terms of concepts and definitions as well as positioning.

The following diagrams show the Tree of Life delineations and the Framework configuration. This is not a hierarchical pattern. Rather, this structure forms a stable and unified geometric system. Each node in the pattern connects to the other nodes. The nodes are arranged in three columns, with each column representing particular emphasis in value. In the Kabbalah, the form illustrates how Creation emerges from the Creator. Kabbalah has the sole use as an esoteric pattern.

The Framework itself is a master plan. It is an intelligent organizing system It depicts the infrastructure for our constitution as well as the operation for our government. This geometric pattern was utilized by our Grand Framers to provide a conceptual structure for framing a government that would give practicality and sustenance to a specific set of ideals.

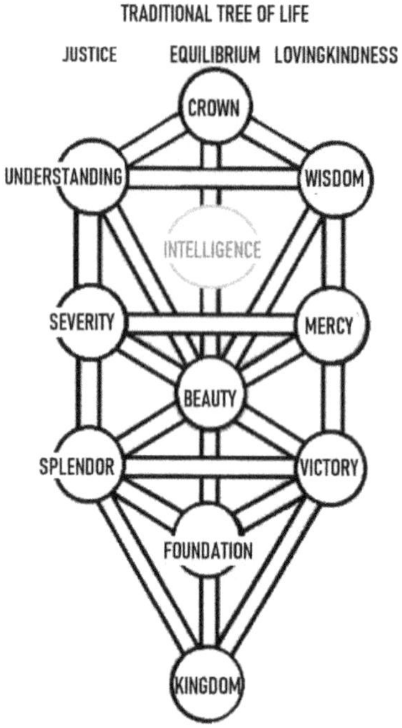

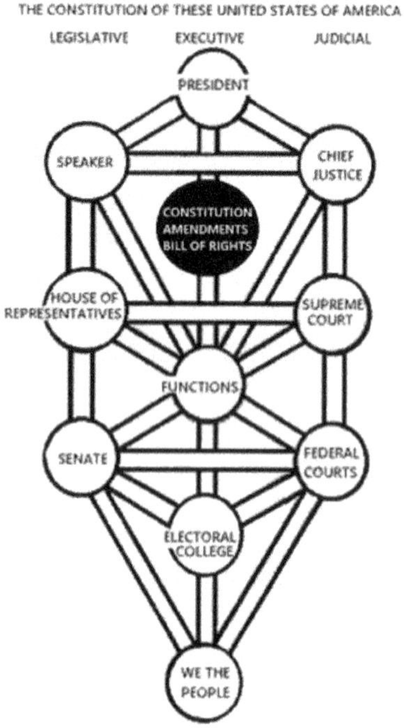

Freemasonry developed from the Society of Stone Masons, who built the great cathedrals in Europe. The Greek philosopher and mathematician, Pythagoras, along with his followers, provided the source material for their work. The Framework is derived from Pythagoras as well as his work and teachings. It is said he was the grandson of Hermes as Hermes was the grandson of Atlas. Regardless of the reality of their connection, the consistent integration and wisdom is of an astonishing dimension. It includes astronomy, geometry, and numbers as well as philosophy.

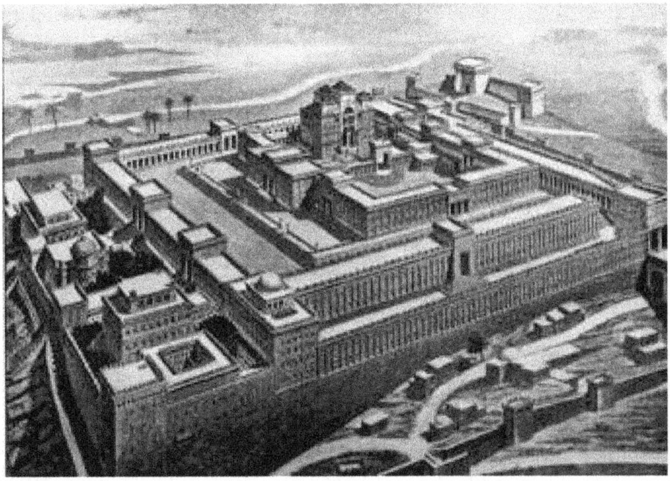

Another source of inspiration for both the Kabbalists and the Stone Masons was King Solomon's Temple. The legend is that due to the fact that King David had been involved in battles, the honor of building the Temple was given to his son, King Solomon. The Temple had precise architectural configurations, but also had rituals, artifacts and rules that were a celebration of purity. The ethics and teachings of the Stone Masons were the foundation of the Freemasons. They kept the teachings without the practical aspect of erecting the magnificent cathedrals. The Temple was built about 1000 BCE and was destroyed in 587 BCE.

Pythagoras lived from 590 to 495 BCE. This overlap indicates Pythagoras can be understood as a continuum of both King Solomon and Jewish knowledge as well as that of Hermes.

The political and religious teachings of Pythagoras were well known in Magna Graecia and influenced the philosophies of Plato, Aristotle, and, through them, Western philosophy. This is discussed in a later chapter. It is known that these people were directly connected to Jewish scholars of their time.

When a person understands the pattern of the Tree of Life (Etz Chaim in Hebrew), it is not difficult to recognize the hidden Framework in our Constitution. The three Grand Framers camouflaged the system by writing the entire document in a more haphazard manner. However, with the Tree of Life in mind, it is easy to discern the Framework when reading the Constitution.

Importantly, the patterns from Hermes move up and down, so there is a natural fit with what was indicated as the Tree of Knowledge of all things. Movement begins at the base in free will and is available to all people on our planet regardless of beliefs. The Tree of Life is covenantal and brings information FROM God into our planet based on vows at Mount Sinai.

The configuration for our Framework is an ancient, universal format. It is a perfect technology system. The purpose of each application signifies the usage. Definitions of the components determine whether it is sacred or secular in implementation. As a secular system from Hermes, it flows freely.

Our Framework is a specific application and not connected to other applications. It is most definitely based on "We the People" as a free will choice. The movement always ascends from "We the People," not otherwise.

Having planned the Framework before the convention, Franklin, Washington, and Rutledge saw how the Great Seal was distorted as it was being designed. A pyramid in ancient systems is revered as mathematically perfect, not broken. There is no door for entry. A pyramid without supporting documentation would have been seen by them as a sign of oppression, not of overcoming tyranny. It indicates precisely the commitment of these three Framers to keep sacred knowledge a secret.

As the leader of the Constitutional Convention, George Washington began by establishing The Committee of the Whole. Nothing passed in this committee was binding prior to ratification of the final document and, then, ratification by the states.

The Constitution was actually written in the Committee of Detail, led by John Rutledge. The members were carefully chosen by Franklin, Washington and Rutledge, the three grand Masons, who initiated the convention itself. Edmund Randolph had a strong Masonic relationship with Washington and was a Grand Mason. Oliver Ellsworth was likewise a Mason and a constitutional scholar. Gorham was a General from the North, but most importantly the president of the Committee of the Whole in the convention, Wilson was chosen on his own merit as an acknowledged constitutional scholar. All were dedicated to a Federal democracy.

From this, it follows that Rutledge closely oversaw the writing of the document, ensuring the intended Framework was preserved. From there, it went to the Committee of Style, where the same format was followed. This team, including Hamilton, polished the words, but left the design intact.

Our Constitution is our guiding light, illuminating the path for the governance of our nation and shaping the experience of every citizen. It is not connected to a person, place, or thing. It is not connected to political or social divisions. It embodies a set of unifying principles that provide for the well-being of us all.

In understanding the Framework, we know the structure and interconnectedness of the components of our government. Once we learn the three pillars of the system, it becomes obvious that the United States of America is not structured like a pyramid. The Executive Branch is not supreme. It is located on the center pillar and directly connected to the Electoral College and the people. There are no direct leadership paths between the Executive Branch and the other branches of our government. The President is not in charge of the other two pillars. Claiming preemptive authority is precisely what our Constitution is against. The Legislature is required to be the check and balance against an authoritarian Presidency. All three branches are connected to We the People as the whole and as determined by the voters.

In the long process of studying the Framework as a deliberate organizing system, based on ancient patterns and concepts, it became obvious that these three men undertook the careful work of establishing this structure in secret. Though an open discussion concerning content took place within the broader group of delegates, the deliberate construction of the organizational Framework by these three men was done in private. It was never mentioned. Most of it was done prior to even calling the convention. No one discusses how this convention was conceived and called. They called it a revision of the Articles of the Continental Congress so as to keep the Anti-Federalists engaged. They did not mention their actual intention, which was to create a Federal democracy.

As soon as the Constitutional Convention was called to order by George Washington, he changed the format. The open discussion referred to by Washington as The

Committee of the Whole, was non-binding until ratification, allowing the Grand Framers to ensure the details of content developed within their intended structure throughout the process.

It was these three leaders who announced that there was a Framework and that the delegates were called "Framers." However, they never defined or explained these terms.

Chapter 9 | Franklin, Washington & Rutledge

Benjamin Franklin was the guiding force behind our Federal Government. According to WIKIPEDIA, Franklin was an American polymath and one of the Founding Fathers of the United States. Franklin was a leading writer, printer, political philosopher, politician, Freemason, postmaster, scientist, inventor, humorist, civic activist, statesman, and diplomat. (WIKIPEDIA COMMONS) This is an absolutely valid list supported by his biographies.

His greatest achievement is virtually unnoticed. He was the Founder of the Founders, the initiator, and the leading force for the Constitution of the United States of America. The first action of John Hancock in the Continental Congress was to appoint Jefferson, who wrote the Declaration of Independence, along with Benjamin Franklin and John Adams, who edited the Declaration, to serve as the committee to design our great seal.

From the time of the imposition of Pierre Eugene du Simitiere as a heraldist to the committee, the pattern of his process becomes clear. As soon as he encounters a block going forward, Franklin retreats without making his viewpoint known. Then he finds another path forward. He cares passionately about good results. In reviewing his actions, he is not controversial. He can be seen with wavering policies, his objectives are apparent when he reaches accord. His modesty regarding awareness for his achievements should be legendary.

There are numerous biographies of Brother Benjamin Franklin written by Masonic Brothers. They are particularly insightful because they provide the context for everything he mastered. They understand the bedrock of his life.

Universal Freemasonry states "Franklin held a deep respect for the institution of Freemasonry. He explained his trust of Freemasons to his skeptical mother in a letter: "I assured her that they are in general a very harmless sort of people and have no principles or practices that are inconsistent with religion and good manners." He respected his Brothers for their peaceful ways, strong morals, and dedication to self-betterment. Benjamin Franklin also possessed a strong faith in God, "the Great Father," and worked towards a universal Brotherhood of all mankind. (Universal Freemasonry)

These quotes credit his achievements, while always referring to his personal attributes from the perspective of the Craft. A few of those insights follow:The Masonic Towel states: "Most of his biographers agree that Franklin's genius showed the greatest advantage in his philosophical concepts and his abilities as an ambassador. The one pictures the man as he was "in his heart" which is not only good Masonic ritual but also good scripture, since, "as he thinketh in his heart, so he is; "the other paints him a master of tact, of homely wit, and fair-mindedly keen in an age when wit had a rapier edge; as skilled in the arts of diplomacy in a time when intrigue and deceit were the very backbone of bargaining between nation and nation.

His whole life of service exemplifies the practice of toleration on the one hand and a non-dogmatic, non-credic religion on the other. We cannot prove that he received the inspiration for these from Freemasonry he loved and practiced, but neither can anyone prove the contrary. It is difficult to associate Masonic ideas with such thoughts as Franklin so often expressed, and not see a connection between. (Masonic Quotes)

The non-confrontational pattern of Franklin is shown in the two tasks delegated to the three committee members: Jefferson, Franklin and Adams: The Declaration and the Great Seal. The third Principle Document of our foundation, Our Constitution, was quietly and purposefully initiated by Benjamin Franklin himself. Without fanfare.

He was alarmed as the First Continental Congress began with the heraldist incorporating images and icons for the very ideas he was against. As a dedicated Grand Mason, he enlisted two other Grand Masons; George Washington, and John Rutledge. These three were dedicated to creating a federal government aligned to ancient precepts. It would take a decade to bring the constitutional convention into being in 1787. The three Grand Masons put everything into motion without divulging their purpose.

THE CONNECTION BETWEEN FRANKLIN AND WASHINGTON

The bond between Washington and Franklin is clearly significant in the founding of America. It is important to see that from a Masonic Perspective.

George Washington, a young Virginia planter, becomes a Master Mason, the highest basic rank in the secret fraternity of Freemasonry. The ceremony was held at the Masonic Lodge No. 4 in Fredericksburg, Virginia. Washington was 21 years old and would soon command his first military operation as a major in the Virginia colonial militia. Freemasonry evolved from the practices and rituals of the stonemasons' guilds in the Middle Ages. With the decline of European cathedral building, "lodges" decided to admit non-stonemasons to maintain membership, and the secret fraternal order grew in popularity in Europe. In 1717, the first Grand Lodge, an association of lodges, was founded in England, and Freemasonry was soon disseminated throughout the British Empire. The first American Mason lodge was established in Philadelphia in 1730, and future revolutionary leader Benjamin Franklin was a founding member.

There is no central Masonic authority, and Freemasons are governed locally by the orders, many customs and rites. Members trace the origins of Masonry back to the erecting of King Solomon's Temple in biblical times and are expected to believe in the "Supreme Being," follow specific religious rites, and maintain a vow of secrecy concerning the order's ceremonies. The Masons of the 18th century adhered to liberal democratic principles that included religious toleration, loyalty to local government, and the importance of charity. From its inception, Freemasonry encountered considerable opposition from organized religion, especially from the Roman Catholic Church. For George Washington, joining the Masons was a rite of passage and an expression of his civic responsibility. After becoming a Master Mason, Washington had the option of passing through a series of additional rites that would take him to higher "degrees." In 1788, shortly before becoming the first president of the United States, Washington was elected the first Worshipful Master of Alexandria Lodge No. 22.

JOHN RUTLEDGE

The third man in this esteemed group was John Rutledge, who was clearly the front person for Franklin in the third Committee for the Great Seal and had prominent position is the Constitutional Convention

John Rutledge became a Grand Master in London in 1760, where he studied law at the Middle College or Middle Temple. Franklin was on a Mission for the colonies in London from 1757 to 1762. His son, William Franklin, was also at Middle Temple and, therefore, a classmate of John Rutledge, who was there from 1757 to 1760.

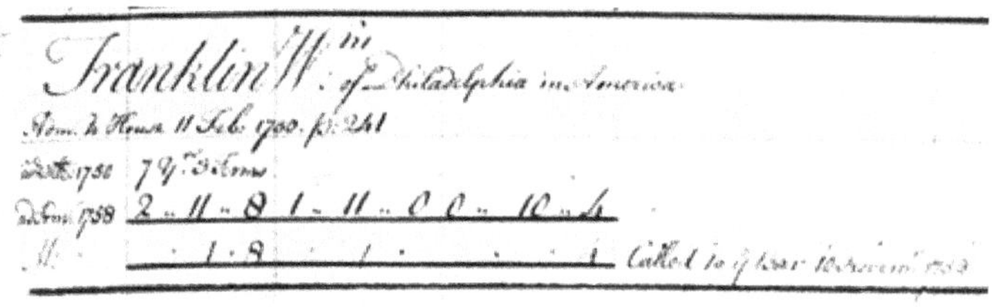
Franklin Wm of Philadelphia in America

The enrollment document for William Franklin in 1760

On the 17th of November 1760, Franklin was present at the Crown & Anchor in London, England's Grand Lodge. According to legend, he spoke there. It is probably the Lodge he attended during his years in London.

Regardless, Franklin would have met Rutledge through his son, William. That connection leads to the understanding of the sponsorship and trust Franklin and Rutledge had for each other. William was older than Rutledge. His own son, William Temple Franklin, was born in London in 1762 and assisted his grandfather for many years, including during the Constitutional Convention. William became a Loyalist and was not involved with Franklin during the long years of the Revolution and the founding of our country. Rutledge's father, Dr. Rutledge, also became a Loyalist and returned to England. Having similar family dynamics could have contributed to the bond that Benjamin Franklin and John Rutledge forged. To reiterate, Benjamin Franklin and his grandson became Patriots, while his son moved back to England. John Rutledge and his younger brother, Edward, were Patriots, while their father was a devout Loyalist, who returned to England. Passions within families ran very high in those decades. We do know that Rutledge participated strongly with Franklin and the Iroquois during those years.

It is apparent that Franklin commanded authority and respect from those in both the Continental Congress and the Constitutional Convention. He guided members privately, behind the scenes. Rutledge was a strategic ally in the third committee for the Great Seal. Later, he had these Committee Assignments: First Committee of Representation, Second Committee of Representation, Third Committee of Representation, Chairman of Committee of Detail, and Chairman of Committee of State Commitments.

Chapter 10 | Broad Aspects of Freemasonry in the Eighteenth Century

According to the Masonic Philosophic Society, approximately 28 of the 40 signers of our Constitution were Masons. Since membership was secret, it is not possible to know how many members were during the convention. Some, such as James Madison, joined later.

The American Enlightenment was a period of intellectual ferment in the thirteen American colonies in the 18th century, which led to the American Revolution, and the creation of the United States of America. The American Enlightenment was influenced by the 17th-century European Enlightenment and its own native American philosophy. According to James MacGregor Burns, the spirit of the American Enlightenment was to give Enlightenment ideals a practical, useful form in the life of the nation and its people. (WIKIPEDIA) Virtually all colonists dedicated to our constitution held this mindset, which covered several generations.

In 1682, John Skene, born in Scotland, was recognized as the first Freemason residing in America. However, many Jews immigrating from England in the late 1600s were also Freemasons. The lodges in America were formed later.

The earliest existing Lodge minutes are from Edinburgh Lodge No. 1 in Scotland and are dated 1599. The Grand Lodge of England, from which most of the Grand Lodges in existence today have descended, was formed in 1717. The first officially warranted lodge on record in America is St. John's Lodge of Boston founded in 1733.

In 1733, Henry Price, the Provincial Grand Master over all of North America for the Grand Lodge of England, granted a charter to a group of Boston Freemasons.

In addition, many men with learning also had the multigenerational mindset of Enlightenment during the 18th century. The Enlightenment was an intellectual movement in the eighteenth century that emphasized reason and science. There are also astronomical concepts. Many of our Mason founders had this mindset as well. However, Jefferson, John Adams, Hamilton, Madison and James Wilson were considered Enlightened, but were not Masons.

Freemasonry in their own concepts is most assuredly not a religion. The Identifiers of a specific god, religion and associated practices of each Mason are their own choice. Religions are considered belief systems. One could recognize religions as teachings and rituals focused on "What to believe.

From Webster's Dictionary of 1828: "*religion* in its most comprehensive sense, includes a belief in the being and perfections of God, in the revelation of his will to man, in man's obligation to obey his commands, in a state of reward and punishment, and in man's accountableness to God; and also true godliness or piety of life, with the practice of all moral duties. It therefore comprehends theology, as a system of doctrines or principles, as well as practical piety; for the practice of moral duties without a belief in a divine lawgiver, and without reference to his will or commands, is not *religion. (Webster, N)*

Freemasons all have an oath and concept of a Supreme Being. The Supreme Being is not delineated. Freemasonry is considered an ethical or moral system. They want wisdom, higher consciousness, and brotherhood.

Washington, Franklin, and Rutledge were all born as Episcopalians. Franklin became a Deist and Washington remained an Episcopalian, at least in name. Rutledge was a dedicated Episcopalian his entire life.

Statements regarding Freemasonry are frequently written by outsiders with their own perspective. Thus the following excerpts regarding Freemasonry and Religion is from the United Grand Lodge of England June 12, 1985

BASIC STATEMENT—Freemasonry is not a religion, nor is it a substitute for religion. It demands of its members belief in a Supreme Being, but provides no system of faith of its own. Its rituals include prayers, but these relate only to the matter instantly in hand and do not amount to the practice of religion. Freemasonry is open to men of any faith, but religion may not be discussed at its meetings,

THE SUPREME BEING—The names used for the Supreme Being enable men of different faiths to join in prayer (to God as they see Him) without the terms of the prayer causing dissension among them. There is no Masonic God: a Freemason remains committed to the God of the religion he professes. Freemasons meet in common respect for the Supreme Being, but He remains Supreme in their individual religions, and it is no part of Freemasonry to attempt to join religions together. There is therefore no composite Masonic God.

VOLUME OF THE SACRED LAW—An open Volume of the Sacred Law is an essential part of every Masonic meeting. The Volume of the Sacred Law to a Christian is the Bible; to Freemasons of other faiths it is the book held holy by them.

FREEMASONRY COMPARED WITH RELIGION— Freemasonry lacks the basic elements of religion:

It has no dogma or theology (and by for-bidding religious discussion at its meetings will not allow a Masonic dogma to develop). (b) It offers no sacraments. (c) It does not claim to lead to salvation, by works, secret knowledge or any other means (the secrets of Freemasonry are concerned with modes of recognition, not with salvation).

FREEMASONRY SUPPORTS RELIGION—Freemasonry is far from indifferent to religion. Without interfering in religious practice, it expects each member to follow his own faith, and to place his duty to God (by whatever name He is known) above all other duties. Its moral teachings are acceptable to all religions. (grandlodgeofiowa.org)

FREEMASONS BEYOND THE CONSTITUTION

The following list is composed of Freemasons of this era, who were not founders of our constitution, but made a notable impact on our country. The purpose is to indicate the extensive impact masonry had on our society as a whole in that period.

MOHAWK CHIEF JOSEPH BRANT, MASON

Evidence of Native American Masons is, perhaps, best illustrated by this obituary for Mohawk Chief Joseph Brant, who was a Mason and a Tory, and undoubtedly supported by other Native American Masons, who were Tories and English Tories.

On November 24, 1807, Mohawk Chief Thayendanegea, also known by his English name, Joseph Brant, died at his home in Burlington, Ontario. Before dying, he reportedly said, "Have pity on the poor Indians. If you have any influence with the great, endeavor to use it for their good."

Brant ranked among Britain's best commanders during the American War for Independence. He was an educated Christian and Freemason who studied directly with Eleazer Wheelock at Moor's Indian Charity School, the parent institution of Dartmouth College. His older sister Mary was founding father Sir William Johnson's common-law wife and also played a significant role in colonial and revolutionary Indian affairs.

The Iroquois, an alliance of Native Americans including the Mohawk, attempted to maintain neutrality at the beginning of the War for Independence, but by 1777, Joseph Brant had led the

Iroquois into an alliance with Britain. He, like most Native Americans, saw Great Britain as their only defense against the colonial settlers who were encroaching into their ancestral territory.

PRINCE HALL, Worshipful Master of the Black Masons

The Boston Massacre was a riot that occurred on March 5, 1770, on King Street in Boston. This is widely recognized as the event that escalated anti-British sentiment in the Colonies and events that triggered our American Revolution.

A month after the Boston Massacre, Colonist William Hall freed Prince, who thereafter used Hall as his surname. His certificate of manumission read that he was "no longer Reckoned a slave, but [had] always accounted as a free man.

In 1775, Prince Hall and fourteen other free blacks joined a British Masonic Lodge. They were soldiers who were stationed in Boston. After the war, they formed their own lodge, the African Lodge of the Honorable Society of Free and Accepted Masons of Boston, the world's first lodge of black Freemasonry and the first society. Hall became the lodge's first Grand Master. Hall was active in the affairs of Boston's black community, using his position as "Worshipful Master" of the black Masons to speak out against slavery and the denial of black rights.

Of primary importance is that he protested the lack of schools for black children. He established a school in his own home. This is a particularly important factor. The most common opinion of that time was that blacks could not be educated.

WILLIAM PENN, QUAKER AND MASON

William Penn was greatly affected by the preaching of Quaker minister Thomas Loe. Expelled from Oxford University in England in 1662 for refusing to conform to the Anglican Church, Penn joined the Quakers. After his father died in 1670, Penn inherited the family estates and began to frequent the court of King Charles II, campaigning for religious freedom.

ILLUMINATI

Some mistakenly refer to our founders as Illuminati. Historically, the name usually refers to the Bavarian Illuminati, an Enlightenment-era secret society founded on 1 May 1776. Thus, the Illuminati were based on the Freemason concepts at the precise time of our American Revolution. The society's goals were to oppose superstition, obscurantism, religious influence over public life, and abuses of state power. They wanted to influence rather than dominate those who were unjust. The Illuminati were preceded by the significant history of Freemasonry in Scotland, England, France, as well as the colonies.

The point is Freemasonry in our colonies could have had some influence on Illuminati through our diplomats, particularly to England and France. Furthermore, the anti-masonry prejudice did not become an issue until President John Quincy Adams, our sixth president. As his father's son, he was in Europe during the Revolutionary period. While the constitution was being written, he was a diplomat in Germany and Eastern Europe. Thus, he dealt directly with multiple small monarchies and the Catholic church as well as the influences of Martin Luther, whose influence began in the 15th century in Germany. The Illuminati were being formed at that time, so he would have had the prejudice from both the Catholic church and the monarchies.

Importantly, Illuminati accept the Great Seal as designed by Charles Thomson.

At the time of our Constitutional convention, he served as an envoy to Prussia and other Eastern European Countries. As such he was aligned to the monarchies and to the Catholic Church. Both groups were antithetical to our constitution at the close of the 18th century.

Today, the Illuminati accept the final version of the Great Seal as the legitimate representation of their beliefs. By publishing this image, they are accepting the adopted version with the bounded eye. This clearly indicates the Illuminati were not sourced by Franklin, Washington, and Rutledge during the design phase. They were extremely upset at the violation of the spiritual side of the Great Seal.

This also demonstrates that they do not consider the patterns of the StoneMasons.

MASONS REGARDING WOMEN

Masons are a fraternal order, composed of high-principled men regardless of race or religion. However, there is an aligned order for Master Masons and women associated with Masons. The Order of the Eastern Star is a Masonic appendant body open to both men and women. It was established in 1850 by lawyer and educator Rob Morris, a noted Freemason, but was only adopted and approved as an appendant body of the Masonic Fraternity in 1873. The order is based on teachings from the Bible, but is open to people of all religious beliefs. It has approximately 10,000 chapters in twenty countries and approximately 500,000 members under its General Grand Chapter. Members of the Order of the Eastern Star are aged 18 and older; men must be Master Masons and women must have specific relationships with Masons. (Wikipedia contributors. "Order of the Eastern Star."). It warped to demand concepts of our times without comprehension of the timeline of history basic concepts of each period individually.

The point of this is that there are steps in everything that progresses. Sometimes, we have to retreat before continuing. Our Founding Fathers created a democracy without the interference of church and monarchs. We are shown that in the Framework with the ability to amend the rules as society shifts and changes. There is a fundamental orderly configuration.

Senior leadership by women is, from all indications, an Aquarian Age concept.

From the late 1600s until 1800, the Age of Enlightenment was a thriving intellectual movement in Europe and the colonies. The "great ideas" concerning God, reason, nature, and humanity were the focus of the intellectual elite. The goals of rational humanity were considered to be knowledge, freedom, and happiness. (Duignan)

Since Freemasonry was a secret fraternal society, there are no precise records showing how many signers of the Declaration of Independence and the Constitution were Masons. At least 28 out of the 40 Signers were Masons, but it is likely that others joined after the Constitutional Convention.

Freemasons are often Christians. The Masonic teachings are very ancient. Masonic teachings are compatible with the teachings of Judaism, Christianity and Islam as well as other religions and traditions). It is important to note that each Mason must believe in a Supreme Being and can only join the fraternity of their own free will. It is not a birthright, but rather a choice. Being a Christian is not mandatory for Masons, but it is an option, one of the most common options in both Europe and America.

Chapter 11 | Freemasonry as a Society Concepts in 1776

Just as understanding the definitions of the words, it is important to understand the decade beginning in 1776, and the mindsets and ideas of the founders. For instance, understanding the process of creating the Great Seal is important as context for the ideas and values of our new country. This book places a high value on the patterns that emerge and stories that are in the same time period and give insight.

The following chapters are included as the backstory, the history, and context for our Framework. The three Grand Master Framers were dedicated against the establishment of a system that paralleled the hierarchical monarchies and church systems. The three major influences were the Freemasons, the Iroquois, and the Jewish connections. Of course, Freemasonry was predominant since all three were Grand Master Masons. However, Franklin and Rutledge had significant interactions with the Iroquois and Washington had significant connections to Jewish Masons during the

Revolutionary War. These relationships were active precisely when the three men were studying and making decisions about the new government, a constitutional republic that had no direct precedent. They wove the patterns for the structure of our constitution directly from the Stonemasons. These events set the tone for our government. The philosophical ideas from the European Monarchies, the Greeks, and Romans were interwoven as appropriate. These ideas were inserted into the Framework itself.

The Reverend Dr. James Anderson, a Scotsman and Freemason, was the Master of a Masonic lodge, and the Grand Warden of the Grand Lodge of London and Westminster. In 1723, he wrote a document called "The Constitutions of the Free-Masons," which became the defining document for all Freemasons. It was given to all members as soon as they joined. Benjamin Franklin published the American Edition in 1734. Clearly, George Washington and John Rutledge would also have known its contents well. (Anderson, James)

Included below are passages from the beginning of the tract, as well as passages regarding Pythagoras. These excerpts are intended to give some understanding of the depth and scope of the Founding Fathers. The 18th Century was called the Age of Enlightenment, when philosophical, intellectual, and rational ideas were the focus. Just reading a few passages like this can give us more appreciation for the level of dialogue and insight that shaped the thinking of our Founding Fathers.

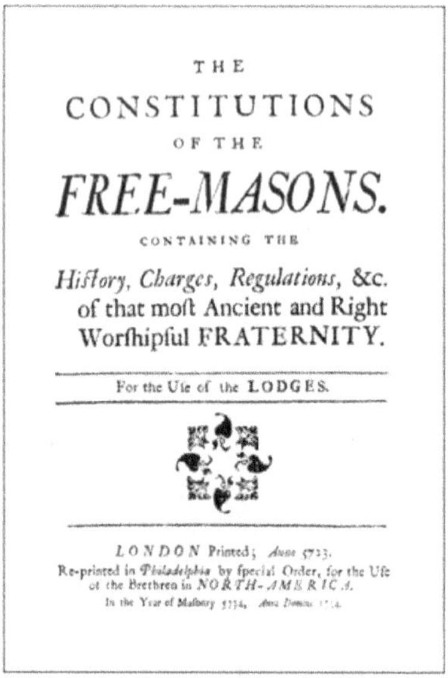

THE
CONSTITUTIONS
OF THE
FREE-MASONS.
CONTAINING THE
History, Charges, Regulations, &c.
of that most Ancient and Right
Worshipful FRATERNITY.

For the Use of the LODGES.

LONDON Printed; *Anno* 5723.
Re-printed in *Philadelphia* by special Order, for the Use of the Brethren in *NORTH-AMERICA*.
In the Year of Masonry 5734, *Anno Domini* 1734.

This is the cover of the Masonic treatise written by James Anderson and published by Benjamin Franklin.

The Constitution, History, Laws, Charges, Orders, Regulations, and Usages OF THE Right Worshipful FRATERNITY OF ACCEPTED Free-Masons;

Collected from their general R E C O R D S , and their faithful T R A D I T I O N S of many Ages.

ADAM, our first Parent, created after the Image of God, the great Architect of the Universe, must have had the Liberal Sciences, particularly Geometry, written on his Heart; for even since the Fall, we find the Principles of it in the Hearts of his Offspring, and which, in process of time, have been drawn forth into a convenient Method of Propositions, by observing the Laws of Proportion taken Year of the World 1. (Anderson, James)

As this book continues we find a comprehensive list of people in Genesis and notable leaders and scholars beginning 5780 years ago.

God is the Great Architect of the Universe

Thus all Freemasons are monotheists. This concept and terminology provide the basis for separating Freemasonry from specific religions. Thus Freemasonry created a sphere of fellowship wherein men could strive for social good and public values without having distinctions and separations because of religions. Therefore, the concept of the Great Architect enabled men of all races to come together for the common good of their communities. Character was an essential component, religion was not. Masons included

Christians, Jews, Muhammadans (as they were called), Blacks, Native Americans, and others. Therefore, there was a strong positive, purposeful unifying factor in Freemasonry. This led to a considerable contribution to the positive American Spirit, as well as dedicated anti-Masonry from those who were not accepted into initiation.

Freemasonry is one of the world's oldest secular fraternal societies. The explanation may correct some misconceptions. Freemasonry is a society of men concerned with moral and spiritual values. Its members are taught by a series of ritual dramas, which follow ancient forms and use stonemasons' customs and tools as allegorical guides.

Masonry is a fraternity, not a religion. Masonry acknowledges the existence of God, but Masonry does not tell a person which religion he should practice or how he should practice it. That is a function of his house of worship, not his fraternity. (AtlasPythaagoras)

These verses from Ecclesiastics provide insight into the concept of

The EYE OF ILLUMINATION

OMNISCIENCE

The eyes of the Lord are far brighter than the sun, beholding round about all the ways of men, and the bottom of the deep, and looking into the hearts of men, into the most hidden part.—*Ecclesiasticus* xxiii. 28.

THERE is an eye that, everywhere,
All, evermore, surveys :
Unseen, yet, ever on us fixed,
Beholding all our ways.

Through traffic's crowded way, alert,
That Eye observes us press :
It marks us, from the unheeding throng
Emerge, companionless.

If the "more important truths of morality" are, as stated:

1. Existence of Deity.
2. Immortality.
3. Love of God for his children:

Then geometry can be said to demonstrate the first, thus: 1. There is no plan without a planner - geometry proves that the universe runs according to a plan, which follows laws to exact that predictions successfully can be made from them.
2. It is impossible for Deity to be less perfect than his creatures. 3. All his creatures exhibit love, tenderness, and devotion for their children. No human parent but would give indefinite life to his child if he could. 4. Therefore, Deity, infinitely more perfect than the most perfect of His children, has, in His infinite love, provided infinite life for His children.

The attempt to prove that which is known of the soul in terms known only of the mind is more or less fruitless. But it is only by some such process of reasoning that we can follow out the admonitions of the Fellowcraft degree. We are to study geometry, not so much in books and lines and angles and measurements and axiom and theorems and propositions and problems, as in a demonstration of the wonderful properties of nature. From these, we deduce that the universe in general, and the world in particular, exist, move, evolve, live according to definite laws or plans. Knowing that plans cannot create themselves, any more than the watch in the desert could create and wind itself, we are logically compelled to believe in the planner. In the nature of things, as we know them. He who plans must be more perfect than we who were planned. Our virtues, then, must be but pale reflections of His. If we would not deny immortality to those dependent upon us whom we love, then the love of the Great Architect, and His provisions of immortality, are as much proved to us as any processes of the mind can prove the certainty of the soul. (Masonic Geometry)

REGARDING FREEMASONRY

Freemasons, having been founded under the influence of Stone Masons, were focused on mathematical systems and living a purposeful, moral life. This simply means that, in the case of the American Revolution, many brethren, feeling that the actions of the crown warranted revolution and independence, were justified in following their consciences without fear of violating their Masonic obligations or any Masonic law. (Freemasonry and the American Revolution)

Masonic brothers from St. Andrews Lodge in Boston initiated the Boston Tea Party, the first act of rebellion at the beginning of the Revolutionary War. It is one of the primary stories in our history. Thousands of colonists convened at the wharf. Meanwhile, the Sons of Liberty led a vote to refuse to pay taxes on the tea or allow the tea to be unloaded, stored, sold or used. Then, the Brothers, some dressed as Mohawks, got on the boats and threw the valuable cargo overboard. There were 342 chests containing 45 tons of tea. The crew even helped.

Governor Hutchinson followed the rules of the British and was totally ineffectual. He was sent back to England. No trial was possible because anyone on the jury would have been involved in the incident. (Boston Tea Party) . Understanding Freemasonry is critical, because, from the beginning, Masons were leaders in the Revolutionary War, in framing the Constitution, and in leading our government and nation from 1776 until the present day. Fourteen of our presidents were Masons. The most recent was Gerald Ford.

Freemasonry is an ethical and spiritual brotherhood. It is not a religion. The test before becoming a Mason is one of moral behavior. In these times, when politics are so fractious, it is worth noting that President Ford was committed to restoring order and unity after Nixon resigned. It was not a popular action, but, in retrospect, it reflects Ford's moral foundation as a Mason. (AtlasPythagoras)

PYTHAGORAS

Pythagoras is said to be the grandson of Hermes. Hermes had extraordinary insights, which included Mathematics and Astronomy. His work, as well as that of Pythagoras, was widely disseminated. Both had strong interactions with the Jews.

This book reflects the study on the Tree of Life with careful consideration of the pathways. Indications are that Hermes and Pythagoras both actually taught the Tree of Knowledge of All Things as given to Adam. This tree includes Free Will Choice and moves up and down the Tree. The lowest sphere begins with self-awareness. The step reflects Noah and interconnections and relatedness with others.

It goes without saying that the name synonymous with triangles and geometry. that the geometric relationships were philosophical ideas.

Pythagoras is It can be seen the basis for Pythagoras was born in the year 3467 in the Hebrew calendar, which is 580 BCE. He traveled extensively throughout the Middle East studying in Egypt, Persia, Chaldea, and Babylonia. He studied with the Babylonian Jews, in particular. Ultimately, he settled in Greece and began teaching. A preponderance of our major philosophers reflect back to his studies. However, his teachings were primarily oral and directed at his own society. It is likely that his students and those, who have followed, use his teachings for their own work. It is difficult to be certain as to whether Pythagoras or his students had the idea originally. His students followed his dedication to ethical, humane behavior. His discoveries, including mathematical as the basis for all things, of cycles, and of astronomical and musical patterns were all connected to his strict moral codes. He taught the transmigration of souls, wherein a soul never dies but returns through many lifetimes. (Pythagoras)

Pythagoras's followers were commonly called "Pythagoreans." They learned and expanded on his concepts. It is not possible to determine with any accuracy, which theories were instigated by

Pythagoras and which were expanded and clarified by his followers. It is an entire body of intelligent thought. These works contain the keys to universal knowledge without the secularized religious precepts of the Age of Pisces. The Theory of the Transmigration of Souls, for instance, is consistent with many Eastern religions as well as spiritual quests. They performed purification rites and rituals based on concepts of their soul journey. They had a monastic lifestyle that incorporated these rituals within their daily lives. They were focused on enabling their own souls to achieve a higher rank in the heavenly realm. They had idyllic precepts that could not be incorporated into a family lifestyle.

Metempsychosis or transmigration of the soul into a new body after death is important. They believed that relationships of numbers were the basis of everything in the universe. Pythagoras is thought to have devised the doctrine of Musica Universalis, which holds that the planets move according to mathematical equations and thus resonate to produce an inaudible symphony of music.

Pythagoras and his students believed that everything was related to mathematics and that numbers were the ultimate reality and, through mathematics, everything could be predicted and measured in rhythmic patterns or cycles.

These teachings were the basis for the buildings and rituals in the great Stone Masons. The magnificent cathedrals are a physical construct following the ancient mathematical patterns. Their societies enabled them to travel from country to country erecting their magnificent buildings. It is probable that they did not have family lives to bind them to specific locations.

The Freemasons directly incorporated mathematics and the universal systems into their rituals and wisdom, while not adhering to the same precepts in their daily lives. In addition, they were not erecting great buildings. Freemasonry was considered wisdom based on idealistic concepts and rites. The Brotherhood was distinctly separated from the secular lives they all had. The Framework of our Constitution was precisely based on the mathematical patterns and interconnected, yet integrated concepts. Our Framework is a precise application of this ancient wisdom. The basic Framework is one unit, the core design, of these sacred precepts.

The universal patterns from Hermes and Pythagoras provide a system that goes up and down as taught in Jacob's ladder. They were the core mathematics in the foundation in King Solomon's Temple. At the same time, the clear precepts of Jews in the Tree of Life were incorporated. Thus the Two Trees in the Garden of Eden are the fundamental union of movement within the whole. In addition, the Jewish vows at Mount Sinai establish an enduring, consistent connection to receiving direction to higher consciousness. The free-will choice of Adam and Eve was not a sin, but rather the mandatory step in a circle of relatedness to the higher realms.

We are now entering a new age, wherein our highest level choices enable harmony and balance for humankind as a whole.

THE FORTY-SEVENTH PROBLEM OF EUCLID.

"This was an invention of our ancient friend and brother, the great Pythagoras, who, in his travels through Asia, Africa, and Europe, was initiated into the several orders of priesthood. and raised to the sublime degree of Master Mason. This wise philosopher enriched his mind abundantly in general knowledge of things and more especially in Geometry, or Masonry. On this subject he drew out many problems and theorems; and, among the most distinguished, he erected this, which, in the joy of his heart, he called EUREKA, in the Grecian language signifying *I have found it, and* upon the discovery of which he is said to have sacrificed a hecatomb. It teaches Masons to be general lovers of the arts and sciences. "(Sacred-Texts)

THE THREE STEPS

Usually delineated upon the Master's carpet, are emblematical of the three principal stages of human life, viz:—YOUTH, MANHOOD, and AGE. In Youth, as Entered Apprentices, we ought industriously to occupy our minds in the attainment of useful knowledge; in Manhood, as Fellow-Crafts, we should apply our knowledge to the discharge of our respective duties to GOD, our neighbor, and ourselves; that so, in Age, as Master Masons, we may enjoy the happy reflection consequent on a well-spent life, and die in the hope of a glorious immortality. The morning is the youth of the day; youth is vigorous till noon; then comes the age of man; to which succeeds the evening of old age; sunset follows the evening or death of the day. Frugality is a great revenue, but nowhere greater than in this case. (Sacred-Texts)

FREEMASONRY FROM A NON-MASONIC POINT OF VIEW

William Blake is now considered a seminal figure in the history of the poetry and visual arts of the Romantic Age according to WIKIPEDIA. There are countless books and Papers about him including connections with Freemasonry. Particularly insightful is an article, "Blake, Freemasonry and the Builder's Craft, by Stuart Peterfreund. Peterfreund has provided significant insights about Freemasonry from his particular vantage point in relation to Blake. Individual clergy and those of class backgrounds inimical to Freemasonry egalitarian background, kept the hostility and suspicion alive with virulent, though misinformed anti-Masonic propaganda. Both as a consequence and as a cause of some of Enlightenment's most radical and influential tendencies, Men of a variety of religious and political persuasions... found meaning in the new science and by the early eighteenth century, British Freemasonry gave institutional expression to this new scientific culture. The official Masonic lodges stand as a new metaphor for their age. Ruled by grandmasters drawn from the peerage, strictly hierarchical in structure, yet curiously egalitarian in their meetings and banquets, governed by 'charges' or rules constitutionally enforced yet indifferent to religious affiliation, the lodges mirrored a larger social and ideological consensus. By the 1770s when Blake came to maturity, Freemasonry played a vital role in the artistic and intellectual life of most radicals, but of others as well... In England, itself, it was virtually an indigenous intellectual force.

Internationally, the brotherhood included among its members Voltaire, Mozart, Goethe, and Franklin; and the attractiveness as a system of thought suggested by the thought that Freemasonry continues to flourish in the face of the hostility and opposition of the uninitiated. In its extreme form, this opposition was mounted by the Catholic Church to the Bavarian Electorate and the Austrian Monarchy. To a lesser extent, individual clergy inimical to Freemasonry's egalitarian leanings kept the hostility alive with violent though misinformed anti-Masonry propaganda.

Craft, rebirth into higher wisdom, fellowship - all three of these are characteristic of the Masonic enterprise and equally of Blake's vision. Blake took freemasonry as one of the social institutions that were his cultural endowment and transformed it through a visionary poetic critique that resulted in Blake's conception of the Builder's Task.

FREEMASONRY AND OUR FOUNDING FATHERS & LEADERS

Benjamin Franklin had been introduced to Masonry when he was in Paris and then became a Grand Master in Philadelphia in 1734. He published "The Constitutions" in the same year. During that time he began learning the principles of the Six Nations, which were, in fact, a democracy.

John Rutledge, likely the son of a Mason from Scotland, was born in South Carolina, went to England to study law, and became a Grand Mason while there. It was in 1760. Interestingly, Franklin was entered upon the minutes as the provincial Grand Master during the Grand Lodge of England's meeting in Crown & Anchor, London, a position he was elected into in June 1760.

Middle College in London, where John Rutledge studied law and became a Grand Master

It is clearly possible that they became bonded at that time. Thus, Rutledge would have followed Franklin's dedication to the Great Law of the Iroquois as well as being Franklin's collaborator in establishing the Framework in the Constitutional Convention. They were bonded in 1760 in the absolute debacle of our Great Seal. The two of them in all probability developed the plan for the Framework and the convention. Then, Franklin enlisted the cooperation of Washington in bringing it and our government into reality. Appendix I in this book by Donald G brings excellent research and relevance to this topic. The bond between Franklin and Rutledge from their connection at Middle College is essential to understand. The strong, enduring bond between them is overlooked.

There were significant Signers of The Declaration of Independence in 1776, who had studied at Middle Temple or Middle College, as it was alternatively called, in London. They were Thomas Heyward, Thomas Lynch, Thomas

McKean, Arthur Middleton, William Paca and Edward Rutledge. Edward Rutledge (John's younger brother).

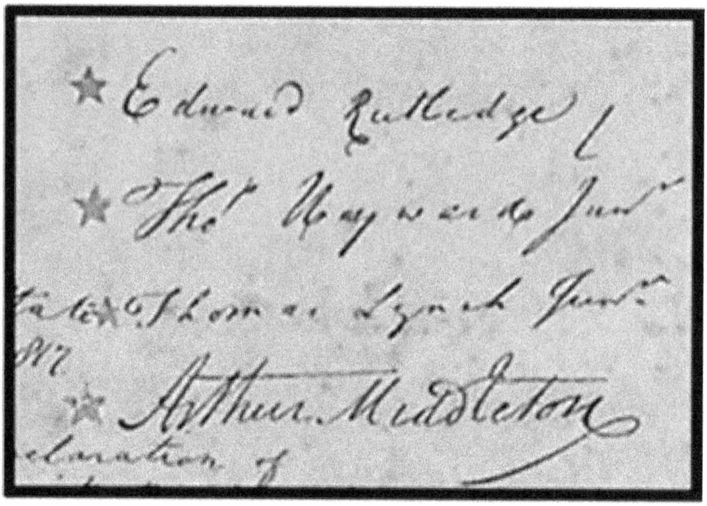

Signers of the Declaration who studied at Middle College and were Masons Edward Rutledge was a younger brother of John

The Framers, as differentiated from the Signers, were not the identical set. The Framers were John Blair, John Dickenson, Jared Ingersoll, William Livingston, Charles Pinckney, Charles Cotesworth Pinckney, and John Rutledge. Middle College would have been the preeminent institution for legal studies as indicated by the number directly involved with both documents.

The Continental Congress focused on state's rights, but public opinion was developing in favor of a strong central government. After Virginia and other states elected delegates to attend the Philadelphia convention, Congress issued a call for a convention to meet at the same place and time to consider the revision of the Articles of Confederation.

Fifty-five delegates assembled in accordance with the call, of this number, thirty-one listed below were Masons:

Abraham Baldwin, Gunning Bedford, John Blair, William Blount, David Brearley, Jacob Broom, Daniel Carroll, William R. Davie, Jonathan Dayton, John Dickinson, Oliver Ellsworth, Benjamin Franklin, Eldridge Gerry, Nicholas Gilman, William Houston, William Samuel Johnson, Rufus King, John Langdon, John Lansing Jr., James McClung, James McHenry, Alexander Martin, Robert Morris, William Paterson, William Pierce, Charles Pinckney, Edmund Randolph, George Read, Roger Sherman, George Washington, George Wythe (Dryfoos) He incorrectly includes Thomas Jefferson and Alexander Hamilton

Six of this group were Grand Masons: Franklin, Washington, Rutledge, David Brearley, Gunning Bedford, Jr., John Blair

The Presidents of the Congress of the Confederation

Peyton Randolph VA Sep. 5–Oct. 22, 1774
Master Mason and Uncle of Edmund Randolph

Henry Middleton SC Oct. 22–Oct. 26, 1774
Mason. 4 day term. His Son Arthur was Signer.

Presidents of the 2nd Congress of the Confederation

Peyton Randolph VA May 10–May 24, 1775
Second Term as President

John Hancock MA May 24,1775–Oct. 31, 1777
Master Mason. Prominent early leader

Henry Laurens SC Nov. 1, 1777–Dec. 9, 1778
Mason See List of readings: stance on slavery.
Also Story following this list..

John Jay NY Dec. 10, 1778–Sep. 27, 1778
Mason. Signer, 1st Chief Justice.

Samuel Huntington CT Sep. 28, 1779–Mar. 1, 1781
Grand Mason, Signer

Under the Articles of Confederation, convened on March 2, 1781

The Presidents of the Confederation Congress

Samuel Huntington CT Mar. 2–July 6, 1781
Extended term under new system

Thomas McKean DE July 10–Oct. 23, 1781
Mason, Signer, Chief Justice, Governor,

John Hanson MD Nov. 5, 1781–Nov. 3, 1782 Hanson was chosen to be President under Articles of Confederation unanimously by Congress (which included George Washington). In fact, all the other potential candidates refused to run against him, as he was a major player in the revolution and an extremely influential member of Congress. Some consider his position to be the FIRST President of the United States. He created the operating system of our government through all the initial appointments he made. **He appointed 2nd**

Great Seal Committee

Elias Boudinot NJ Nov. 4, 1782–Nov. 3, 1783
He Appointed 3rd Great Seal Committee. Significant patriot from New Jersey. His great-grandfather, a Hugenot, came to America in 1687. He had no interest in Heraldry because of his religion, even though our Great Seal was passed in his term. He went to College of New Jersey along with Oliver Ellsworth and others. Interestingly, he wrote the first Thanksgiving Proclamation under Washington. He and Franklin were activists for the education of slaves,

Thomas Mifflin PA Nov. 3, 1783–Nov. 30, 1784 Convention delegate. First governor in PA. Definitely not a MasonSee Story following this list: Masonic Connections

Richard Henry Lee VA Nov. 30, 1784–Nov. 4, 1785 Signer, Early significant leader for Revolution. Author of Independence Resolution:" Resolved, That these United Colonies are, and of right ought to be, free and independent States, that they are absolved from all allegiance to the British Crown, and that all political connection between them and the State of Great Britain is, and ought to be, totally dissolved. (2) That it is expedient forthwith to take the most effectual measures for forming foreign Alliances. (3) That a plan of confederation be prepared and transmitted to the respective Colonies for their consideration and approbation. See Story following this list: Masonic Connections

John Hancock MA Nov. 23, 1785–June 5, 1786
Second Term

Nathaniel Gorham MA June 6, 1786–Feb. 2, 1787
Chairman of Committee of the Whole. Member of Committee of Detail. Not a Mason

Arthur St. Clair PA Feb. 2–Oct. 5, 1787
Mason, Governor, Northwest Territory

Cyrus Griffin VA Jan. 22, 1788–Mar. 2, 1789
Mason, Judge

It is essential to note that John Hanson, who appointed the Second Committee to design our Great Seal, and Elias Boudinot, who appointed the Third Great Seal, were not Freemasons.

STORIES OF NOTE

THE MASONIC CONNECTIONS
OF "WASHINGTON'S SECRET WAR"
by John Parsons

While Washington was encamped at Valley Forge, there was a move afoot by the New England faction in Congress to replace him with Gates. Gates was very good at self-promotion, and used Thomas Muffin, the Quartermaster General whom Washington had fired for incompetence, and Thomas Conway, an Irish soldier of fortune, to advance his cause to Congress. Henry Laurens, the President of the Congress, smelled a plot, and asked his son Henry, who was a Major serving on Washington's staff, what he thought about the individuals involved. The younger Laurens informed his father that they were all a bunch of scoundrels, mistrusted by the Army and that Washington was a fantastic leader. (Parsons, J)

Over the next several months as the plot played out, Washington's allies effectively scuttled the efforts of Congressional radicals, and got Conway, Lee, Muffin, and ultimately Gates, removed from any positions of power. Fleming's book does a superb job of demonstrating how they did it.

While Fleming really doesn't go into the motivations of most of the actors, it is apparent that the ties of Masonic brotherhood played a probable, but non-obvious role, in Washington maintaining his position as Commander-in-Chief. (Parsons, J)

MASONS, WHO SIGNED OUR CONSTITUTION

Gunning Bedford, Jr. (Grand Master of the Grand Lodge of Delaware)

John Blair

David Brearly (Grand Master of the Grand Lodge of New Jersey)

Jacob Broom (Wilmington Lodge, Delaware)

Daniel Carrol

John Dickinson

Oliver Ellsworth

Benjamin Franklin

Rufus King

William Richardson Davie, Jr. (Grand Master of the Grand Lodge of NC)

Jonathan Dayton

Dr. James McHenry (Spiritual Lodge No. 23, Maryland)

John Francis Mercer (Grand Master of the Grand Lodge of VA; (1784-6)

William Paterson

Edmund Randolph, (Grand Mason New Jersey) non-signer

John Rutledge

Daniel of St. Thomas

Jenifer

George Washington

This group is strategically important during the writing of our constitution. They established the first federal constitutional democracy in modern history. They incorporated the capacity for amendments and changes in the rules. They did not consider that our Framework itself would be vulnerable.

The following illustration shows the fourteen Masons, who became Presidents of the United States. (Illustration Masonic Presidents)

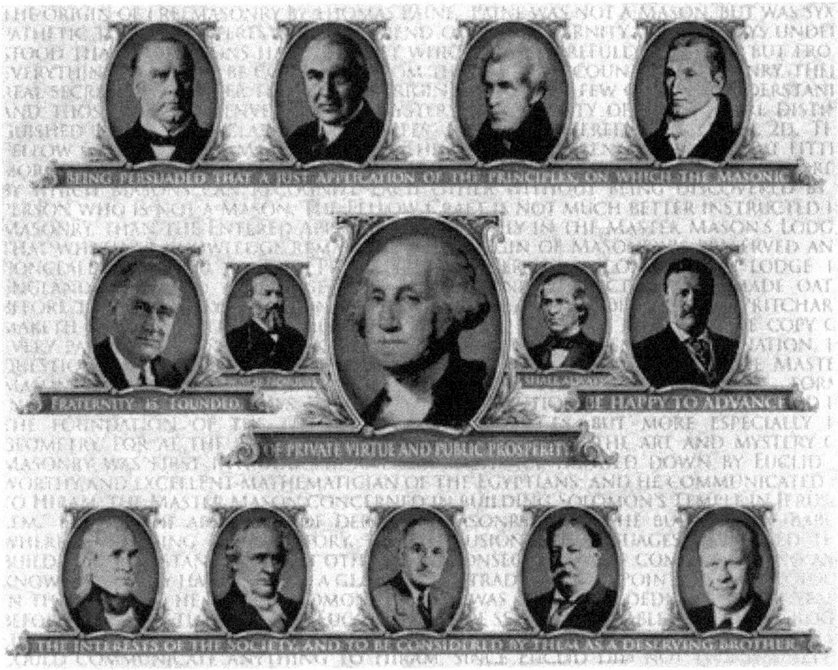

Presidents who were Freemasons were: George Washington, James Monroe, Andrew Jackson, James K. Polk, James Buchanan, Andrew Johnson, James A. Garfield, William McKinley, Theodore Roosevelt, William Howard Taft, Warren G. Harding, Franklin D. Roosevelt, Harry S. Truman, and Gerald R. Ford.

In addition to the individuals listed above, Lyndon B. Johnson was "Entered Apprentice", but did not advance

Ronald Reagan was made an honorary Freemason, Bill Clinton was a member of the Order of DeMolay (for boys).

The following image is an interesting relic. It contains pictures of the 15 Presidents of the United States who were also Freemasons. However, James Madison became a Freemason after he completed his terms of office as President. There are assertions that Jefferson became a Mason, but that has been disproven. He was in the company of Masons, but was not one of their society.

MASONIC PRESIDENTS
"Let there be Light"
Faith Hope and Charity
SEAL OF THE PRESIDENT OF THE UNITED STATES

The symbols on this image include the unbounded eye, which was important to Franklin, in particular. Therefore, we can begin to understand how upset he was with the altered Great Seal.

The following chart lists the Supreme Court Justices who are identified by one or more sources as having been Freemasons. The first column shows the chronological order in which that Justice joined the Supreme Court. The numbers not listed are for Supreme Court Justices who are not indicated by any source as having been Freemasons.

Supreme Court Justices who were or are Free-Masons

#	Name		Dates
1	John Jay	Chief Justice	1789-1795
2	John Rutledge	Chief Justice	1789-1791, 1795
3	William Cushing		1789-1810
5	John Blair, Jr.		1789-1796
8	William Paterson		1793-1806
10	Oliver Ellsworth	Chief Justice	1796-1800
13	John Marshall	Chief Justice	1801-1835
16	Thomas Todd		1807-1826
18	Joseph Story		1811-1845
20	Robert Trimble		1826-1828
21	John McLean		1829-1861
22	Henry Baldwin		1830-1844
26	John Catron		1837-1865
29	Samuel Nelson		1845-1872
30	Levi Woodbury		1845-1851
35	Noah H. Swayne		1862-1881
37	David Davis		1862-1877
38	Stephen J. Field		1863-1897
44	John M. Harlan		1877-1911
45	William B. Woods		1880-1887
46	Stanley Matthews		1881-1889
48	Samuel Blatchford		1882-1893
60	William H. Moody		1906-1910
63	Willis Van Devanter		1910-1937
64	Joseph R. Lamar		1910-1916
65	Mahlon Pitney		1912-1922
68	John H. Clarke		1916-1922
69	William H. Taft	Chief Justice	1921-1930
76	Hugo L. Black		1937-1971
77	Stanley F. Reed		1938-1957
79	William O. Douglas		1939-1975
81	James F. Byrnes		1941-1942
82	Robert H. Jackson		1941-1954
83	Wiley B. Rutledge		1943-1949
84	Harold H. Burton		1945-1958
85	Fred M. Vinson	Chief Justice	1946-1953
86	Tom C. Clark		1949-1967
87	Sherman Minton		1949-1956
88	Earl Warren	Chief Justice	1953-1969
92	Potter C. Stewart		1958-1981
96	Thurgood Marshall		1967-1991
97	Warren Burger	Chief Justice	1969-1986

(Chart of Supreme Court Justices)

Warren Burger was a member of Bench in Middle Temple. Warren E Burger, Chief Justice of the US 1969-1986, was Called in 1971 - He visited the Inn on many occasions, and also spearheaded a movement in the 1970s and 1980s to establish Inns of Court in the US, in the image of their Old World counterparts. At a ceremony in Washington DC in 1988, Burger signed a 'Declaration to commemorate and celebrate the perpetual friendship and brotherhood' between the London and American Inns. (Friendship & Revolution)

In addition, Chief Justice John Roberts is an honorary member of the Bench. Category: Honorary Benchers Bench Call Date: 19.7.2007 Full Title: The Hon Chief Justice John G. Roberts Jr

Chief Justice John Roberts (Masonic Matters)

Interestingly his ceremony was held at the Middle Temple, where John Rutledge studied and became a barrister and a Grand Mason.

The Masters of the Bench, or Benchers, are responsible for the governance of the Inn. Masters are elected by their peers from the Inn's members who have been Called to the Bar. The Inn also elects Honorary Masters of the Bench, distinguished individuals from other walks of life who have excelled in their respective professions. Currently, the Inn has 154 Honorary Benchers.

Chapter 12 | Benjamin Franklin, John Rutledge, and the Iroquois

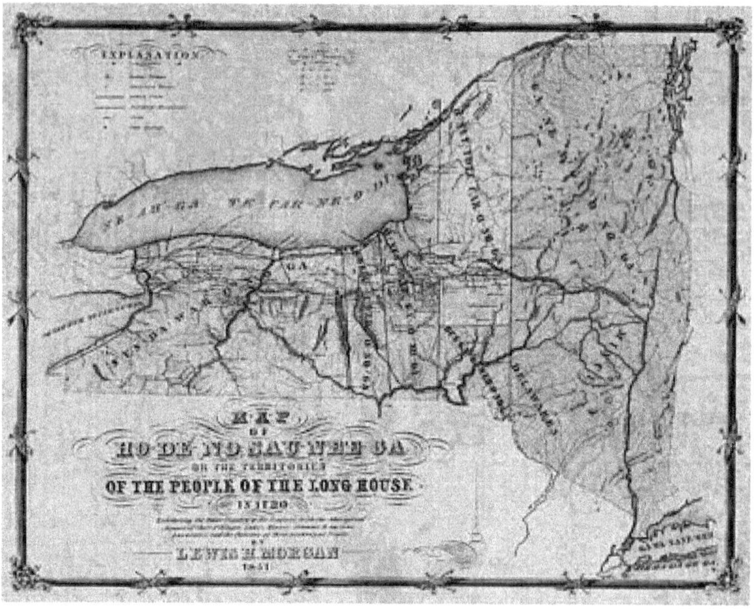

1720 map of New York State showing the Iroquois Nations

Deganawidah, the Great Peacemaker, led the Native American nations in the region that is now New York to form a commonwealth many generations in the past. It is believed to be before the year 1500. It was his intention to establish a legal system to serve as a stop for the violence that was exacerbated by codes of honor. He stated his vision that *"Thinking shall replace killing, and there shall be one commonwealth."* Haudenosaunee was the original name of the Iroquois. (Deganawida and Hiawatha)

The Haudenosaunee, known today as the Six Nations Iroquois. Haudenosaunee means, "People who Build Houses," and the term has come to designate the League of the Iroquois.

The Longhouse was not simply a dwelling. It was an idea: Hereabouts are five nations, each with its own council fire, yet they shall live together as one household in peace.

Deganawidah, known as the Great Peacemaker, was the founder of the confederacy, made the joint commitment for peace with Jikonhsaseh, the Mother of Nations. The Great Law of Peace establishes: "They shall be the Kanonsionni, the Longhouse. They shall have one mind and live under one law. Thinking shall replace killing, and there shall be one commonwealth.

The Nations began as five, then expanded to six and, finally, seven. All were adjacent in upstate New York. The Great Law of the Iroquois is recognized in our Great Seal primarily for the ideas. The system of the Tree of Knowledge and the Tree of Life came from Pythagoras and the Jews. It is easy to consider they were all inspired in the ancient past.

THE IROQUOIS

Benjamin Franklin introduced the Albany Plan for Union in 1754 during the French and Indian War. It was intended to establish a union between the colonies, which would benefit the colonies, which would continue as British colonies. It did create cooperation between the Indians and the British. That shift in loyalty from the French to the English was a major event in the history of the Revolutionary War and in establishing our government.

The primary objectives in the Albany Plan were for defense and commerce between all the colonies. Concerning the states that rejected the plan, Franklin wrote, "The colonial assemblies and most of the people were narrowly provincial minded in outlook, mutually jealous, and suspicious of any central taxing authority."

That was a telling comment that continued through our constitutional convention. During the debates over the plan for union, Franklin pointed to the strength of the Iroquois Confederacy and stressed the fact that individual nations of the Confederacy maintained internal sovereignty, managing their own internal affairs, without interference from the Grand Council.

When Franklin published his "Short hints toward a scheme for uniting the northern colonies," his Albany Plan proposed that each colony could govern its internal affairs and that a Grand Council consisting of a different number of representatives from each colony would provide for mutual defense. This proposed council closely resembled the Grand Council of the Iroquois nations. While the colonies and the Crown were not ready for a colonial union and the Albany Plan was not ratified, Franklin gained recognition as an advocate of colonial union and a place in history as an originator of the federalist system of government.

The Albany Plan contained the core concepts for the Second Continental Congress, which produced the Articles of Confederation in 1777 during the American Revolution. These articles were the first constitution of the newly declared United States of America. Ratified in 1781, it laid the foundation for the current U.S. Constitution. (Albany Plan)

The Albany Plan, based on Iroquois ideas, is the primary source for the ideas in our Constitution. In this book, the sacred aspects connected to our Framework is the focus. One can observe parallel patterns reaching far back in time. The Mediterranean concepts evolved into systems containing calendars, writing systems and mathematical patterns. The Native American continuum has been connected to nature as source for understanding all things..

THE GREAT SEAL OF PEACE OF THE IROQUOIS

The influence of the Iroquois is significant in the obverse side of our Great Seal. We include many of the Iroquois symbols that were known to Franklin and Rutledge before the design of the Great Seal. It is readily apparent to any s

Among the Haudenosaunee are groups of people who come together as families called clans. As a matrilineal society, each clan is linked by a common female ancestor with women possessing a leadership role within the clan. The number of clans varies among the nations with the Mohawk only having three to the Oneida having nine. The clans are represented by birds and animals and are divided into the three elements: water, land and air. The bear, wolf and deer represent the land element, the turtle, eel and beaver represent the water element and the snipe, hawk and heron represent the air element. (Haudenosaunee confederacy)

SYMBOLS OF THE IROQUOIS

Author's Rendition

These are the clan animals found on the Great Seal of the Iroquois with their meanings. This is fascinating to consider in the context of Universal Systems.

The Tree of Knowledge and the Tree of Life use Hebrew traits to form a set of positions on the tree differentiated by values. The Symbols of the Iroquois are likewise positioned on their Tree of Peace.

Eagle: Divine Spirit, Connection to Higher Authority. Coyote: Prankster, insight, playful

Elk: Strength, agility, freedom

Beaver: Builder, gatherer

Hawk: Messenger, stopper of time

Turtle: Creative, source, self-contained

Wolf: Loyal, success, perseverance

Deer: Love, gentleness, kindness

Bear: Power, Adaptability

Heron: Solitude, independence

Snake: Shrewdness, Transformation

Snipe: Always busy

Other aspects

A CLUSTER OF ARROWS: Recognized from the creation story the cluster of arrows is a symbol of unity for the Haudenosaunee. The Peacemaker used this symbol to point out how if the nations joined together they could not be broken. This symbol represents the strength that results from the joining of the nations.

EAGLE: Said to be a messenger to the Creator the eagle is the protector of peace. Placed atop the Tree of Peace it alerts members of the confederacy if danger approaches. Eagles are known for their sharp vision, a keen sense of perception, powers of intuition, Eagles represent action, resolve, and grace. They fly higher than any other animal.

WHITE PINE TREE, GREAT TREE OF PEACE: The white pine tree was the tree chosen by the Peacemaker as a symbol of the unity of the nations of the Haudenosaunee confederacy. Its needles which always grow in clusters of five are symbolic of the uniting of the nations. The white pine also has broad branches that can provide shelter and it is beneath the tree that the Peacemaker asked the Chiefs to join him.

FOUR WHITE ROOTS: The roots at the base of the Great Tree of Peace are said to be the four white roots which represent the points north, south, east and west. Following these roots other nations can find the Great Tree of Peace and seek to join the nations of the Haudenosaunee Confederacy. (Note the connection to the four worlds.)

LONGHOUSE: Symbolic of the traditional territories held by the Haudenosaunee. Within a longhouse, families all live together in harmony. With the nations united they are all one family living territorially in one long house.

CIRCLE: The circle is a widely used symbol in many cultures and nations. For the Haudenosaunee it represents unity, strength and the cycles of life. Gathering the original Chiefs in a circle around the Tree of Peace the Peacemaker had them hold hands to make their circle strong. He showed them that if they kept their circle united, they would always be able to keep the Tree of Peace standing. If they let go of their grip to each other and broke the circle the Tree could fall to the ground and then so too would the peace.

SKY WORLD: A pattern of a semicircle is often seen in many beaded designs or quill work and represents a huge overhead dome to recognize the Sky World from where life came.

TURTLE: Symbol for North America as it is said that the turtle carries it on its back. From the creation story it was the turtle that carried sky woman on his back.

This list is compiled from many sources but includes those cited on our bibliography.

An interesting pursuit would be to associate the symbols in association with the definitions on the Framework found in Chapter 12. It is not difficult to coordinate the definitions and placement of the spirits and animals of the Iroquois with Framework, the Tree of Knowledge, and The Tree of Life. They all seem to be derived from the same ancient source. Franklin likely could have perceived these concepts.

In late July, 1787, twenty years after the Stamp Act Congress, John Rutledge found himself chairing the Committee of Detail at the Constitutional Convention. The Committee was charged with taking all of the resolutions that had been passed in the Convention and drafting a document that could be polished and refined through the debate on the floor of the convention. Rutledge's biographer states that he opened the meeting with some passages from the Great Law of the Iroquois. The main passages relate to the sovereignty of the people, peace, and unity. Rutledge had asserted earlier that a great empire was being created, so it must be firmly rooted in American soil.

As far as I can determine, the Great Law of the Iroquois was the basis for ideas, rather than patterns. Ultimately, they made their final selection of symbols. Charles Thomson recorded the symbols of the final set for the Great Seal of the United States of America. What we do not know is whether these three men recognized similarities as a universal system between the Tree of Life and the Great Seal.

Terri Hansen wrote an excellent paper on the PBS blog. Her chart follows:

Iroquois Confederacy and the Great Law of Peace affected our United States Constitution specifically

Restricts members from holding more than one office in the Confederacy: Article I, Section 6, Clause 2, also known as the Ineligibility Clause or the Emoluments Clause bars members of serving members of Congress from holding offices established by the federal government, while also baring members of the executive branch or judicial branch from serving in the U.S. House or Senate.

Outlines processes to remove leaders within the Confederacy: Article II, Section 4 reads "The President, Vice President and all civil Officers of the United States shall be removed from Office on Impeachment for, and the conviction of, Treason, Bribery, or other High Crimes and Misdemeanors."

Designates two branches of the legislature with procedures for passing laws: Article I, Section 1, or the Vesting Clauses, read "All legislative Powers herein granted shall be vested in a Congress of the United States, which shall consist of a Senate and House of Representatives." It goes on to outline their legislative powers.

Delineates who has the power to declare war: Article I, Section 8, Clause 11, also known as the War Powers Clause, gives Congress the power, "To declare War, grant Letters of Marque and Reprisal, and make Rules concerning Captures on Land and Water;"

Creates a balance of power between the Iroquois Confederacy and individual tribes: The differing duties assigned to the three branches of the U.S. Government: Legislative (Congress), Executive (President), and Judicial (Supreme Court) act to balance and separate power in government. (Hansen, Terry)

Scholars of our constitution have concentrated on ideas and details, while not seeking a structure. Franklin led the trio during the convention to include the components of the constitution as a system, while always maintaining the Committee of the Whole, wherein there were no votes regarding the specifics.

Dr. Donald Grinde gave an important speech at Cornell University, which is included in its entirety as Appendix II. It is essential reading in understanding the significance of The Great Law of the Iroquois in our Constitution. He wrote extensively about both Franklin and Rutledge. This paragraph about Rutledge is particularly appropriate:

"In late July 1787, twenty years after the Stamp Act Congress, John Rutledge found himself chairing the Committee of Detail at the Constitutional Convention. The Committee was charged with taking all of the resolutions that had been passed in the Convention and drafting a document that could be polished and refined through the debate on the floor of the convention. Rutledge's biographer states that he opened the meeting with some passages from the Great Law of the Iroquois. The main passages relate to the sovereignty of the people, peace and unity. Rutledge had asserted earlier that a great empire was being created so it must be firmly rooted in American soil. With this said, Rutledge bent over and began the task of drafting the Constitution." (Grinde, D.)

Chapter 13 | George Washington and Jewish Connections

Washington's backstory is quite different from Franklin's and Rutledge's. He is not the scholar crafting the constitution, but rather the skilled leader, who could inspire people continually. He carefully communicated and paid attention to the thoughts, words, and ideas of everyone. He could galvanize and motivate people to our American cause. People were loyal to him and, thus, to our new republic. His extraordinary ability to make new connections based on trust, competence and ethics is unparalleled. He is, for all times, our iconic hero.

TIMELINE FOR PRINCIPAL JEWISH RABBIS & THEIR WORK

From 900 until 1090 CE there was a great Jewish culture in Spain. Abd-ar-rahman III became Calif of Spain in 912 CE. There was tolerance and positive interaction between Christians, Muslims, and Jews.

Rashi (1040 to1100) wrote important commentaries on almost the entire Tanakh (Hebrew Bible) and Talmud. Maimonides (1135 - 1204) wrote an influential code of law (The Mishneh Torah) as well as the most influential philosophical work (Guide for the Perplexed) in Jewish history.

Moses de Leon, of Spain (1250 – 1300) authored the Zohar (Book of Splendor) which contains mystical interpretations of the Torah. This begins the modern form of Kabbalah (esoteric Jewish mysticism).

Isaac Luria (1534 - 1572) developed the modern form of esoteric Jewish mysticism AKA Kabbalah.

The Ba'al Shem Tov (1700 - 1760) founded Hasidic Judaism (Timeline)

The point of this list is to recognize concurrent timelines. During this same period the StoneMasons, then the Freemasons were developing esoteric philosophies. Possible fields of study with respect to concurrence and timing could include Rupert Sheldrake's extensive work. "Morphic Resonance" is a process whereby self-organizing systems inherit a memory from previous similar systems. He studies Cosmic Consciousness and other related fields. (Sheldrake, Rupert)

Both Jewish and Puthagorean, thus Masonic traditions, stem from King Solomon's Temple. It is important to note that Hasidic Judiasm and Freemasonry concurrently has the same patterns and focus in the 18th century. It is not a stretch of reasoning to see that traditional Jews would find the precepts and patterns in FreeMasonry consistent with their beliefs.

The connection between our Framework and the Tree of Knowledge stemmed from being asked the right question. Both systems were well known, but the right question opened the connection instantly for this author. Timewise, it was 200 years after the convention that ratified the Constitution.

It is notable that while George Washington was a practicing Episcopalian, he maintained relationships with both Jews and Catholics. There are letters to both groups.

As President, Washington was in communication with Touro Synagogue in Rhode Island, as well as the Portuguese Synagogue in New York City. He also noted "going to the Papists" during the Constitutional Convention. He was dedicated to accommodating and respecting everyone, regardless of religious belief.

At Valley Forge, Washington was ready to cede victory to the English. The frigid and damp winter had left his troops thread-bare and starving. One evening while walking the camp, he saw Haym Salomon, a practicing Jew, lighting the Chanukah candles. Salomon had made a vast fortune since coming to the colonies. His contributions to fund the revolution were exceeded only by Robert Morris. Their extraordinary generosity made the revolution possible. In the end, they both died penniless.

Solomon belonged to the New York branch of the Sons of Liberty, a Masonic Lodge. They led the Boston Tea party rebellion against the Stamp Act. However, he is listed also with the Maryland Lodge No.2, Ancient York Rite.

The ever-curious Washington asked Salomon to explain his candles. According to the Jewish Encyclopedia: *Mattathias Maccabeus was already old when the religious persecution under Antiochus Epiphanes broke out. The king's soldiers under Apelles, who is mentioned by Josephus but not in the Book of Maccabees, came to Modin, a small city in Judea. They set up an altar to the heathen god, and ordered Mattathias, as the most influential citizen, whose example would be followed, to sacrifice in accordance with the king's command. But Mattathias said: "Though all the nations that are under the king's dominion obey him, . . . yet will I, and my sons, and my brethren, walk in the covenant of our fathers" (I Macc. ii. 19-20). And when a certain Jew was about to obey the command, Mattathias, who was filled with holy wrath, killed the offender and destroyed the altar, while his sons cut down the king's officer. Thereupon Mattathias called out: "Whoever is zealous for the Law, and maintaineth the covenant, let him follow me." His countrymen, abandoning all their possessions, followed him and hid in the mountains and desert places. Others, who had hidden themselves before, joined them.*

When Mattathias learned that the pious ones would rather be cut down by the king's soldiers than defend themselves on the Sabbath he commanded them to fight, when necessary, on that day. (Gottheil, R., & Krauss, S.)

Despite being substantially outnumbered, the Maccabees prevailed against the Greeks, who had ravaged The Holy Temple. Now, having reclaimed the Temple, the Maccabees prepared a sacred service, finding only one small vial of purified olive oil that was uncontaminated by the Greeks. The miracle of Chanukah is that this one-day supply of oil lasted the entire eight days it took to obtain a supply of new oil. The Festival of Chanukah occurs each year to celebrate this miracle. The Chanukah candelabrum has eight candles for each day the oil lasted, plus the Shamash, which is used to light these candles.

Menorah

This story of the few vanquishing the many enthralled Washington. Rather than surrender to the British, he returned to his tent determined to proceed with the revolution. According to legend, Washington noted this moment as a significant turning point.

The eagle's tail feathers indicate the massive effect on Washington. Washington insisted on the inclusion of this symbol. It is the sole symbol in our Great Seal not based on the number thirteen. Note that the tail feathers indicate the practice of having a Shamash of a different length. Regardless, we have the nine tail feathers on the Eagle in our Great Seal. The middle candle is longer. The image fits the legend. There are no other legends to fit the image.

A noteworthy story was written By Donald Moran and is posted in the site for the Sons of Liberty Chapter of the Sons of the American Revolution.

In August of 1781, our Southern forces had trapped Lieutenant General Charles Cornwallis in the little Virginia coastal town of Yorktown. George Washington and the main army and the Count de Rochambeau with his French army decided to march from the Hudson Highlands to Yorktown and deliver the final blow. But Washington's war chest was completely empty, as was that of Congress. Washington determined that he needed at least $20,000 to finance the campaign. When Morris told him there were no funds and no credit available, Washington gave him a simple but eloquent order: "Send for Haym Salomon". Haym again came through, and the $20.000 was raised. Washington conducted the Yorktown campaign, which proved to be the final battle of the Revolution, thanks to Haym Salomon. (Donald Moran)

Hyam Salomon Jew. Freemason, Patriot. He dedicated his life to funding the cause for Independence along with Robert Morris.

Washington's primary network of spies was also composed of Jews. Their history in England had been so adverse for centuries, they knew precisely which side the English colonists were on.

Some background is essential.

Around the Year 1000 CE, the steel nose for plows and the steel rim for wheels were invented. For the first time in history, people could produce more than they could use, and expanded trade began. Common sense would indicate that international trade would be the obvious domain for Jews. Their religion and language surpassed geographic barriers as well as fear of strangers.

"The history of Yiddish is usually divided into four periods: Earliest Yiddish (up to 1250), Old Yiddish (1250-1500), Middle Yiddish (1500-1750), and Modern Yiddish (since 1750). Because many Jews were literate when Yiddish came into being, literary documents of each period have survived, with the exception of the earliest period." In addition, Yiddish vernacular extends beyond Rabbinic Hebrew to include common words from other languages. It is, in fact, a fusion language. (Yiddish)

Thus, trade was not territorially limited. With their newly found wealth, they became money lenders to the rich and powerful. By the year 1200, the debts to Jews by the royals and nobles of England were immense.

The Magna Charta, "The Great Charter," is a charter of rights agreed to by King John of England at Runnymede, near Windsor, on 15 June 1215. These debts were one of the principal purposes of the Magna Charta in this respect. Debts held by the Jews were forgiven. Jewish families were forced to leave and only a few traders were allowed to pass through the market towns.

These two aspects of the Magna Carta are critical to understand.

10. *If one who has borrowed from the Jews any sum, great or small, die before that loan be repaid, the debt shall not bear interest while the heir is underage, of whomsoever he may hold; and if the debt falls into our hands, we will not take anything except the principal sum contained in the bond.*

11. *And if anyone die indebted to the Jews, his wife shall have her dower and pay nothing of that debt; and if any children of the deceased are left under age, necessaries shall be provided for them in keeping with the holding of the deceased; and out of the residue the debt shall be paid, reserving, however, service due to feudal lords; in like manner let it be done toughing debts to others than Jews.*

Arguably, these rules affect England to this day.

In the year 1232 Pope Gregory IX established the Inquisition to suppress heresy against the Catholic Church. Jews were targeted. By the late 1400s, this had intensified in Spain when the Jews were forced to leave on the Days of Awe in 1492. It was the very date that Columbus sailed on his explorations replete with Jewish crew members.

There are many assertions, particularly among genealogists, that after the Inquisition, many Jews with money moved into the market towns in England with a new identity as Christians, but continued to practice Judaism secretly in their homes. The Jewish traders were able to facilitate the purchase of land and establish a new identity. It is apparent in the family research of these surnames that they all began after the Inquisition. Suddenly, a man had a huge estate with no prior history. Brewster, Howland, and Hall were a few of the names. There are no records as far as I know, just a smattering of blog posts. The blog wherein I first heard this concept no longer exists. However, I checked many of the names from the Mayflower and the ships that came between 1620 and 1629. The pattern was nonexistent or existed for only a few generations for them all.

Some moved to Holland, where there was more tolerance, but were afraid their descendants would lose their Jewish identity. Some relocated to America, beginning on the Mayflower, as separatists from the Church of England. They were particularly numerous from 1620 to 1629, settling south of Boston and on the Cape. Interestingly, these families remained quite private and had very good relationships with the Wampanoags. Many ultimately became Quakers. It goes without saying that Jews do not keep track of Jews, who leave Khal Israel regardless of the reason.

In 1630 the Winthrop Fleet landed and the mass migration of non-separatists began. The two groups were privately independent but publicly co-operative. The non-separatists settled in Boston and areas north and west. The Non-Separatists had long family lineages. As a result of the laws of primogeniture, the younger children of the great families intermarried and had no significant inheritance and no titles.

In 1654, six Jewish families moved to New Amsterdam. They had left Holland for Recife, Brazil, but were refused entrance. They, then, traveled to New Amsterdam and established the Portuguese Synagogue, which is still in existence.

It was not easy under Peter Stuyvesant, the son of a Dutch Reformed Minister, who was bigoted against everyone, who was not Dutch Reformed. Jews were no exception. He was against the Colonial Swedes, the Quakers in Queens, the English of other religions, Lutherans, and the Dutch as well. When the English took over in 1665, the Jews began to move northerly to the areas still inhabited by the Dutch.

Peter Stuyvesant was the son of a Dutch Reform minister. He was venomous to Peter Jochimsson, a Colonial Swede from Delaware, who traveled to meet with Stuyvesant. He apparently had Jochimsson killed. Stuyvesant sent the native, who had come with Jochimsson, back to Delaware with a bill for burial fees.

John Bowne, a Quaker from Flatbush, Queens, invited George Fox to speak to the crowds on his property. Stuyvesant was particularly obsessed with his opposition to the Quakers. He put Bowne in a dungeon and later sent him to Holland for trial by the Dutch West Indies Company. The Company purpose was trade, so they sent John Bowne back to America. Browne's stance remains a standard for religious freedom in America.

As the English increased in influence, the Dutch and the Jews spread out, particularly along the Hudson, forming an intense, dedicated network. For centuries, their own survival required them to keep track of the activities and allegiances of the people around them. They knew precisely who they could and could not trust. This proved to be an invaluable asset to Washington.

Secondly, Rabbi Gershom Mendes Seixas was given great honor at Washington's inauguration as one of either 13 clergymen or as representative of one of 13 states. He was apparently not a Freemason. (Oppenheimer)

The Ratification of our Constitution by the State of Rhode Island did not happen until May 29, 1790. Citizens balked at joining the union. They had to be threatened they would be a foreign country if they did not join. Our Founders were adamant about the mystical aspect of the number 13. Vermont and Kentucky were ready to join. The threat worked so Rhode Island became the 113th State.

As soon as they ratified, President George Washington made an official visit to Newport Rhode Island on August 17th, 1790. It was his first state visit. He received two letters of tribute from Moses Seixas, the brother of Gershom Seixas: One on behalf of his synagogue, the other on behalf of his lodge

Moses Seixas was also the presiding Master of Newport's King David's Lodge. On behalf of his lodge he delivered to Brother Washington a written masonic address:

ADDRESS

Of the Master, Wardens and Brethren of King David's Lodge, to George Washington, President of the United States of America.

Sir.
We the Master, Wardens, and Brethren, of King David's Lodge, in Newport, Rhode Island with Joyful hearts embrace this Opportunity, to greet you as a Brother and to hail you welcome to Rhode Island. We exult in the thought that as Masonry has always been patronised by the wise, the good, and the great; so hath it stood and ever will stand as its fixtures are on the immutable pillars of faith, hope, and Charity.

With unspeakable pleasure we Gratulate you as filling the Presidential Chair with the applause of a numerous and enlightened people, whilst, at the same time, we felicitate ourselves in the honour done the Brotherhood by your many exemplary Virtues and emanations of Goodness proceeding from a heart worthy of possessing the Ancient Mysteries of our craft; being persuaded that the wisdom and Grace with which heaven has endowed you, will ever square all your thoughts, words, and actions by the eternal Laws of honour, equity, and truth, so as to promote the advancement of all good works; your own happiness, and that of mankind.

Permit us then Illustrious Brother cordially to Salute you with Three times Three and to add your fervent supplications that the Sovereign Architect of the Universe may always encompass you with his holy protection

---

*Washington's response to his Masonic brotherhood To the Masons of King David's Lodge, **Newport, Rhode Island***

[Newport, R.I., 18 August 1790]

Gentlemen,

I receive the welcome which you give me to Rhode-Island with pleasure—and I acknowledge my obligations for the flattering expressions of regard contained in your address1 with grateful sincerity.

Being persuaded that a just application of the principles, on which the masonic fraternity is founded, must be promotive of private virtue and public prosperity, I shall always be happy to advance the interests of the Society, and to be considered by them a deserving Brother.2

My best wishes, Gentlemen, are offered for your individual happiness.

Go: Washington

Note that Washington wrote his reply the next day. He was speaking to his own brother and notably, this was his first statement to any Lodge. Moses Seixas was among thirteen Jewish members of the Lodge and would later serve as Grand Master of the Grand Lodge of Rhode Island and Providence Plantations in 1802 until his death in 1809.

King David's Lodge was chartered in 1778 by the Grand Lodge of New York. Moses Michael Hays (1739–1805) served as its first Master. An important banker in Boston, Hays was one of the first, if not the first, American to receive the degrees of what would become known as the Scottish Rite of Freemasonry. He served as the Grand Master of the Grand Lodge of Masons in Massachusetts between 1788 and 1792.

Two months after Washington's visit, King David's Lodge merged into St. John's Lodge on October 19. St. John's Lodge helped form the Grand Lodge of Rhode Island and Providence Plantations in 1791 and continues to work in Newport to this very day.

Furthermore, Moses Seixas, as an official of Touro Synagogue, wrote an entirely different message. He became a Rabbi subsequently.Sir,

Permit the children of the stock of Abraham to approach you with the most cordial affection and esteem for your person and merits — and to join with our fellow citizens in welcoming you to NewPort.

With pleasure we reflect on those days — those days of difficulty, and danger, when the God of Israel, who delivered David from the peril of the sword, — shielded Your head in the day of battle: — and we rejoice to think, that the same Spirit, who rested in the Bosom of the greatly beloved Daniel enabling him to preside over the Provinces of the Babylonish Empire, rests and ever will rest, upon you, enabling you to discharge the arduous duties of Chief Magistrate in these States. Deprived as we heretofore have been of the invaluable rights of free Citizens, we now with a deep sense of gratitude to the Almighty disposer of all events behold a Government, erected by the Majesty of the People — a Government, which to bigotry gives no sanction, to persecution no assistance — but generously affording to all Liberty of conscience, and immunities of Citizenship: — deeming every one, of whatever Nation, tongue, or language equal parts of the great governmental

Machine: — This so ample and extensive Federal Union whose basis is Philanthropy, Mutual confidence and Public Virtue, we cannot but acknowledge to be the work of the Great God, who ruleth in the Armies of Heaven, and among the Inhabitants of the Earth, doing whatever seemeth him good.

For all these Blessings of civil and religious liberty which we enjoy under an equal benign administration, we desire to send up our thanks to the Ancient of Days, the great preserver of Men — beseeching him, that the Angel who conducted our forefathers through the wilderness into the promised Land, may graciously conduct you through all the difficulties and dangers of this mortal life: — And, when, like Joshua full of days and full of honour, you are gathered to your Fathers, may you be admitted into the Heavenly Paradise to partake of the water of life, and the tree of immortality.

Done and Signed
by order of the Hebrew Congregation in NewPort, Rhode Island
Moses Seixas, Warden
August 17th 1790

Response to Touro Synagogue by President George Washington

President Washington took this task extremely carefully. It took four days of dedicated thought. On August 21st, 1790, President George Washington responded with a letter to Moses Seixas and the Hebrew congregation of Newport, Rhode Island that expressed hope that the newly formed United States would accord respect and tolerance to all of its citizens. Washington's response promised not only tolerance but full liberty of conscience to all, regardless of background and religious beliefs.

Gentlemen

While I receive, with much satisfaction, your Address replete with expressions of affection and esteem; I rejoice in the opportunity of assuring you, that I shall always retain a grateful remembrance of the cordial welcome I experienced in my visit to Newport, from all classes of Citizens.

The reflection on the days of difficulty and danger which are past is rendered the more sweet, from a consciousness that they are succeeded by days of uncommon prosperity and security. If we have wisdom to make the best use of the advantages with which we are now favored, we cannot fail, under the just administration of a good Government, to become a great and happy people.

Citizens of the United States of America have a right to applaud themselves for having given to mankind examples of an enlarged and liberal policy: a policy worthy of imitation. All possess alike liberty of conscience and immunities of citizenship. It is now no more that toleration is spoken of, as if it was by the indulgence of one class of people, that another enjoyed the exercise of their inherent natural rights. For happily the Government of the United States, which gives to bigotry no sanction, to persecution no assistance requires only that they who live under its protection should demean themselves as good citizens, in giving it on all occasions their effectual support.

It would be inconsistent with the frankness of my character not to avow that I am pleased with your favorable opinion of my Administration, and fervent wishes for my felicity. May the children of the Stock of Abraham, who dwell in this land, continue to merit and enjoy the goodwill of the other Inhabitants; while every one shall sit in safety under his own vine and fig tree, and there shall be none to make him afraid. May the father of all mercies scatter light and not darkness in our paths, and make us all in our several vocations useful here, and in his own due time and way everlastingly happy.

The singular fact stands out that in Newport the Jewish Master of the Masonic Lodge delivered, on behalf of his lodge, the first Masonic address to Washington as President, at the same time that he delivered his address on behalf of his congregation. They are totally different in tone and substance

In consideration of what has been said herein shows the probability of Jews having been the first to introduce Masonry into the Colonies, and that the period of their greatest activity as Masons in the early history of the Republic was between 1780 and 1810. The Jews described in this paper were men of parts and character and distinguished in the early American annals of their people. Their connection with the Order was no doubt of benefit to their coreligionists, as it was to themselves, and brought them into relations with many not of their race, prominent in the official and civil life of the country, who were also members of the fraternity. Nearly all were members of the Hebrew congregations in the cities where they resided.

Though it is not maintained that because they were Masons they arranged during 1790 for the addresses of their various congregations to Washington, yet the facts presented herein may very well be considered in support of a theory that their connection with the Order made them feel doubly desirous to join in the welcome to the head of the nation, who like themselves was a Mason.

Pres. Washington would reply to the brothers of King David's Lodge after extremely careful consideration. He wrote on August 22nd.

Jews apparently introduced Freemasonry to America before Benjamin Franklin. Freemasonry was the vehicle wherein the finely educated Jewish leaders could interact with highly educated leaders of other religions on the same positive, purposeful level. Samuel Oppenheim has written a mind-opening book "The Jews and Masonry in the United States before 1810." The early Jews came in at a highly functional level. This a far different story than those, who were oppressed, immigrating more than a century later. to Ellis Island. When John Quincy Adams became our sixth president, he was part of a movement against Freemasons. Public attitude changed along with the strong presence of Masonic leadership decreasing. Freemasons are dedicated to being the best men they can be. They do not lead by dominance, but by demonstrating their highest values in action. Opposition comes from judgments by those outside their brotherhood.

Chapter 14 | The Constitution

Our Constitution is our guiding light, the common factor for our government and our lives. It is not connected to a person, place, or thing. It embodies a set of unifying principles, rather than bringing separation or division, a context for the well-being for all of us.

Benjamin Franklin, along with two other Grand Masons, George Washington, and John Rutledge, carefully planned our Constitution Convention. They wanted a Federal Government organized according to the ancient teachings they knew so well. They did want a debate. They did not want changes. They announced terms, but never divulged what they meant. They carefully crafted the document in the Committee of Detail led by John Rutledge Benjamin Franklin felt passionately about achieving that goal, which embodies the Eye of Illumination.

The Structure of Our Constitution

Definition of Constitution in Noah Webster's Dictionary of 1826.

CONSTITUTION, noun

1. *The act of constituting, enacting, establishing, or appointing.*

2. *The state of being; that form of being or peculiar structure and connection of parts which makes or characterizes a system or body. Hence the particular frame or temperament of the human body is called its Constitution We speak of a robust or feeble Constitution; a cold, phlegmatic, sanguine or irritable Constitution We speak of the Constitution of the air, or other substance; the Constitution of the solar system; the Constitution of things.*

3. *The frame or temper of mind, affections or passions.*

4. *The established form of government in a state, kingdom or country; a system of fundamental rules, principles and ordinances for the government of a state or nation. In free states, the Constitution is paramount to the statutes or laws enacted by the legislature, limiting and controlling its power; and in the United States, the legislature is created, and its powers designated, by the Constitution*

5. *A particular law, ordinance, or regulation, made by the authority of any superior, civil or ecclesiastical; as the Constitutions of Justinian and his successors.*

6. *A system of fundamental principles for the government of rational and social beings. The New Testament is the moral Constitution of modern society.*

Webster's definition was written thirty years after our Constitutional Convention and ratification. His definitions reflect our constitution in action. Franklin and others slid the term Framework into the terminology without comments. The term was most assuredly a reference to Freemasonry being sourced by the Sacred Order of the Stone Masons.

The Federal Convention of 1787: The Constitutional Convention

When you study the creation of our Great Seal, three people emerge who were dedicated to forming a government aligned with deep spiritual patterns. Though designed by people involved in heraldry, these leaders were committed to ancient patterns, symbols, and numbers. These three men were George Washington, Benjamin Franklin, and John Rutledge. It appears they were the guiding force in calling the convention. The objective was stated to be amending the Articles of Confederation. In reality, that was near to impossible. However, under that guise, it would be possible to obtain representation from all of the states. Respect, thus participation, came from having the leader be George Washington.

Once you see the patterns, their actions make sense within that context. You will not find those patterns by studying the words. In fact, they jumbled the content of the document to keep the ancient wisdom intact.

The Federal Convention, now known as the Constitutional Convention, began on May 25, 1787. It took weeks to reach a quorum of seven states. George Washington was elected president of the convention. The convention was tasked to revise the Continental Constitution since several states would never agree to a new centralized government.

Washington's direction, however, ensured that the convention functioned as a continuation of The Committee of the Whole. This procedure facilitated topical debate and discussion before they came to a vote. This vital interchange would have otherwise been limited by the formality of voting procedure. The point was to allow free debate without those constraints.

The American Continental Congress previously used a committee of the whole concept "to take into consideration the state of America. This was, in fact, the problem. There were thirteen states, plus "the state of America." There was no strong, centralized government.

This is the definition of a committee of the whole from Wikipedia. A committee of the whole is a meeting of a deliberative assembly according to modified procedural rules based on those of a committee. The committee includes all members of the assembly, except that some 0officers may be replaced. As with other committees, the activities of a committee of the whole are limited to considering and making recommendations on matters that the assembly has referred to; it cannot take up other matters, nor can it vote directly on the assembly's business. The purpose of a committee of the whole is to relax the usual limits on debate, allowing a more open exchange of views without the urgency of a final vote. Debates in a committee of the whole may be recorded, but are often excluded from the assembly's minutes. After debating, the committee submits its conclusions to the assembly (that is, to itself) and business continues according to the normal rules. (Committee of the Whole)

This system enabled the establishment of many ad hoc committees. Most of all, there could be secrecy until the final votes. I assert there was still secrecy throughout the whole convention and ratification process. By every indication, Franklin, Washington, and Rutledge were totally dedicated to their carefully constructed plan. The Committee of the Whole procedure enabled every topic to be introduced and debated without voting. They could also add elements that had not been introduced. There would be ample discussion, but, ultimately, the three Grand Framers retained control of the outcome.

There were more than fourteen Masons in this convention. The lists vary because they were an oral tradition and did not keep good records. Five were possibly Grand Masters, including Franklin. As far as we know, they never met as a group of delegates. They never voted as a block, in fact, they had several heated arguments. They all, however, would all have recognized the patterns within the Framework, whether stated or not. Numbers and patterns mattered at the core of their teachings. Ideas varied, patterns were known.

In July, a Grand Committee formed, which included Elbridge Gerry, Oliver Ellsworth, Robert Yates, William Paterson, Gunning Bedford, Jr., George Mason, William Davie, John Rutledge, Abraham Baldwin, and Benjamin Franklin. In its report to the Convention on July 5, they offered a compromise, allowing the work to form the Constitution to begin.

Chapter 15 | The Committee of Detail

It was but one line in Madison's notes for July 24, 1787: "On a ballot for a Committee to report a Constitution conformable to the Resolutions passed by the Convention, the members chosen were Mr. Rutlidge, Mr. Randolph, Mr. Ghorum, Mr. Elseworth, Mr. Wilson."

It is significant that neither Madison, who wrote the Virginia Plan, nor Paterson, who wrote the New Jersey Plan, were chosen. Considerable time had been spent in the convention debating the two plans. The delegates did not want further debate. This was a popular vote and the delegates wanted results. They wanted a constitution. Madison, who kept prodigious notes, thought they were merely putting the ideas in order.

George Washington had written in his diary that the delegates needed to "draw into method and form the several matters which had been agreed twas time to start collecting the various parts, what the delegates called "resolves" (and twenty-three had been passed to this point), along with other proposals and amendments, into some kind of order." This discretely introduces the framework.

Beginning on July 27, these five men crafted our government with Franklin and Washington selecting them and privately advising them. This was the significant proceeding in the convention. They constructed and wrote our constitution.

Historian David Stewart calls the committee's work "the most important single undertaking of the summer and that it required "precision where the agreement was clear, equivocation where it had been elusive." He also notes that "missing parts would have to be drafted, ambiguities dispelled, the whole thing knitted into a coherent document," and that "from one perspective, their draft was a remarkable cut-and-paste job" because it copied provisions from the Articles of Confederation, the convention resolutions, and even Charles Pinckney's plan. However, Stewart argues that they did much more, they added provisions that the convention never discussed, they changed critical agreements that the delegates had already approved. Spurred by Rutledge, they reconvened the powers of the national government, redefined the powers of the states, and adopted fresh concessions on that most explosive issue, slavery. It is not too much to say that Rutledge and his committee hijacked the Constitution. Then, they then remade it. (Wikipedia Contributors: Committee of Detail)

This paragraph succinctly describes the work of the Committee of Detail. There were no notes taken. My observation is that Stewart recognized the content, but missed the pattern of the Framework, which was the basis for this entire document. Rather than "Cut and Paste," it was superbly crafted with wisdom of the highest order.

The selection of members of this committee was of strategic importance to Franklin, Washington and Rutledge. We can be sure that Franklin and Washington let their choices be known quietly, but clearly. There is no other likelihood that Rutledge would have received the most votes. John Rutledge, who received the most votes, became Chairman. As a Grand Master, Rutledge had the highest Masonic rank of all five delegates. He worked with Franklin to create this convention. They convinced Washington to join them in the endeavour. Rutledge was considered preeminent, as was Madison, in his knowledge of constitutions throughout history.

Randolph and Ellsworth were also Masons, who had the correct capabilities and were from large states. Randolph, Wilson and Ellsworth were likewise outstanding lawyers with vast expertise in constitutions.

Randolph, also a Grand Mason, and closely connected to Washington, wrote the second, the final draft. He would have known the plan.

Ellsworth was a Mason with a great independent mind. In the final consideration, he made the most significant stance.

James Wilson was a genius with originality. He also had a mentor of great significance, John Dickenson. He had a talent for bringing people together. In addition, he was from Pennsylvania as was Franklin, who carefully assessed him over the other state delegates. He wrote the first draft.

Second to Washington, Gorham had the most prestigious position in the convention as leader of the Committee of the Whole. Gorham offered a different perspective. He had been the President of the Assembly under the Articles of Confederation the preceding year. Being from Massachusetts he understood Shay's uprising very well. Thus he knew the problems of having a weak central government, particularly with respect to taxation and having an army. Gorham had been president of the "Committee of the Whole," as the meetings in the convention were formed. This procedure allowed greater flexibility and discussion than the rules of order for meeting in the Convention as a Whole.

All five had perfect attendance records in the convention.

The Committee of Detail operated within the Committee of the Whole. The point of operating within the Committee of Whole is that it was not obligatory. The Committee added and omitted ideas at their own will. They quoted from a wide variety of sources to attain agreement. However, they did not identify their own format. Thus, these five strategically important delegates designed our constitution. However, no one seems to have known there was a carefully crafted plan for the Constitution and for our government. The Constitution is a Framework. The design is geometric and integrated. Each specific use determines the context, be it scientific, corporate, personal, or mystical. I understood the format because I applied our Constitution as the context. Then I chose each element to fit the Framework. In my work, I identified the primary components related to the context and proceeded to organize those elements. The context for our Constitution was ideal for me since I already knew it well and was familiar with the Tree of Life as an organizing system. Ultimately, the purpose of this book is to reveal the significance of the words Framework and Framers.

In the process, however, it became obvious that while historians have looked at the ideas in countless ways, the relationships are not considered in depth. The bonds provide great insight as to the entire history.

Beginning on July 27th these five men literally crafted our government.

Rutledge and Randolph may very well have utilized the Tree of Life from King Solomon as the format or "Framework" as the blueprint for the government. The design clearly shows three pillars of government.

"The tree" is an organizing principle, a relationship model, for any set of data. The design is not a mystical system in itself. It is generally known as a mystical system, but it is the data set, not the design, that is Jewish and spiritual. It was also passed down from the ancient masters, Hermes, Pythagoras and Euclid. Interestingly, the pathway system used for Kabbalah is not appropriate for an organizational, mathematical or technical system. They use two distinctly different pathways and focus on the Lightning path from God.

Purpose

Randolph's statement in the preamble of the Committee's report is often cited as evidence for the proposition that the Constitution was deliberately written to be broad and flexible to accommodate social or technological change over time:

In the draught of a fundamental constitution, two things deserve attention:

1. *To insert essential principles only; lest the operations of government should be clogged by rendering those provisions permanent and unalterable, which ought to be accommodated to times and events:*

2. *To use simple and precise language, and general propositions, according to the example of the constitutions of the several states, the decision to use "simple and precise language, and general propositions," such that the Constitution could "be accommodated to times and events," is often cited as the "genius" of the Constitutional framers, and is one of the main arguments for the Living Constitution framework. Wikipedia*

The Committee of Detail was created to write the Constitution. Because all these ideas had been discussed and voted upon in the Committee of the Whole, led by Nathaniel Gorham, nothing was obligatory. All had been active and involved. Not one of them had a passionate advocate for any aspect. They were all knowledgeable and capable of compromise as well as not divulging anything that happened in the committee. Franklin and Washington were very deliberate in the group they appointed for this task. There were no discussions.

Unlike other quests to understand the history of our Constitution, this book began with knowing the Framework. One assumed Madison was the most significant. He was clearly not. It became obvious his notes were about his issues. He loved the clash of debate on ideas. There was no understanding there is an organizing system. Actually, he made scant notice of the Committee of Detail and he was rather dismissive of the Committee of Five as he called it. It is quite probable that had he known this was such a significant committee, he would have been making demands for himself rather than putting his notes in order.

Professor William Eward made this observation, which becomes obvious to all who investigate the Committee of Detail or the Framework itself. *"Madison's Notes contain a lengthy gap, encompassing ten days at the end of July and the beginning of August. During this time the Convention stood adjourned while the Committee of Detail re-worked the miscellaneous Convention resolutions into a single document. The gap itself is well known; but its significance, in my view, has been underestimated. The Committee is typically treated in a page or two, as an interlude between the more dramatic events on either side. My first claim is that this widespread view is a mistake. This ten-day gap in Madison's Notes was arguably the most creative period of* constitutional drafting of the entire summer. Certainly, day for day, it was the most intensive. Far from being a mere interlude, at least in certain respects, and for certain fundamental issues, it was the main event. " (Evard)

To repeat: "It was the main event."

Ewald continues: "The Committee of Detail offers a striking illustration of these points, and of the way in which the seemingly mundane details of archival research and textual editing can influence our understanding of the drafting of the Constitution."

Ewald then discusses the records of the Committee. A haphazard history of retaining the few documents are then discussed *At this stage, a warning is in season. It is important not to leap from these facts to a tempting and obvious conclusion. Almost all of the early drafts of the Constitution are in Wilson's hand. Even the Randolph draft contains Wilson's check marks.He was a powerful member of the Convention, a skilled legislative draftsman, and possessed remarkable energy. Many historians have inferred that he must have utterly dominated the proceedings: in Brant's phrase, that it was a Committee of "Wilson and four others." But that is too hasty. In the first place, from the fact that most of the surviving documents are in Wilson's hand, nothing whatsoever can be inferred; and indeed, many provisions that he strongly and consistently opposed appear for the first time in his drafts. It was Rutledge, not Wilson, who ultimately presented the* Committee's report to the Convention; and as we shall see, on many issues, Wilson, far from being dominant, appears to have been outflanked by Rutledge and the others. But there is a further point. Anybody who has attempted to work with the manuscripts quickly comes to recognize Randolph's legible but uneven scrawl and to dread the wild and idiosyncratic jottings of Rutledge. Wilson, in contrast, displays excellent penmanship. He wrote an elegant cursive: quite possibly, for this reason, he was chosen as the Committee amanuensis."(Evard)

In the Reading List, the link to Eward's paper on the Committee is included. The issues here are complex and require careful analysis.

J. E. Pfander reviewed William Ewald's paper, "The Committee of Detail"

"Ewald begins his analysis of the Committee's work by situating it as one of three important acts in the

Constitution's development. Act I precedes the Committee's appointment in late July 1787; it includes the initial introduction of the Virginia Plan, the Convention's deliberations on that plan in Committee of the Whole, and the eventual decision to commit the resolutions in that plan, as amended, to the Committee of Detail for elaboration. Act III includes the Convention's work following the Committee of Detail's report in early August 1787. In that piece of the drama, delegates worked through the text line by line, suggesting changes and adding new provisions. Ewald observes that historians, drawing on Madison's notes, devote most of their attention to Acts I and III.

They virtually ignore Act II, the interlude during which the convention adjourned to let the Committee of Detail hash out particulars. Ewald sets out to reclaim the importance of the Committee's work and to highlight its contributions to the document."

Ewald proceeds with an excellent review of the Committee of Detail. However, he does not address the quest regarding the Framework itself.

It is significant that neither James Madison, who wrote the Virginia Plan, nor William Paterson, who wrote the New Jersey Plan, were chosen. Neither were Alexander Hamilton, who wrote the British Plan, or Charles Pinckney, who also designed a' plan, or Roger Sherman, who wrote the Connecticut Compromise. It is apparent that Washington, Franklin, and Rutledge were dedicated to the members chosen to be on this committee. With Rutledge at the helm, they wanted all the members to be amenable to their plan, knowingly or not.

That Madison was not selected is particularly interesting. He studied at the College of New Jersey, which became Princeton. He spent a fifth year studying with John Witherspoon, President of the college, who had the most extensive library in America. Madison studied all the ancient masters. His specialty was Hebrew. He was also one of the greatest scholars of various European Constitutions.

Washington, Franklin, and Rutledge, the three most notable Masons in the Convention, did not want to duplicate any aspects of previous plans or Constitutions. They wanted the Albany Plan and the Iroquois Constitution. They did not want further debate. This was a popular vote, and the delegates wanted results. They wanted a Constitution.

When studying this Committee, a new alliance becomes quite evident. Edmund Randolph dominates this committee. He is a Grand Mason from Washington's Lodge. Randolph is to Washington as Rutledge is to Franklin. Rutledge's comments on Randolph's Draft is the basic constitution. These four men were the core of writing our constitution right in the open for everyone to see. Ellsworth and Wilson were chosen for their independent, original thinking. In today's terms, they were both geniuses, geniuses without alliances and without dedication to specific concepts. Gorham, as president of the Committee of the Whole, gave credence to the committee.

The constitution establishes the system of Governance itself. There is a framework. This committee felt that a Bill of rights was an issue for each state. It was Madison who wrote the nine proposals for the Bill of Rights. Then he added a tenth.

One wonders how Franklin, Washington, and Rutledge devised the Bill of Rights and thus all the amendments in the same format as an addition to our Constitution. These were personal factors, not components of governance.

They expected these to be issues for each state. Then, in the ensuing debate to ratify the Constitution, Madison offered a set of nine. This was a popular idea nd James WIlson had proposed a set during the Committee of Detail.

The rights and amendments were properly a distinct and separate set. Who had that Eureka moment? Just add one right and make it aligned to the Framework. I think it was Franklin, who may well have been the functional Framer the whole time, while never showing his hand.

John Rutledge opened their meetings by acknowledging the Great Law of the Iroquois, the founding Constitution of the Haudenosaunee in Confederacy. Twenty years before, He attended meetings with the Iroquois when the colonists were negotiating with the Native Americans regarding the Stamp Act of the English. He knew the principles of their confederation, the Tree of Peace, and the significance of circles within their culture. The Great Law of the Iroquois is based on the sovereignty of the people, peace, and unity. "A great empire is being created so it must be firmly rooted in American soil." (Grinde)

Franklin and His protegee, John Rutledge, had put everything in place after seeing the debacle of the Great Seal, which overruled all their spiritual precepts. Franklin convinced Washington to join them. These three men were united in establishing a spiritual framework based on ancient wisdom. Secrecy was a mandate. This team was comprised of the best minds to develop the constitution without political bias. Gorham provided the stature. Rutledge as leader could lead everything into their ancient order and pattern without discussion. He knew it. He put it in place without debate.

Commentaries on Members of the Committee of Detail

John Rutledge

John Rutledge, who received the most votes, became Chairman of the Committee of Detail. Please note that John Rutledge was also chosen on the Third Committee to design the Great Seal, which ultimately is quite significant.

John Rutledge, elder brother of Edward Rutledge, signer of the Declaration of Independence, was born into a large family near Charleston, South Carolina, in 1739. He received his early education from his father, an Irish immigrant and physician. Dr. John Rutledge, Sr. died in 1850 leaving his widow with seven children. Fortunately, John Sr. had great respect as the first doctor in that area. He was very close friends with both Jefferson and Washington. Also importantly, his widow, Sarah Hext, had noteworthy lineage.

Historian Flanders waxed ecstatic for almost two pages as to her unparalleled qualities. "All accounts concur in her praise. Nature bestowed upon her liberal endowments, and her gifts were improved and cultivated by education. She was distinguished by fortitude and wisdom." Flanders tells an anecdote that on the day Rutledge enrolled in the Bar upon returning from London and Middle Temple "he threw what money he had into his mother's lap that it might be said he had begun life without a guinea in his pocket." (Flanders)

To be widowed at age 26 and raise two sons to be outstanding leaders in our Revolution and Constitution is noteworthy.

John Rutledge was educated at the Middle Temple in London. As we noted earlier Rutledge became a Masonic Grand Master while still in the London Lodge. When there he met Franklin and apparently became his Protégée. His designation of this committee is one of the leading indicators that Franklin was leading this entire operation.

His viable loyalty to Franklin is a major component in his life. He became very devoted to Franklin when he was a Middle Temple and became an attorney and a Grand Mason. He continued during his years with Franklin and Iroquois.

His private connection to one of the heraldists, William Barton, in the Third Committee made a great impact on Barton so that no diagrams of the final description were made. In the Committee of Detail, the main event of the Constitutional Convention, he engineered the Framework as well as the components as determined with Washington and Franklin. He precisely followed Franklin's modus operandi. He was right there with Franklin, while never violating their personal relationship. He was in the center of all the action, but he kept his privacy and that of Franklin foremost.

"On the whole, Sir, I cannot help expressing a wish that every member of the convention who may still have objection to it, would with me, on this occasion, doubt a little of his own infallibility, and to make manifest our unanimity, put his name to this instrument" Rutledge signed the Constitution and heartedly recommended it to his constituents.

Franklin died on April 17, 1790. Rutledge's bond of 30 years with Franklin ended. There was no replacement possible. Then, on July 6, 1792, his wife, Elizabeth, died. They had been married for 30 years as well. His world turned upside down as our new government began. He was no longer decisive and eloquent.

He was appointed to be the Second Chief Justice when John Jay resigned. Rutledge served but was not confirmed. It can be assumed that he had aged.

QUOTES

"So long as we may have an independent Judiciary, the great interests of the people will be safe. By doing good with his money, a man, as it were, stamps the image of God upon it, and makes it pass current for the merchandise of heaven."

"By doing good with his money, a man, as it were, stamps the image of God upon it, and makes it pass current for the merchandise of heaven"

"I consent, Sirr, to this Constitution because I expect no better and because the opinions I have had of its errors I sacrifice to the public good. I have never whispered a syllable of them abroad. Within these walls they were borne and here they will die... (Flanders)

Edmund Randolph

First of all, let us consider the strong Masonic relationship between Randolph and Washington. After moving to Mount Vernon, Washington began the transfer of his Masonic membership from the Fredericksburg Lodge No.4 to Alexandria Lodge No.39. Washington announced his intention to attend the St.John's day meeting. Signed:

"Mount Vernon, June 19, 1784" Washington was made an honorary member that day.

The Lodge applied for a new Charter with Washington as Charter Master. On April 28, 1788, the then Grand Master Edmund Randolph signed a charter for Alexandria Lodge No. 22, Naming, George Washington and others. Since this included the time period for our Constitutional Convention, their bond was uniquely strong.

Thus, Franklin, Washington, Rutledge, and Randolph were all Grand Masons with highly significant bonds as brothers. The Committee of Detail was the dedicated focus for all four men. They did not explain their bonds or their purpose. They announced nothing, but installed the Framework and all the components. Edmund's father, John Randolph, remained Loyal to the King, forever dividing the two men. Peyton Randolph, Edmund's uncle, was a colonial leader, who had been the President of First Continental Congress. He was considered by many to be the most prominent leader of his generation. Since he was childless, Edmund became the son he never had as well as his heir.

Young Edmund sided with his uncle and quickly signed up for the Continental Army. He was immediately appointed as an aide-de-camp to General Washington, a family friend.

Early into his army service, Edmund's uncle, Peyton, passed away. He had been considered the most probable man to be President. Now the patriarch of the Randolph family, Edmund returned home to take care of his uncle's will.

Randolph spent most of the next decade in private law practice, though he did sit for three years in the Continental Congress.

What is interesting about Randolph is, despite his large amount of participation in creating the Constitution, he refused to sign the document upon its completion. He had several fears about the new government, most notably the ability of the Supreme Court to override the laws of the States.

Because he was still Governor, Randolph was responsible for calling together and sitting as chairman of the Virginia Ratifying Convention. He oversaw a hotly contested debate and, along the way, changed his mind about the document and decided to support it. This change assisted in swaying the vote to approve ratification.

As a delegate from Virginia for the Constitutional Convention, he introduced the Virginia Plan as a foundation for a new government for the country. Edmund Randolph argued against the importation of slaves and was in favor of the new government having a strong central government. He also supported a plan that had three chief executives from different areas of the country. The Virginia Plan also suggested two houses, wherein both of these houses delegates were picked based on the state population. Edmund Randolph additionally suggested and was supported with unanimous approval by the Constitutional Convention's delegates, that having a national judiciary branch should be necessary. Article III of the United States Constitution created the federal court system, which did not exist under the Articles of Confederation.

"The general object was to produce a cure for the evils under which the United States labored; that in tracing these evils to their origins, every man had found it in the turbulence and follies of democracy."

"A people who mean to continue free must be prepared to meet danger in person; not rely upon the fallacious protection of mercenary armies."

Oliver Ellsworth

Oliver Ellsworth was the deal maker who saved our Constitution and our Republic from the brink of failure during the convention. He was critical in the Ratification. As first leader of the Senate he pushed for adoption of Hamilton's proposals. One can only wish he had served in Congress longer.

During the Committee of Detail, Oliver Ellsworth renewed a term from our Declaration of Independence, namely "The United States." He replaced the term "National" with the term "United." He solidified this in our national consciousness forevermore. Gouvenor Morris added "of America."

His grandfather had come to the colonies as a tavern keeper. In those days, our money changers were the tavern keeps, the blacksmiths and the millers. Oliver's parents had high hopes that he would become a minister.

He transferred from Yale after two years to the College of New Jersey, which became Princeton. There, the President of the university was Dr. Findley, a minister. Ellsworth was far more interested in College policies than in religion. He was dedicated to Bacon's Abridgement and to Jacobs' Law Dictionary.

Ellsworth was a founding member of St. John's Lodge in Princeton, New Jersey. The following letter may give an indication of the status of Ellsworth as a Mason.

> PRINCE TOWN NEW JERSEY Sept. 24th 1765.
> To JEREMIAH GRIDLEY Esqr.
> Right Worshipful.
>
> Whereas we the Subscribers being desirous of being formed into a regular and lawful Lodge, do now make Application to you for a Warrant to Constitute the same, also to appoint the first Master which I nominate Richard Stockton of the said Place ; Pray let it be sent by the bearer of this, safely enclosed, and the said bearer will Satisfy you for the same.
>
> NB : let it be nominated for St. Johns. Pray Sir, (if you can conveniently), empower us to give Warrants for the Constituting ELSWORTH, of Lodges RICHARD STOCKTON, OLIVER SOVEREIGN SYBRANDT, SOLOMON KELLOGG, AUGUSTUS DIGGENS, THEODRICK ROMEYN, BENJAMIN HEINS

Jeremiah Gridley served as "Grand Master of the Masons in North America" around the 1760s From Proceedings, Page I-99, after 10/25/1765 Quarterly Communication. Richard Stockton, the signer of the Declaration of Independence, was the son of John Stockton, one of the founders of Princeton University.

After graduation, he continued religious study, but ultimately, his father agreed that Oliver could proceed in a career in the law. It was quite some time before he procured clients, although he went to court as an observer daily.

During this period, he decided the best method was to study one topic at a time until he mastered it. Ultimately, this became his modus operandi. He would determine the core component of every issue. He would relentlessly focus on that one issue. It was said that "Ellsworth had great tact, great power of logic, great energy and earnestness of elocution. He stood at the head of the Connecticut Bar." (Flanders - p64)

Flanders went on to say "He had the penetration, the powers of discernment and analysis that enabled him to unfold with precision and perspicacity the difficulties of a question, to strip sophistry of its disguises, and maintain the view he wished to enforce" (Flanders p64)

The superlatives continue for pages. When reading them as a set, a solid picture of his unique outlook and capabilities emerges. Franklin, Washington and Rutledge would have valued his focus on excellence while maintaining his personal point of view on all things. He had no alliances, associations or commitments that would deter him from his personal best view.

During debate on the Great Compromise, Ellsworth proposed that the basis of representation in the Legislative Branch remain by state, as under the Articles of Confederation. He was active in the concept that one house would be based on population and the other, by equal representation of all states. The Connecticut Compromise is, arguably, the critical issue in the formation of our government. It became the issue wherein a federal government would be enacted. Otherwise, things would remain in the Articles of Confederation and states rights. The holdouts were North and South Carolina and, most importantly, Georgia. If the new Constitution failed, the states would once again be under British rule and separated. It was a stalemate.

Ellsworth was the deal maker. He agreed to support slavery issues to the states. This meant that slavery was not a Federal Constitutional issue. He kept his word. He left the convention without voting, which indicates the personal stress this was for him.

This was the strategic item in the entire convention and, then, in the ratification. Without a federal system, the British would have undoubtedly prevailed in the War of 1812. So Ellsworth understanding that the government of these United States could not have begun with slavery as a Federal issue

"All good men wish the entire abolition of slavery, as soon as it can take place with safety to the public, and for the lasting good of the present wretched race of slaves. The only possible step that could be taken towards it by the convention was to fix a period after which they should not be imported." (Ellsworth,O p163)

Thus, his stance on slavery was in his determination, a step in the process toward "lasing good." It also implies the commonly held idea in that era wherein slaves could not be educated.

The huge step forward was that every freeman have the right to vote. Every freeman soldier would vote. This was

a major step forward in history. There were no requirements for property or status or religion.

He also was adamant concerning Judicial review rather than Legislative review.

His work indicates always a commitment to a strong Federal Government. That commitment appears to be the defining characteristic of all five members of this committee. By establishing the Committee of the Whole, they could create our constitution based on their decisions. In the Committee of the Whole, aspects were debated. However, nothing was obligatory. In fact, the committee added aspects they thought important..

In the new government Ellsworth had a position that can be recognized as second only to that of Washington. He was the first in the role that became the Senate Majority Leader. He deftly engineered passage of all Hamilton's proposals. He led with dedication, intelligence and critical knowledge of our constitution itself. .

Ellsworth was the main author of the Judiciary Act of 1789, which established the structure and jurisdiction of the federal court system and created the position of Attorney General. Ellsworth's specification in Section 25 of Article III gave the federal government its only effective authority over state government at the time.

He was a master politician. Had he continued for a second term and possibly more, the spirit of the constitution would have had sound roots. Instead, we had factionalism, while he went on the serve in ways that had no endurable impact.

Interestingly, in his retirement, he became focused on theology. It came full circle.

According to his biographer, when asked about Washington concerning a eulogy, Ellsworth said that Washington had little influence on the constitution itself, Ellsworth said that he was on a committee of five that actually wrote the constitution. (Jayne) He did, in fact, write the last draft. In that statement, he clearly means all five were partners in this magnificent achievement.

Oliver Ellsworth could, rightfully, be recognized as The Master of Our Constitution. He prioritized the critical matters and followed them through to completion.

"Liberty is a word, which, according as it is used, comprehends the most good and the most evil of any in the World. Justly understood, it is sacred next to those which we appropriate in divine adoration, but in the mouths of some, it means anything, which enervates a necessary government, excite a jealousy of the rulers, who are our own choice, and keep society in confusion for want of a power sufficiently concentrated to promote good."

"The right of the judges to inflict punishment gives him both power and opportunity to oppress the innocent: yet none but crazy men will from thence determine that it is best to have neither a legislature nor judges."

"The charge of being ambiguous and indefinite may be brought against every human composition, and necessarily arises from the imperfection of language. Perhaps no two men will express the same sentiment in the same manner and by the same words; neither do they connect precisely the same ideas with the same words."

"The powers of congress must be defined, but their means must be adequate to the purposes of their constitution. It is possible there may be abuses and misapplications; still, it is better to hazard something than to hazard at all."

"All good men wish the entire abolition of slavery, as soon as it can take place with safety to the public, and for the lasting good of the present wretched race of slaves. The only possible step that could be taken towards it by the convention was to fix a period after which they should not be imported."

"The sole purpose and effect of it is to exclude persecution and to secure the important right of religious liberty."

"Legislatures have no right to set up an inquisition and examine the private opinions of men. Test-laws are useless and ineffectual, unjust and tyrannical."

Nathaniel Gorham

While the other four members of this committee were focused on the content, Gorham delivered the prestige and status to the group. He was the President of the Confederation and, therefore, was the highest elected official in the convention. Coming from Massachusetts, he led balance to the issues of North and South.

Nathaniel Gorham was a clearly strategic choice to be a member of this committee by both Washington and Franklin. One can easily imagine Franklin chatting amicably with the delegates as they arrived and casually dropping his hint that Gorham be the leader of the Committee of the Whole.

Gorham was an active participant from the onset of the Revolution. He was a delegate to the Massachusetts' Provincial Congress in 1774 and 1775. During the war he was a member of the Massachusetts board of war, which oversaw the State's military strategy, logistics and recruitment. (gorham nathaniel)

In Western Massachusetts in 1786 Shay's Rebellion and other act arose in refusal to pay debts. Gorham had conviction that this was only the beginning of such acts. The Confederate Constitution gave no strength to the government to resolve these problems. He felt the country would unravel without a powerful federal government. He had the first hand experience to push federalism.

James Wilson wrote "Shays' Rebellion in western Massachusetts in 1786 convinced many Americans that a stronger, centralized national government was necessary, and that anarchy would result if the Articles of Confederation remained the only thing uniting the states. When western Massachusetts debtors took up arms, refused to pay their debts, and closed the courts, Gorham predicted worse would follow - his feelings were focused by the fact that he was acting in 1786 as president of the Confederation government. (Wilson, James)

During the War, Gorham took a leadership role in the economic management of military affairs in Massachusetts. He had great support for his integrity and common sense. He was dedicated to a strong central government, which he thought would benefit the nation economically. He was also determined that the size of each state would not dictate preference and domination. His personal characteristics as well as his convictions were in sync with their practical ideas and plans. (Gorham, Nathaniel)

At the same time, he was skillful in the art of compromise. While he was not an authority on the finer aspects of drafting our constitution, he was a great pragmatist. He was a fine common-sense leader and was skilled in everyday business affairs. He was a trusted leader for all of New England. It is likely that he was Washington's choice, rather than Franklins' due to his significant leadership regarding banking and money, interstate commerce to establish long term stability in all aspects of life. (Gorham, Nathaniel)

It is noteworthy that in 1779 Gorham served as a delegate to the Massachusetts' Constitutional Convention. His leadership then gave him credibility to serve in this committee. He was not merely a figurehead.

A timeline for the government and the Convention.

John Hancock, the duly elected President since November of 1785, had not come to serve. He never showed up. David Ramsay, a Delegate from South Carolina, had reluctantly agreed to serve as the Chairman of Congress in Hancock's absence. He resigned on May 15 and Gorham took his place as Chairman..

On May 27, 1787, The Constitutional Convention was convened with a quorum of seven states. The stated purpose was to revise the Articles of Confederation. Eventually, all states except Rhode Island were represented. George Washington easily was elected to serve as Chairman of the Convention.

Gorham was immediately chosen to be Chairman of the Committee of the Whole in the Convention. This procedure allowed full discussion of all topics without making any decision permanent.

On June 5 President John Hancock resigned from the Continental Congress. with six months remaining in his term of office. The next day, June 6, Nathaniel Gorham, who was Chairman of Congress and Chairman of the Committee of the whole, was elected President of the United States in Congress Assembled, known as the Continental Congress.

The significant aspect after this chaotic period was that Nathaniel Gorham held the respect of both the Congress and the Convention at this tumultuous time.

According to Colonial Hall, "In 1787, Mr. Gorham was a member of the grand convention which formed the federal constitution. In this august body, he sustained a high reputation for his knowledge and integrity. He stood high with all parties for his wisdom and prudence, and eloquence in debate. He was on this account one of the most influential members of the State convention, which adopted the constitution. (Gorham, Colonial Hall)

He was dedicated to a strong central government, which he thought would benefit the nation He was a trusted leader for all of New England. In other words, he was the common sense member of this august committee.

In 1787, Mr. Gorham was a member of the grand convention which formed the federal constitution. In this august body, he sustained a high reputation for his knowledge and integrity. He stood high with all parties for his wisdom and prudence, and eloquence in debate. He was one of the most influential members of the State convention and adoption of the constitution.

Personal responsibility or Individual Responsibility is the idea that human beings choose, instigate, or otherwise cause their own actions. A corollary idea is that because we cause our actions, we can be held morally accountable or legally liable. Personal responsibility can be contrasted to the idea that human actions are caused by conditions beyond the agent's control. Since the late 19th-century, personal responsibility has become increasingly associated with political conservatism and libertarianism. More recently, personal responsibility has been associated with the reform of social welfare programs (e.g. in the Persona 1996). The earliest known English use of the phrase is by Massachusetts Rep. Nathaniel Gorham at the U.S. Constitutional Convention on July 18, 1787. (Projects, C)

Washington's first act was to choose the Chairman of the Committee of the Whole. This process had started in 1745. The entire membership of a legislative body would sit in a deliberative rather than a legislative capacity. The purpose was informal debate and preliminary consideration of matters awaiting legislative action. Nothing discussed or agreed upon would be binding. It was the ideal format for Franklin, Washington and Rutledge. After all, they had just been locked out of the Great Seal choice.

From Nathaniel Gorham
Charles Town April 16 1789

My Dear Sir (James Madison)

Your election to a seat in the new Government I think you can entertain no doubt was pleasing to me. I sincerely hope your attendance will be as pleasant to yourself as beneficial to your Country. It is suggested here that you intend to pass a short Resolve requesting the several States to collect a Revenue for you until you can have time to digest & prepare a system. Suffer me to suggest for your consideration whether a plan like the foregoing will not have a tendency to lessen the dignity of Government. It appears to me that one of the greatest mistakes the old Government ever made was the frequent applications to States and in some instances when there was no real necessity for it; the Congress itself having sufficient power in the case—the consequence was that at length they became afraid to use some of their Constitutional Powers. It appears to me that the loss of one or two Months collections although in a favorable season is not an object to induce a departure from a dignified conduct—besides I think a Resolve like the one I have heard mentioned would infringe the President's prerogative—this ought carefully to be avoided at the outset. It has always appeared to [me] that Parliamentary forms should be observed as much as possible and that all you[r] doings except in some trivial case should be in the form of an act rather than a Resolve— the latter being a kind of slovenly practice of doing business, which has for the sake of expedition or to serve a purpose crept into use in the Legislatures of America—but I believe seldom or never known in G Britain. You know the State Legislatures will encroach upon the National Government wherever they can—be careful therefore how you set out. Excuse my suggestions mention not my name as having written on the subject—& believe me to be

Your sincere Friend & Humble sert
Nathaniel Gorham

(Founders Online: To James Madison from
Nathaniel Gorham)

"Any person chosen governor, or lieutenant-governor, counsellor, senator, or representative, and accepting the trust, shall before he proceed to execute the duties of his place or office, take, make and subscribe the following declaration, viz. 'I, __________, do declare that I believe the Christian religion, and have a firm persuasion of its truth.' "

JAMES WILSON

JAMES WILSON

James Wilson was a highly contributory member of the Committee of Detail. He was always an advocate for a strong federal government, which was the mandatory qualification for all five members.

Born in Scotland, Wilson studied at the universities of St Andrews, Glasgow and Edinburgh, so his foundation was the Scottish Enlightenment thinkers, including Francis Hutcheson, David Hume and Adam Smith. He had a brilliant mind educated at the very apex of the Scottish Enlightenment movement.

In 1766 at age 23, he immigrated to America and began studying law under John Dickinson. Dickenson wrote the first draft of the 1776-1777 Articles of Confederation and Perpetual Union. He was the author of "Letters from a Farmer in Pennsylvania. He had studied in Middle Temple in London and was a Freemason. Both Dickenson and WIlson were delegates to both the Declaration and the Constitutional Conventions.

Since Wilson was born and educated in Scotland. He understood the British government directly. He contributed a masterful understanding to the Executive branch of our constitution. He also was significant in having a popularly elected Electoral College. In these turbulent times currently regarding the Electoral College, it is important to understand that significance. He did not want a hierarchical group dominating our elections.

It is, therefore, quite understandable that Wilson would be a powerful member of this august committee. It is also unlikely that he had knowledge of the Framework itself. He was vastly important in the philosophy of the law.

Wilson had close ties to the philosophers as well as to the Masons, but he was not a joiner. He, therefore, would have been an appropriate selection for this committee. He was an absolutely brilliant intellectual with similar constitutional concepts and with a clear practical perspective. He is the author of our constitution.

"Congress Powers and Limits Wilson's first recorded comment at the U.S. Constitutional Convention indicates both his belief in democratic accountability and his hope for a stronger government. He thus observed on May 31, in defending the idea of popular election of members of the House of Representatives, that he was for raising the federal pyramid to a considerable altitude, and for that reason wished to give it as broad a basis as possible. No government could long subsist without the confidence of the people. In a republican Government this confidence was peculiarly essential. He also thought it wrong to increase the weight of the State Legislatures by making them the electors of the national Legislature. received a thorough exposure to the most advanced philosophical and legal thought of the age." (Ewald)

Immediately after the ratification of our Constitution, Wilson was the first to speak out and importantly, used his proper name. It is called the State House Speech.

It ends with these words:

After all, my fellow citizens, it is neither extraordinary or unexpected, that the constitution offered to your consideration, should meet with opposition. It is the nature of man to pursue his own interest, in preference to the public good; and I do not mean to make any personal reflection, when I add, that it is the interest of a very numerous, powerful, and respectable body to counteract and destroy the excellent work produced by the late convention. All the offices of government, and all the appointments for the administration of justice and the collection of the public revenue, which are transferred from the individual to the aggregate sovereignty of the states, will necessarily turn the stream of influence and emolument into a new channel. Every person therefore, who either enjoys, or expects to enjoy, a place of profit under the present establishment, will object to the proposed innovation; not, in truth, because it is injurious to the liberties of his country, but because it affects his schemes of wealth and consequence. I will confess indeed, that I am not a blind admirer of this plan of government, and that there are some parts of it, which if my wish had prevailed, would certainly have been altered. But, when I reflect how widely men differ in their opinions, and that every man (and the observation applies likewise to every state) has an equal pretension to assert his own, I am satisfied that any thing nearer to perfection could not have been accomplished. If there are errors, it should be remembered, that the seeds of reformation are sown in the work itself, and the concurrence of two thirds of the congress may at any time introduce alterations and amendments. Regarding it then, in every point of view, with a candid and disinterested mind, I am bold to assert, that it is the best form of government which has ever been offered to the world.

As President, Washington appointed James Wilson as Associate Justice of the Supreme Court.

"Liberty and happiness have a powerful enemy on each hand; on the one hand tyranny, on the other licentiousness [anarchy]. To guard against the latter, it is necessary to give the proper powers to the government; and to guard against the former, it is necessary that those powers should be properly distributed." ~ James Wilson.

In giving a definition of the simple kinds of government known throughout the world, I have occasion to describe what I meant by a democracy; and I think I termed it, that government in which the people retain the supreme power, and exercise it either collectively or by representation. This constitution declares this principle, in its terms and in its consequences, which is evident from the manner in which it is announced. "We, the People of the United States."

At a time when most essays about the Constitution (both

Federalist and Anti-Federalist) were published anonymously,

Wilson had the courage to sign his name to his beliefs.

Wilson felt by going to the highest ideals and principles, and spread to the greatest number of people the government could be a Democratic, Federal, National Reepublic.

This constitution declares this principle, in its terms and in its consequences, which is evident from the manner in which it is announced. "We, the People of the United States.

PART TWO |THE FRAMEWORK AS AN ORGANIZING SYSTEM

Chapter 16 | DEFINITIONS

Definitions by Noah Webster in his 1828 Dictionary. Referring to Webster's first dictionary is the best connection to the definitions of the concepts as our government began.

DEMOCRACY, *noun* [Gr. People, and to possess, to govern.] Government by the people; a form of government, in which the supreme power is lodged in the hands of the people collectively, or in which the people exercise the powers of legislation. Such was the government of Athens.

FED'ERAL, *adjective* [from Latin faedus, a league, allied perhaps to Eng. wed. Latin vas, vadis, vador, vadimonium. See Heb. to pledge.] 1. Pertaining to a league or contract; derived from an agreement or covenant between parties, particularly between nations. The Romans, contrary to *federal* right, compelled them to part with Sardinia. 2. Consisting in a compact between parties, particularly and chiefly between states or nations; founded on alliance by contract or mutual agreement; as a *federal* government, such as that of the United States. 3. Friendly to the constitution of the United States. [See the Noun.] NATIONAL, *adjective* 1. Pertaining to a nation; as *national* customs, dress or language. 2. Public; general; common to a nation; as a *national* calamity. 3. Attached or unduly attached to ones own country. The writer manifested much *national* prejudice. He was too *national* to be impartial.

Chapter 17| The Structure and Concepts

Just as understanding the definitions of the words, it is important to understand the decade after the colonies won the Revolutionary War and the Constitutional Convention. Understanding the process of writing, The Great Seal is important in understanding the ideas and values of our new country. The patterns that emerge and stories that give insight deserve high respect. This Chapter is dedicated to the spiritual/intelligent underpinnings that led to THE FRAMEWORK as the organizing system of our Constitution and or government. It is unsurpassed as a whole set of meaningfulness and integration of all factors. It was intelligent, balanced, and harmonious at its foundation. It is kind. It is wise. It is universal. It is comprehensive.

Our calendar given to us through Noah has four seasons.

Each Season has 13 weeks of seven days. of 24 hours.

There is one Jubilee Day of 30, New Year Eve.

In Genesis, thirteen is counted as Jacob and his 12 sons or Jacob's 12 sons and his daughter, Dina. In the New Testament, it is counted as Jesus and his 12 disciples.

In the Tree of Knowledge the twelve sons of Jacob are indicated on the diagonal lines. Jacob is featured on the center horizontal line, connecting them. In Torah, Jacob is depicted on the center of the tree because he is described as the center of the universe. Dina's placement with the twelve sons is in the position called Da'at on the Tree of Life and the sphere without form on the Tree of Knowledge. It signifies Spirit and Inspiration. It is designated as Understanding in the Tree of Life and can also be comprehended as Intuition.

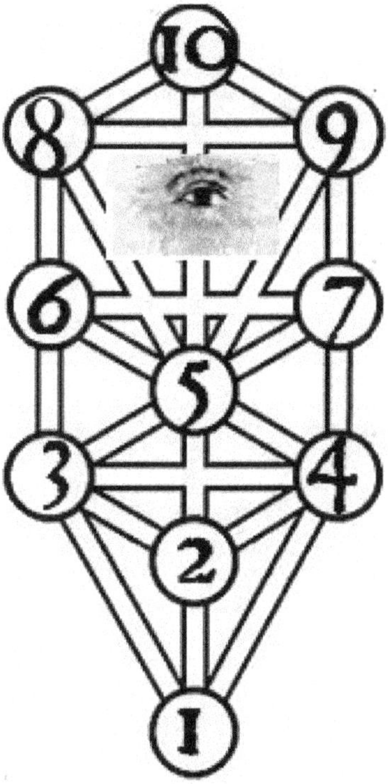

Our Founding Fathers considered Twelve as a full set. However, the thirteenth aspect related to God. Thus, it was called the Eye of Providence. Our ancestors thought this to be beyond human in origin. One might consider this the Soul of our Nation.

These diagrams show circles containing only full circles and a counting method for the number 13.

These diagrams show the source material for the medallion on the Great Seal of the United States. Having this seal comprised of thirteen small stars was inspired. That it is also the Star of David was coincidental.

Designation of the Seven Aspects in the Jewish Star

Later, when the seamstress Betsy Ross designed our flag, she suggested to Washington that a five-point star could be folded so that only one cut was needed. It was a practical suggestion, not a spiritually symbolic idea.

There are two biblical references that give insight. One is from knowing there are two trees: The Tree of Knowledge of All things and the Tree of Life. The other is Genesis 28:12 wherein the angels go up and down the ladder. Thus there are two directions for the configuration of the two trees: One goes up and the other comes down. Jews vow to receive direction from God directly on the lightning flash coming down the tree.

Since Adam and Eve made a free will choice to leave, they must begin the return at the bottom rung. These thoughts are clues to the Framework, which begins at the base? The numbers work. There are seven days in a week. Of the ten attributes designated on the Tree of Knowledge, seven are achievable by humans. The upper three are comprehensible but rarely achieved.

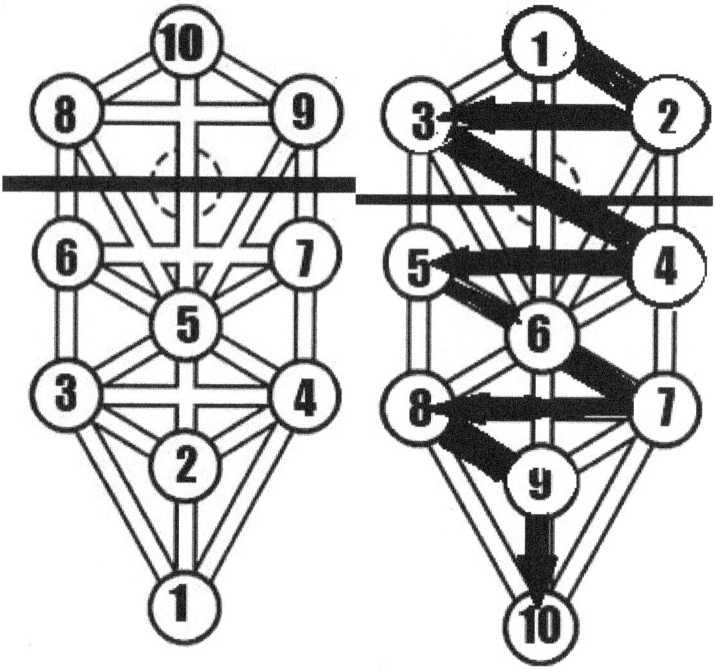

Tree of Knowledge Tree of Life with Lightning Path

These two diagrams are a pair, not opposites. Both are valid.

As a student of universal patterns, there are indications from many sources.

In the case of our Framework, the pattern starts from the bottom with All of the People. The upper triad leadership derives their power from the People, specifically those who vote. One can instantly see the rationale to revamp the

Framework to include all the voters and their issues from the Number Two position. The story of this diagram would be that the ascent is the Return to God and anyone in those positions can only continue the quest by serving All the People. We connect to the Eye of Providence through that "O" position.

Throughout this book, the definition of the Term as stated in Noah Webster's Dictionary of 1828. The first aspect in understanding concepts over time is to be clear of the definitions of that time.

More than thirty ago, I was invited to a meeting at the Mayor's office to teach about the Tree of Life (a rabbinical Jewish concept explained later in this work) as an organizing system. I immediately responded "The Framework of the Constitution has the same format." I also realized that no one considered our Framework as the mathematical diagram of an open, stable system with ancient origins (similar to the Tree of Life). The idea was not recognized or respected, not even as a vague theory.

This book is written to show the structure (not just the content) of the Constitution as the Framework— as the structure, the organizing diagram—of our government. Each aspect of the Constitution is connected to all the others in terms of mathematics and meaning. There is an inherent, in-built system that includes a mathematical configuration with integrated concepts, to enable an open, stable format and foundation.

This is a practical and historical compilation of ideas and anecdotal stories intended to introduce that Framework as a vital part of our interpretation and application of the Constitution.

Chapter 18 | Patterns & Numbers

Just as understanding the definitions of the words, it is important to understand the decade after the colonies won the Revolutionary War and the Constitutional Convention. Understanding the process of writing The Great Seal is important in understanding the ideas and values of our new country. The patterns that emerge and stories that give insight deserve high respect..

It is also important to understand that after our Great Seal was established, the symbol itself became quite well known. The primary goal for the seal created by our Founding Fathers was to separate our Nation from religions and monarchies. They took the task of establishing a great seal that would depict and elucidate our country very seriously.

The Number Thirteen

Our Founding Fathers were dedicated to the mysticism of the number thirteen since there were thirteen states in the Revolution. They insisted Rhode Island join the United States to establish that number in our Constitution and a new government.

Thirteen, a prime number, signifies Noah's Jubilee Calendar. There are four seasons of thirteen weeks in the collective set of 364 days. The 365th day, designated as New Year's Eve, is an entirely different set. It separates the years.

February 29th is part of Set 1 and is comprised of the extra 6 hours each year. Every four years this calculated. February 30th contains the extra minutes and should be recognized every hundred years to kept the system accurate.

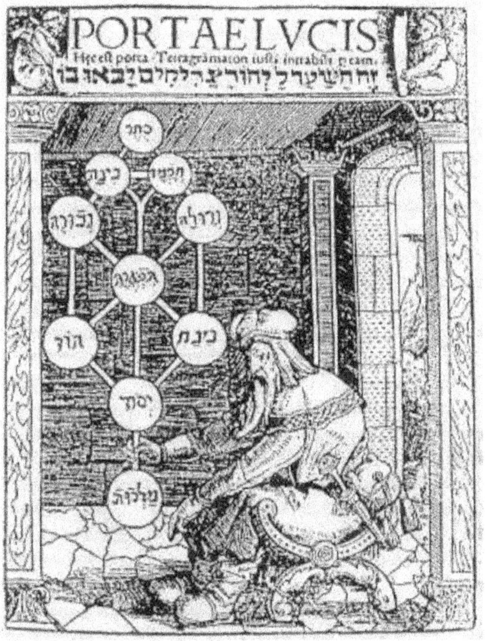

This is an ancient depiction of the Jewish Tree of Life. Note in particular that the pathways descend. There is only one path to return. This explains the difference between the Tree of Life and the Tree of Knowledge. In the Book of Genesis Adam and Eve made their own free-will choice to leave the Garden of Eden. Later Noah established the Way of Return to be one of Relatedness. In their Covenant with God Jews obligated themselves and their descendants to follow directions From God. In Jacob's Ladder we see movement up and down the ladder. The spheres represent attributes, whereas the pathways delineate the connections and relatedness.

Noteworthy also, is the design of the topmost three spheres. According to traditional teachings of the Tree of Life, the seven lower spheres are characterized by the attributes of God that are achievable by people. The upper three may be understood by the wise ones, but rarely attainable.

Thus in the application of our Framework, the mandate is to elect leaders who embody and manifest the highest of attributes possible. There is no place in these positions for our highest officials, who do not manifest the best we can be for the good of all. The very Framework of our Constitution can be totally undermined by any leaders, who are not dedicated to the highest of ideals on which we were founded.

These are common designations for the Tree of Life descending. The upper triad denotes characteristics the leaders at the top of the three pillars should manifest. Beauty is the manifestation of balance and harmony in the Framework as a whole. We can see the Kingdom depicts Jews as a whole Nation. Thus our designations as "We the People" refers to our Nation as a Whole.

The Tree of Knowledge of All Things is formatted in the same system. It is also applicable to our Constitution. While the Tree of Return depicts the journey we have to return to God through acts of kindness and relatedness, the values correspond very well. One can easily understand the constant ebb and flow of our system and our interactions. This pattern is established in the Book of Genesis and no religion is involved. It is an ethical relationship model. It works well for atheists as well as those with a variety of beliefs.

To sum it up:

The Right Pillar: Is it kind?

The Left Pillar: Is it fair?

The Center Pillar: Is there peace?

The universal problem: Ego and self-vested interests.

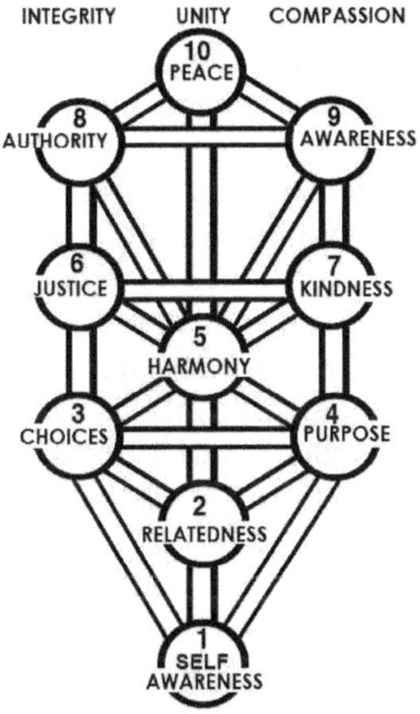

seven days in the collective set of 364 days. The 365th day of 30 hours is the Day of Jubilation.

On March 26, 1781, George Washington wrote: "The many remarkable inter-positions of the divine government, in the hours of our deepest distress and darkness, have been too luminous to suffer me to doubt the happy issue of the present contest." They were fervent in their passions against monarchies, feeling the hand of divine providence strongly.

In Noah Webster's Dictionary published in 1828, this is the definition of Providence as applies to the use in our Great Seal.

3. In theology, the care and superintendence which God exercises over his creatures. He that acknowledges a creation and denies a providence involves himself in a palpable contradiction; for the same power which caused a thing to exist is necessary to continue its existence. Some persons admit a general providence but deny a particular providence not considering that a general providence consists of particulars. A belief in divine providence is a source of great consolation to good men. "By divine providence" is often understood as "God Himself." (Noah Webster's American Dictionary)

In my previous book, *God is a Verb! Selah*, I demonstrated how the unbounded Eye of Providence illustrates God as a verb, where the bounded Eye, in contrast, shows God as a noun. I assert that this side of the Great Seal, influenced by heraldry, is hindered by the use of the pyramid symbol. I do not suggest changing the depiction, but I do believe the shift from Franklin's original concept is significant.

Following is the reverse of the Great Seal, which has the approved design, though never used as an official seal.

The next is taken from our one-dollar bill. This symbolism's function is opposite to Thomas Jefferson's proposal, who sought to signify Israel fleeing Egypt and the pyramids. The steps can still be seen, but the meaning is subverted.

This seal clearly shows gratitude to a god or light or spirit without a reference to any religion.

the very many on the seal is the eye of providence, and the interpretation of it by the designers is different from that used by Masons. S. Brent Morris wrote a paper regarding "The Eye in the Pyramid" The eye on the seal represents Benjamin Franklin proposed another concept from Exodus. His version depicted the parting of the Red Sea. He suggested the motto Rebellion to tyrants is obedience to God.

Franklin and Jefferson would never have approved depicting the pyramid with a bounded Eye of Providence.

The committees and consultants who designed the Great Seal of the United States contained only one Mason, Benjamin Franklin. The only possibly Masonic design element among the very many on the seal is the eye of providence, and the interpretation of it by the designers is different from that used by Masons. S. Brent Morris wrote a paper regarding "The Eye in the Pyramid" *The eye on the seal represents Benjamin Franklin proposed another concept from Exodus. His version depicted the parting of the Red Sea. He suggested the motto Rebellion to tyrants is obedience to God.*

an active intervention of God in the affairs of men, while the Masonic symbol stands for a passive awareness by God of the activities of men. The eye of Providence was par an active intervention of God in the affairs of men, while the Masonic symbol stands for a passive awareness by God of the activities of men. The eye of Providence was part of the common cultural iconography of the 17th and 18th centuries. When placed in a triangle, the eye went beyond a general representation of God to a strongly Trinitarian statement.

It was during this period that Masonic ritual and symbolism evolved; Eventually, the all-seeing eye came to be used officially by Masons as a symbol for God, but this happened towards the end of the eighteenth century after congress had adopted the seal. A pyramid, whether incomplete or finished, however, has never been a Masonic symbol. It has no generally accepted symbolic meaning, except perhaps permanence or mystery. The combining of the eye of providence overlooking an unfinished pyramid is a uniquely American, not Masonic, icon, and must be interpreted as its designers intended. It has no Masonic context. The eye of providence on the seal thus can be traced, not to the Masons, but to a non-Mason consultant to the committee.

He cuts out of the Newspapers, every Scrap of Intelligence, and every Piece of Speculation, and pastes it upon clean Paper, arranging them under the Head of the State to which they belong and intends to bind them up in Volumes. He has a List of every Speculation and Pamphlet concerning Independence, and another of those concerning expertise.

It was a bad fit for our new nation, which was specifically dedicated to distinct governance, a democracy of the people, by the people, and for the people. Symbols of monarchy were abhorrent to these leaders.

du Simitière submitted the first diagram that was heraldic. It contained a shield for each of the six primary ancestral

European Monarchies for the colonists. Franklin, in particular, would have been outraged. In his customary non-confrontational matter, he would have been working to divert the seal from European concepts.

It is also important to note that John Adams placed no value on Freemasonry. His son, President John Quincy Adams, was an adamant Anti-Mason. Adams had depicted Hercules for his drawing for the back side of the Seal. Franklin appears never to confront anyone on concepts that were contrary to his Masonic belief system. He drops the issue and may find a totally different approach.

Just considering Hercules as a half-god, half-human, who becomes a god because of his skills as a warrior, would be radically different from the Stonemason concepts of Pythagoras.

The Second Committee met in 1782 The Articles of the Confederation had been passed. John Hanson was the new President. He was the perfect Administrative Leader. He literally established the w *forms of government."*

(Founders Online: John Adams to Abigail Adams)

This letter shows the problems Franklin and others had with the heraldists. European Monarchies formed the context for their Frances Hopkinson, also a heraldist, was hired by the committee. He contributed some elements, such as a constellation of 13 stars. He also included two figures (a Native American and a woman or a soldier and a woman), a shield of thirteen stripes, an olive branch, and arrows. This design was not even put to a vote.

The Third Committee met in 1783.

John Rutledge served on the Third Committee, which met in 1782. He left during the process. Evidently, there was no path to creating a Great Seal using the ancient symbols that matched the vision of the Three Grand Framers. He would have been outraged by this pyramid and the bounded eye. William Barton was a heraldist on the third committee who first suggested using the pyramid on the Great Seal. It turns out that he was also a member of a fraternal society, The Society of Cincinnati. This was a fraternal society formed from people who served in the Revolutionary War. Twenty-three of the framers were members of this society. More participated. Their members included Washington, Hamilton, and Franklin. (Hume, Edgar)

In this version, the motto *ANNUIT COEPTIS* at the top and the eye is bound. The 13 steps are reduced as well. This begins the shift to depict the steps as a pyramid with a separate top. The eye is bounded.

A second motto was chosen for this side of the seal. *Novus ordo seclorum* (meaning *new order of the ages*) originates from lines by the Roman poet Virgil. Note that this motto has 26 letters, so that the two together have 39 letters, which can be reduced to 13.

Negativists misinterpret this motto as indicating domination and conspiracy. Nothing could be further from the truth. Their conviction was that our democracy would be the first of many.

The Roman numeral at the base of the Pyramid is 1776. Coincidentally, it reduces to the number 3, corresponding to the three pillars of our Constitution.

Now that we understand how upset Franklin, Washington, and Rutledge were, should we change the symbol? Absolutely not! Now it is a long established tradition. We know the contrived explanations. The distortions have a tradition of their own.

It is a long established symbol of the forces our revolution overturned and has contrived meanings. The biblical story of Jews fleeing slavery in Egypt is an ancient story of oppression. The pyramid is the symbol of Pharaoh. It represents hierarchy, with the masses at the bottom and no connection to the eye of illumination, which is contained. Thus the eye is not only limited, but unavailable. The following quotes by three great presidents attempt to make this symbol positive and meaningful

Thus the original meaning has changed through the times to embody thoughts of our leaders. We have made the symbol valid in our terms. Thus it should not be changed. However, it shall always be a symbol Franklin and Rutledge and, probably, Washington opposed strongly as a symbol of European Monarchists.

The Obverse

(The right side of the one dollar)

The reverse side of the Seal uses a single emblem, conceptualized as providence and the divine or the heavenly realm. The obverse side represents the manifested, physical, or practical realm. Consequently, Franklin, Washington, and Rutledge did not find the included symbols problematic. The tail feathers, representing the Menorah, would likely have been included by Washington's express request.

This side of the Great Seal contains ideas designed by Frances Hopkinson, who introduced the eagle. Apparently, no one was committed to Franklin's idea of a turkey. He depicted people such as an Iroquois man paired with a Colonial woman. Another design included a soldier paired with an angelic woman. He envisioned an olive branch for peace, and arrows. He also depicted a constellation of six-sided stars.

E Pluribus Unum became the motto and was translated as *Out of Many, One*. Both the Latin and the English had 13 digits. There were also 13 stripes on the shield, thirteen arrows in one shaft and 13 leaves with 13 berries in the other shaft.

Hopkinson's design never came to a vote, but his ideas influenced future versions.

This diagram contains the 13 original states in order of ratification. The thirteenth state was a mandatory component to our Founding Fathers.

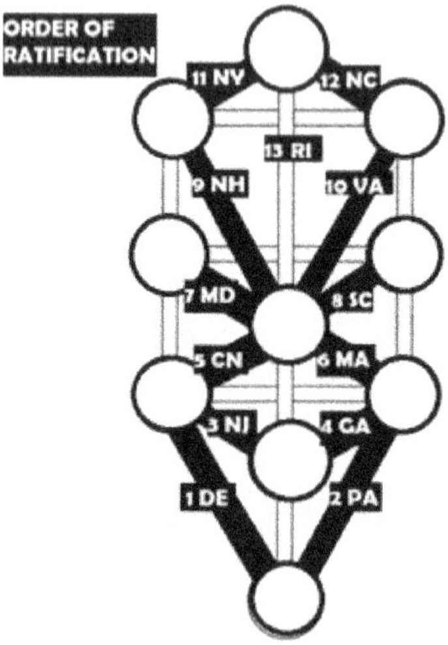

Did Washington, Franklin, and Rutledge know this pattern? Did Franklin discover it in France? Did it come from the Masons? Did Washington get it from the Jews? Did it result from their own intuition? We may never have direct proof. They kept it secret so that others would not disturb their sacred determination and knowledge. What we can know with certainty, by observation, is that their work precisely fits the ancient paradigm.

Franklin and Jefferson would never have approved depicting the pyramid with a bounded Eye of Providence.

The committees and consultants who designed the great Seal of the United States contained only one Mason, Benjamin Franklin. The only possibly Masonic design element among the very many on the seal is the eye of providence, and the interpretation of it by the designers is different from that used by Masons. S. Brent Morris wrote a paper regarding "The Eye in the Pyramid" The eye on the seal represents an active intervention of God in the affairs of men, while the Masonic symbol stands for a passive awareness by God of the activities of men. The eye of Providence was part of the common cultural iconography of the 17th and 18th centuries. When placed in a triangle, the eye went beyond a general representation of God to a strongly Trinitarian statement. It was during this period that Masonic ritual and symbolism evolved; Eventually, the all-seeing eye came to be used officially by Masons as a symbol for God, but this happened towards the end of the eighteenth century after congress had adopted the seal. A pyramid, whether incomplete or finished, however, has never been a Masonic symbol. It has no generally accepted symbolic meaning, except perhaps permanence or mystery. The combining of the eye of providence overlooking an unfinished pyramid is a uniquely American, not Masonic, icon, and must be interpreted as its designers intended. It has no Masonic context. The eye of providence on the seal thus can be traced, not to the Masons, but to a non-Mason

Final design by Charles Thomson

It is important to understand the imagery of the pyramid.

Jefferson wanted to illustrate the Israelites' exodus from slavery in Egypt on the front of the seal. Jefferson wanted the same.

Franklin's idea was similar. He wanted to show Moses parting the Red Sea with the motto Rebellion to tyrants is obedience to God.

An oft-quoted remark attributed to Franklin was that he did not like the use of the eagle. He did write an interesting letter to his daughter, Sarah, but never mailed it. It was made public in the writings of his grandson, William Temple Franklin. Called Temple Franklin, he was born when his father was in Middle Temple in London and his grandfather was on his Mission to London. It had nothing actually to do with our Great Seal. The letter is found in our reading list and, as one might expect, it is yet another of Franklin's fascinating letters. The oft quoted excerpt is "For my own part I wish the Bald Eagle had not been chosen as the Representative of our Country. He is a Bird of bad moral Character. He does not get his Living honestly."

The reader should note that the eagle was atop the pine tree in the Great Seal of the Iroquois.

Negativists misinterpret this motto as indicating domination and conspiracy. Nothing could be further from the truth. Their conviction was that our democracy would be the first of many.

The Roman numeral at the base of the Pyramid is 1776. Coincidentally, it reduces to the number 3, corresponding to the three pillars of our Constitution.

Now that we understand how upset Franklin, Washington, and Rutledge were, should we change the symbol? Absolutely not! Now it is a long established tradition. We know the contrived explanations. The distortions have a tradition of their own. We should all know the story, however.

It is a long established symbol of the forces our revolution overturned and has contrived meanings. The biblical story of Jews fleeing slavery in Egypt is an ancient story of oppression. The pyramid is the symbol of Pharaoh. It represents hierarchy, with the masses at the bottom and no connection to the eye of illumination, which is contained. Thus the eye is not only limited, but unavailable. The following quotes by three great presidents attempt to make this symbol positive and meaningful

"The generation which commences a revolution rarely completes it." - Thomas Jefferson

"American history is not something dead and over. It is always alive, always growing, always unfinished." - John F. Kennedy

"The unfinished work of perfecting our union falls to each of us." - Barack Obama (The Great Seal)

Thus the original meaning has changed through the times to embody thoughts of our leaders. We have made the symbol valid in our terms. Thus it should not be changed. However, it shall always be a symbol Franklin and Rutledge and, probably, Washington opposed strongly as a symbol of European Monarchists.

The Obverse

(The right side of the one dollar)

The reverse side of the Seal uses a single emblem, conceptualized as providence and the divine or the heavenly realm. The obverse side represents the manifested, physical, or practical realm. Consequently, Franklin, Washington, and Rutledge did not find the included symbols problematic. The tail feathers, representing the Menorah, would likely have been included by Washington's express request.

This side of the Great Seal contains ideas designed by Frances Hopkinson, who introduced the eagle. Apparently, no one was committed to Franklin's idea of a turkey. He depicted people such as an Iroquois man paired with a Colonial woman. Another design included a soldier paired with an angelic woman. He envisioned an olive branch for peace, and arrows. He also depicted a constellation of six-sided stars.

E Pluribus Unum became the motto and was translated as Out of Many, One. Both the Latin and the English had 13 digits. There were also 13 stripes on the shield, thirteen arrows in one shaft and 13 leaves with 13 berries in the other shaft.

Hopkinson's design never came to a vote, but his ideas influenced future versions.

We can see the heraldic aspects of the meaning of numbers were aligned with traditional Masonic and Pythagorean concepts. Thus nothing of the Obverse, the practical side, was offensive to the Three Grand Masters.

The final version shows numerous applications of the Number 13

13 stars above the eagle

13 steps on the Pyramid

13 letters in ANNUIT COEPTIS

13 letters in E PLURIBUS UNUM

13 vertical bars on the shield

13 horizontal stripes at the top of the shield

13 leaves on the olive branch

13 berries on the olive branch

13 arrows

The prime number thirteen has two significant geometric aspects

One aspect is called the centered square. In it, circles are arranged in a perpendicular/horizontal base.

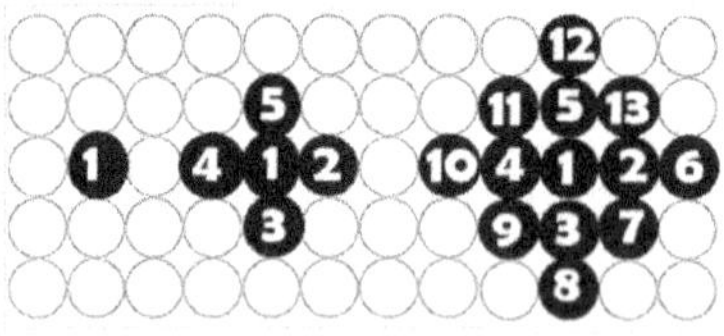

The second aspect indicates the pattern used by King David as well as in our Great Seal. These circles are aligned on the diagonal.

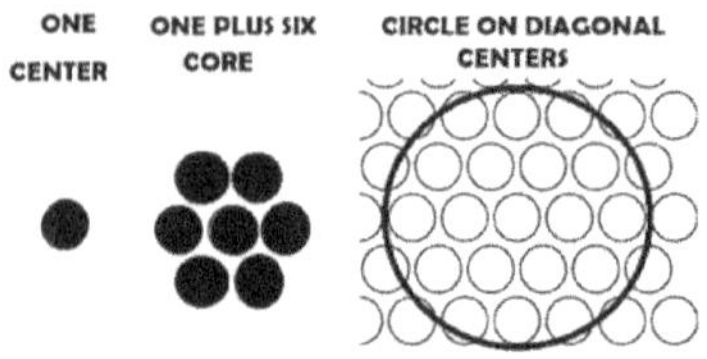

There are two biblical references that give insight. One is from knowing there are two trees: The Tree of Knowledge of All things and the Tree of Life. The other is Genesis

28:12 wherein the angels go up and down the ladder. Thus there are two directions for the configuration of the two trees: One goes up and the other comes down. Jews vow to receive direction from God directly on the lightning flash coming down the tree.

Since Adam and Eve made a free will choice to leave, they must begin the return at the bottom rung. These thoughts are clues to the Framework, which begins at the base? The numbers work. There are seven days in a week. Of the ten attributes designated on the Tree of Knowledge, seven are achievable by humans.. The upper three are comprehensible, but rarely achieved.

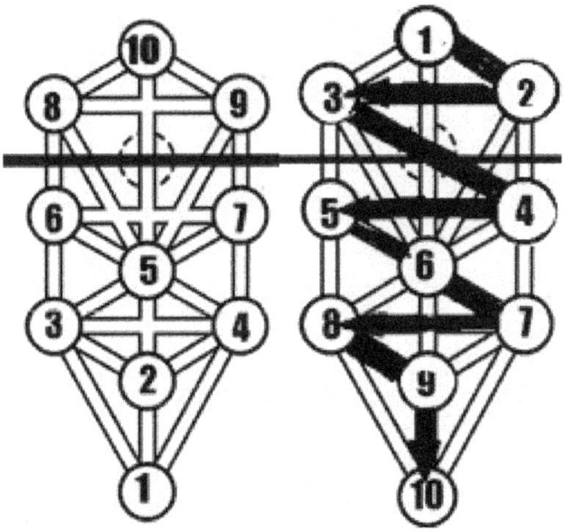

Tree of Knowledge Tree of Life with Lightning Path

These two diagrams are a pair, not opposites. Both are valid.

As a student of universal patterns, there are indications from many sources.

In the case of our Framework, the pattern starts from the bottom with All of the People. The upper triad leadership derives their power from the People, specifically those who vote. One can instantly see the rationale to revamp the Framework to include all the voters and their issues from the Number Two position. The story of this diagram would be that the ascent is the Return to God and anyone in those positions can only continue the quest by serving All the People. We connect to the Eye of Providence through that "O" position.

Chapter 19| Terminology for the Framework Itself

This is a book about the Framework, hence the title. Consequently, the corresponding definitions for the components and their relatedness are appropriate in this chapter prior to discussion about the format itself. These are contemporary definitions on the Tree of Knowledge ascending, based on decades of work, including the calendar given to Noah after the Flood. The definitions are ascending on the Tree of Knowledge. Ascending in comparison with the Tree of Life as an organizing system. There absolutely no validity to using these terms in reference to the Founders or to Freemasonry. The reference would be "God is a Verb. Selah" by the author. These are a layer of the Framework itself.

The Hermetic Tree on the left shows collaboration with the Jews in very ancient times. The Hermetic Tree flows in both directions. Whereas, since their vows at Mount Sinai all Jews through their Jewish mothers adhere to the Lightning Flash. The Lightning Flash is depicted down from G-d. Thus the 21st and 22nd Paths are shifted from the two lowest positions to pathways connecting the upper spheres to the seven lower spheres. The seven lower spheres are considered achievable by human beings. The three upper spheres are more difficult to attain. Each of those spheres contains all the attributes of the lower seven. The Tree of Knowledge of All Things is on the right. It has been overlooked by misinterpreting Adam and Eve in the Garden of Eden.

A positive, purposeful God realized that He could not expect humans to follow the basic principles for human beings without Free Will Choice is fundamental. Thus, He gave them one simple rule that had no moral equivalency. "Don't eat the Apple." They immediately chose to eat the apple.

Thus, Humans have the model of the Tree of Knowledge as an ethical system along with their free-will choice. Their purpose is, therefore, to Return to God in awe, appreciation, and compassion for other Humans. Their Tree is dedicated to a Free-Will choice in Self-awareness and relationships. with a mandate The Preamble James Madison kept the record of our Constitutional Convention, but he was focused on the debates and his vantage point, in particular. After it was ratified, Madison, Hamilton and Jay wrote extensively. They wrote about the ideas. They paid no attention to the Committee of Detail, the actual drafters of the constitution. In fact, they overlooked the guts: The Framework.

No one ever considers whosoever called the convention or why somebody wanted to amend the Articles of Confederation."

Secret # 1 – They wanted to write an entirely new federal constitution.

Secret #2 – They had to have a strategy, since states' rights prevailed.

Secret #3 – Who were the leaders calling this convention?

Secret #4 – Why did they keep it a secret?

Secret # 5 – What did Madison overlook?

Secret # 6 – What did the terms "Framers" and "Framework" mean?

ASPECTS TO CONSIDER REGARDING OUR FRAMEWORK

Unstated objectives - Giving voting rights to every soldier

Source of the Framework - Freemasons, Stonemasons and Pythagoras

Sources of ideas - Iroquois and Jews

Things to avoid - Monarchies and Religious Groups What happens if you eliminate the Electoral College? Was the Electoral College against Slaves?

Why did Washington call the Committee of the Whole?

If Washington knew the Framework, why did he not use it as President?

Why weren't Freemasons involved in our Great Seal?

How important was Franklin? Was he just there because he was old?

Who were the members of the Committee of Detail and why were they chosen?

Did the Committee of Detail make a difference?

Who were the members of the Committee of Style and did they make a difference?

Does the Framework matter now?

I assert the term Vaulting makes all the difference. If you stand in place at this time and jump forward, the distance is small. Consider our times that allows no history, no information.

If you have a running start, your effect going forth begins with your starting point. The stronger and further back to the origination, the further forward with greater significance, the effect goes.

Virtually all studies and applications have started with the records of James Madison and the Federalist Papers. The Committee of Detail is not considered. That committee was the guts of the convention.

Our imperative is to go back past the ratification of our Constitution, past the convention, past the Revolutionary War, and delve as far back as possible to put matters on track as strongly as possible.

Chapter 19 | The Structure of the Constitution

From the Book of Genesis, we learn that God gave Adam and Eve the choice to remain in the Garden of Eden or leave the protection of the Garden. God realized he could not expect humans to adhere to positive traits with each other unless they had made their choice to leave. They left the Garden of Eden with the Tree of Knowledge of all things. Jews became a Nation in the Age of Aries with the mandate to follow the Tree of Life descending from God. Thus there was a double helix formed by the two trees. We can best understand the two trees as a single frame with two directions depicted. A single frame is depicted in this manner.

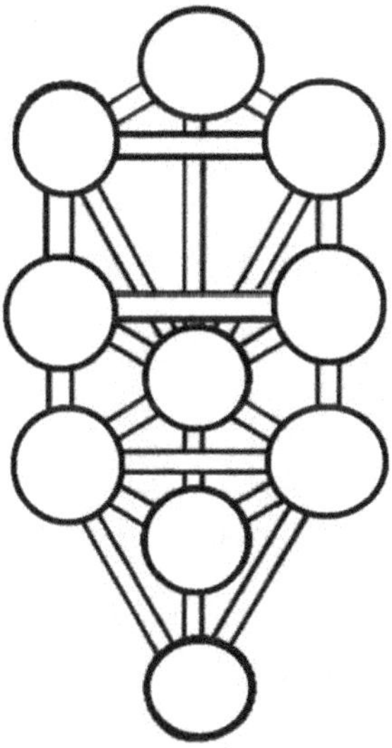

The Universal Framework

This frame or format can be used for a vast array of data and systems. It is said to be a perfect organizational system. All components have a comprehensive set of integrated factors. It can organize businesses and lesson plans, calendars and time, virtually any sset of data. If it has spiritual data, it has spiritual relevance. If it has ordinary, mundane data, it is not. There is nothing superstitious about using the Framework. It is also valid as a method to determine extraneous or missing factors. In later chapters, we discuss some of the methods to include data streams and connections.

Using a simple frame, our Constitution has this organizational format. The first position reflects the American People. The People source our government. Unlike dictatorships and systems sourced by the leader, in America, our democracy is "of, by and for the people." The leadership positions must reflect the people themselves.

This the standard format for the Tree for our constitution

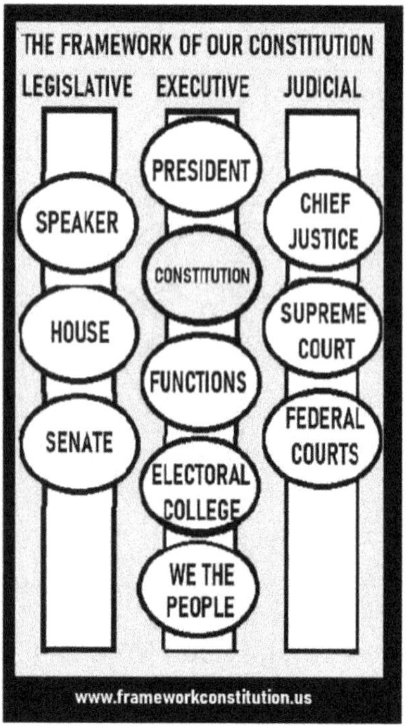

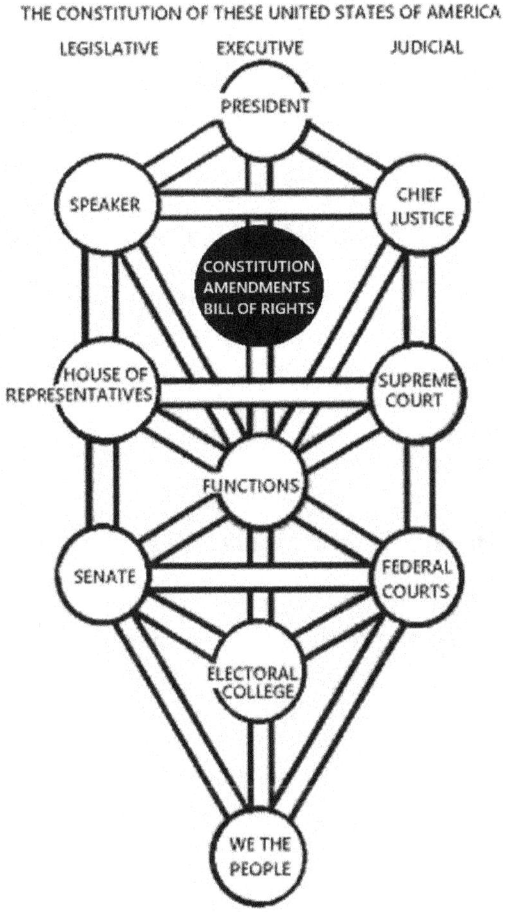

The Three Pillars

The three pillars are exactly as dedicated and enumerated. The pillar on the left is the Legislative Branch. The key context is Integrity. The pillar on the right is the Judicial Branch, and the mindset is compassion. The center pillar is the Executive Branch. The focus is always unity and peace. This is also the leadership position for teamwork. The position for Functions has evolved from the designation of the Army and the Navy. This central position reflects the whole in terms of co-operation as well as operations.

The qualities of the Pillars are:

Legislative: Integrity Executive: Peace Judicial: Compassion

The Left Pillar: The Legislative Branch: Integrity

Integrity is the fundamental principle and context of the Legislative Pillar. The House of Representatives and the Senate are the operational components of this aspect of government. The Framers considered the House to be the senior body of Congress. Therefore, the senior position is the Speaker.

The Right Pillar: The Judicial Branch : Compassion

The Judicial Pillar is on the right side of the Framework. If you were to designate the three pillars in shades of black to white. The left pillar would be black, the right pillar would be white, and the center would be grey, interpreting moderation and harmony. The Judicial Pillar represents The Golden Rule in action. The Chief Justice sets the tone for compassion. I visualize the configuration of Yin and Yang to express the Judicial Function. Practical aspects of this pillar are the Supreme Court and the lower Federal Courts.

The Center Pillar: The Executive Branch: Peace

The characteristics for this pillar are Peace and Unity. Balance is also an objective. This is absolutely not about ruler ship and domination. It is precisely opposite of all hierarchical programs. In the process of putting this organizational plan in place, it is easy to determine where the dysfunction leading to imbalance occurs. This is the center post for the entire Framework. It extends from the basis of "We the People" to the President. Voting and the entire scope of governmental operations belong here.

The President

The President occupies the senior position of the center pillar, chosen to represent "We the People." All the people. The values of this pillar are unity and peace. The President is the team leader for our country. His power is derived from All the People. A President is successful to the degree he or she enables peace and harmony in our country. Therefore all international activities must have the same dedication to keep peace. with all others on our planet. The Constitution positions the President to bring our Constitution into its greatest potential for the benefit of all people. The presidential authority must strive for the benefit of all people. Partisan politics was never a consideration. In his first appointments, he had diversity and included people with opposite opinions. He did not stack his appointments with soldiers and Masons. He did not include Rutledge, in particular. He was dedicated to diversity. How are we doing?

The President is in the senior position. His sphere of operations exists only in his specific sphere. From his sphere is a string of frames all dedicated to his programs and responsibilities. This position is responsible to All the People and these on his extension have no other direct responsibilities. in the other pillars in the framework. He has responsibilities to cooperate with positions on the other two pillars! However, the President is a separate and distinct entity located on the Executive pillar. The energy of this sphere focuses on unity and peace. The Executive connects directly to the voters and people of our entire country. While the President may have party affiliations, as President, he or she is directly responsible to our Constitution and all our people. The purpose of the President is peace and unity for all the people. A depiction of his field is in the Chapter on Extensions.

Upper Triad

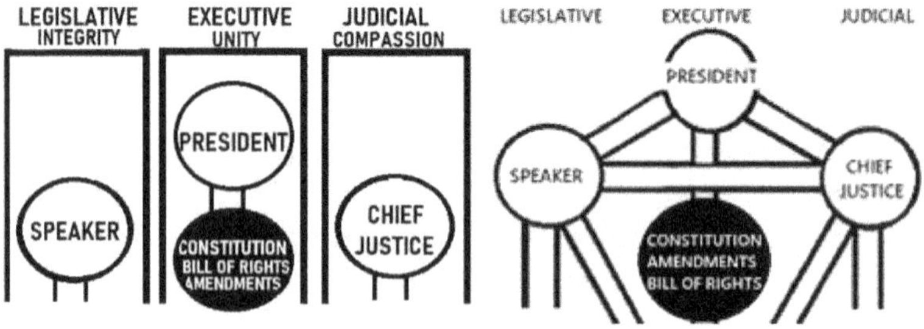

The three key leadership positions of our government align with their respective branches. These three positions perform their duties in the context of leadership on their dedicated pillar specifically. The President is NOT preeminent over the other leaders and has no direct link to their Pillar of authority.

Most of all, this configuration highlights a mandate for three co-equal and distinct branches, each with their own specialized and significant area of responsibility and leadership. None are dominant. They operate independently, yet co-operate in the general functions, operations, and rules. The three leaders have no direct connection or authority to the other two pillars. The President has his/her own distinct tree or line of operations. It is outside the primary framework. The President has no authority or supremacy over operations in the other branches. The President must represent All of the People directly and specifically not through the other branches or pillars.

It is worthwhile to note that the Vice-President operates only in the Executive Branch, with one exception: to be the deciding vote when there is a tie in the Senate. There is no other function designated across the pillars.

The Unbounded Sphere as Context and the connection to the Eye of Illumination or Providence

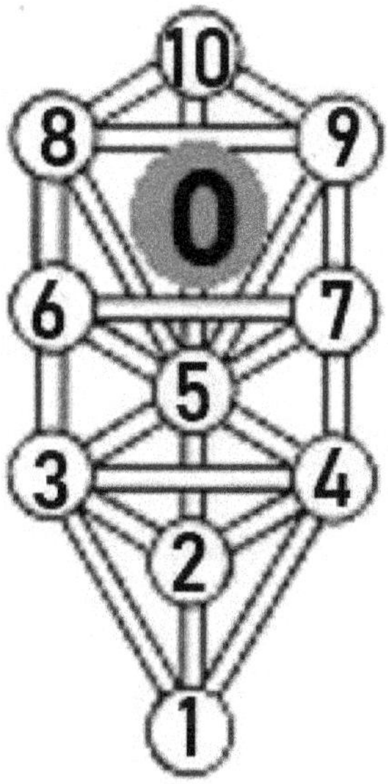

We denote the eleventh sphere as the "All Seeing Eye." It illuminates the whole without specificity. Essentially it is the sphere without bounds. Our Constitution embodies this concept within the Framework of our government. It is found in the Primary Frame. When we extend the Framework, we can denote this position for distinctive functions and positions without the ennobling concept. For instance, in the Presidential Tree, it can connote the Vice-President. It then functions on a par with all the other spheres.

In the Framework of our Constitution, this sphere becomes the Eye of Illumination and thus, the Constitution itself, and the extensions are the Bill of Rights and Amendments. The sphere without physicality—the added dimension—zero on the Framework: The Sphere of Insight & Higher Consciousness. This sphere does not have pathways to the other components. It is the Higher spirit that unites us all.

It is our American Spirit, which is under siege now. It is imperative this component be preeminent.

The Core

The Framework shows the fifth position as Functions and Operations.

In actual operation, the central position, identified as the Army and Navy originally, expanded organically to include all the governmental functions that are core to all operations without details specific to the three branches.

Consider this as a revolving wheel constantly in motion, constantly in change, always with the intention to keep order and balance. Rather than the dedicated relationships of the other components, this position is like a wheel, never stagnant. This is the sphere of debate, of compromise and resolution. The purpose of the Central Pillar is Peace and Unity.

In consideration of the Framework as a whole providing a structure and foundation and the unbounded sphere as the spirit of the whole, this sphere is the continuity and continuum to keep all matters relevant to the present, while honoring the basic system.

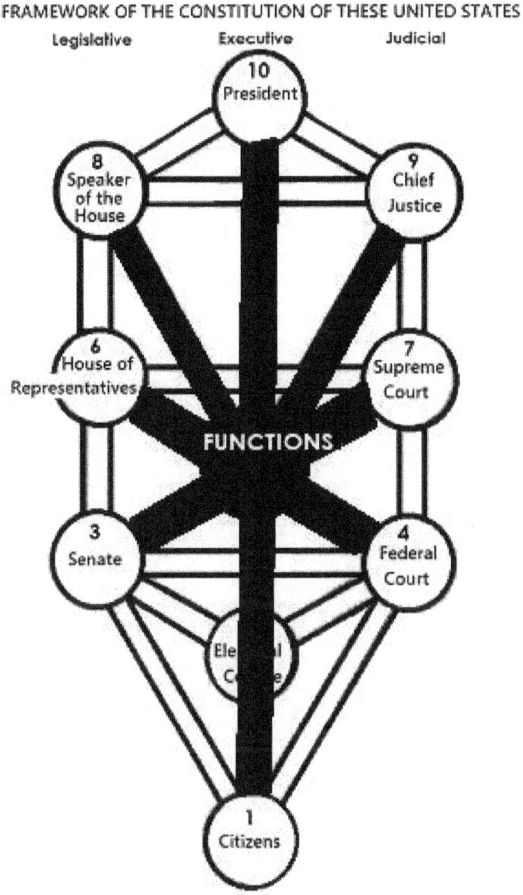

The Core Function

The function in this sphere is to continually keep balance and harmony. It is a wheel in continuous movement. As depicted, this position can connect to all the other spheres.

It has the common core of Government operations. Thus, it is a perfect system for our democracy. There is nothing hierarchical in the tree. Every component has equal value. The Framework of our Constitution is the ideal format for our democracy.

Initially the Army and Navy

The Constitution refers to the Army and the Navy in this position. That aspect has now expanded to include all the military. However, from the visual of this component, it is obvious this refers to governmental functions of every manner. It is a continually shifting position that connects to all three branches, Legislative, Judicial, and Executive, as well as the citizens.

The Major Structure

Vertical beams and crosswise posts form the core of integrated operations in the Framework. These linear connections show the direct links between the branches of our government. The primary concept is that the three primary positions for each pillar do not connect directly with the other pillars other than with each other.

FRAMEWORK OF THE CONSTITUTION OF THESE UNITED STATES

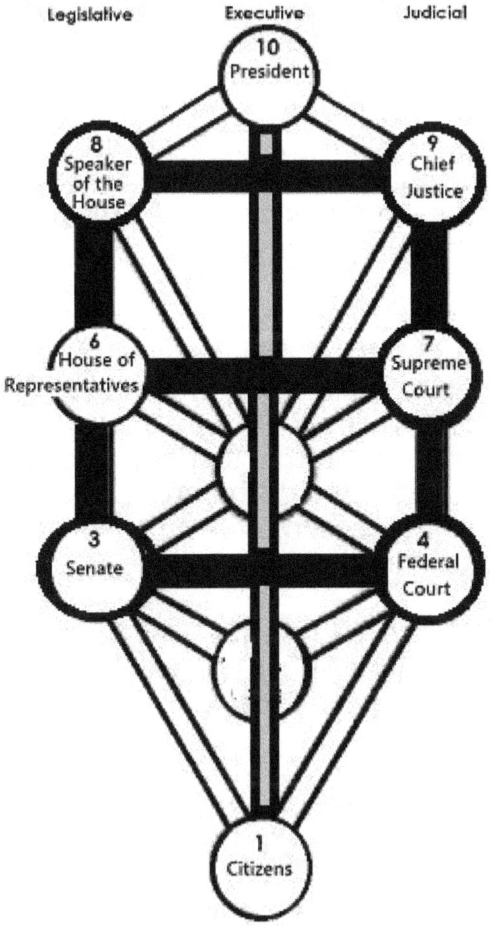

The Electoral College

Voting procedures were the most difficult to establish. Our Founding Fathers wanted all who fought for our freedom to participate in the election of the President and Vice-President. The huge difficulty was that a huge percentage of the soldiers were illiterate white men.

Slaves were part of commerce and a totally separate issue. Slavery was worse and was actually the issue that nearly broke the union.. Slaves had come from Africa and did not speak English or another European language. The written language was not part of their societies. It was not even known that they could be taught. Their traditions of dance, rhythm, and tones. The capabilities of slaves from Northern Africa were not known in the south.

The Federalist Papers, Alexander Hamilton stated that the objective of the Electoral College was to preserve "the sense of the people," while at the same time ensuring that a president is chosen "by men most capable of analyzing the qualities adapted to the station, and acting under circumstances favorable to deliberation, and to a judicious combination of all the reasons and inducements which were proper to govern their choice."

The founding fathers established the Electoral College a compromise between electing the President by a vote in Congress and electing the President by a popular vote of qualified citizens.

In framing our constitution, the problem of elections was very serious. There had never been a constitutional republic. Men - albeit white men - were all going to have the right to vote. This meant that uneducated men were going to be included. Blacks and women were not even a consideration because there was no common knowledge they could be educated. Blacks had come to our continent without any aspect of European literacy. Undoubtedly, they did not speak English when they were brought here. The Civil War gave blacks self-determination and the first thing many did was to become educated. In 2020 there is no question of blacks becoming highly educated and intellectually functional.

Blacks are tested and astoundingly well proven at every level of society and learning. We have had eight years of a superior President, who is black, and had outstanding black members of his team at every level. Two-hundred thirty years ago that was not even a consideration.

Educated women were unusual. There was no thought about any women having the capacity to be qualified in this republic. Now, there are even recommendations that the President and Vice-President both be women.

It is wrong to fault our Founding Fathers for dealing solely and specifically with the problem of uneducated white men. They were dealing with franchisement without the issues of rank, property, assets, religion, education, language, and heritage. Their greatest concerns were illiteracy From Webster's Dictionary of 1828.

ILLITERACY, noun [from illiterate.] The state of being untaught or unlearned; want of a knowledge of letters; ignorance.

PREJ'UDICE, noun [Latin prejudicium; proe and judico.]

1. Prejudgment; an opinion or decision of mind, formed without due examination of the facts or arguments which are necessary to a just and impartial determination. It is used in a good or bad sense. Innumerable are the prejudices of education; we are accustomed to believe what we are taught, and to receive opinions from others without examining the grounds by which they can be supported.A man has strong prejudices in favor of his country or his party, or the church in which he has been educated; and often our prejudices are unreasonable. A judge should disabuse himself of prejudice in favor of either party in a suit. My comfort is that their manifest prejudice to my cause will render their judgment of less authority.

2. A previous bent or bias of mind for or against any person or thing; prepossession. There is an unaccountable prejudice to projectors of all kinds.

3. Mischief; hurt; damage; injury. Violent factions are a prejudice to the authority of the sovereign. How plain this abuse is, and what prejudice it does to the understanding of the sacred Scriptures. [This is a sense of the word too well established to be condemned.

The word "Indoctrination" did not appear in Webster's Dictionary. The greatest fears of the Founding Fathers in establishing voting rights for the uneducated was the great potential they could be influenced by outside forces, nations and religions. Unrestricted voting rights for the uneducated were the greatest leap forward for any government 235 years ago.

In total, around 230,000 soldiers served in the Continental Army, The Continental Army was supplemented by about 145,000 militiamen. It is estimated that around 5,000 African-Americans served as soldiers in the Revolutionary War. (1:71)

The black soldiers served alongside white soldiers, making the Continental Army a desegregated, integrated army, which it would not be again until 1948. More served on the British side. Interestingly, they made very good spies.

Undoubtedly, no one suspected them. (History of Massachusetts)

In the Chapter about George Washington and Jewish Connections, Half-Way Inn owned by John Hendricks was discussed. About 1,000 feet down creek from the barn is a little wooded area. This property was sold off more than a century ago. It was the cemetery for black soldiers in the Revolutionary War. No doubt George Washington arranged this with Inn Keep John Hendricks. As I drove by I always thought that it really is sacred ground that has never been disturbed. Nothing was ever built on that cemetery in 240 years. Trees have taken over and there are no markers, but it is a testimony.

At the time of the Revolutionary War, this inn was the sole structure in the area. When the huge estates with mansions were built in the 1800s, the village was built to house those who worked on the estates. It would have been a remarkably good selection. It was on the major road and on a creek leading to a landing place on the Hudson River. It would have been under the supervision of John Hendricks and, therefore, a safe, permanent site. It has been neglected, but left undisturbed for 240 years.

Remarkably, the slaves fleeing almost a century later would have passed this site by either the road or the creek to the next stop, which was the overshot barn at the former inn.

This is noteworthy in that it shows an aspect of Washington's leadership and concern for black soldiers that has not been challenged or changed in all this time.

There is no instance known wherein blacks were anything other than clearly good soldiers. In reconsidering the vantage point of our Founding Fathers, however, there seems to be no indication that any of the Founding Fathers were aware of literacy of blacks. Thus, there appear to be no advocates for their rights as citizens with voting rights that are in public awareness. Their expansiveness was limited to the possibilities they recognized. Accepting voting rights for all white men was a gigantic leap forward. In our times, this void in knowledge and experience is as incomprehensible as the potential was 235 years ago.

Noah Webster's dictionary of 1828 did not have a term for peasant. One of the definitions for serfs was slave. The terms that would have been appropriate for many soldiers would be a rustic (coarse, plain and simple) or a commoner (One of the lower rank, or common people.

The Founding Fathers were including those who would be called vulgar, the common unlettered people. The Founding Fathers would have considered gentry, people of education and good breeding. It would have been extraordinary to allow the gentry to have equal voting rights with the vulgar, when they would also have been outnumbered. Having a society without class and land ownership was a huge and courageous leap forward. Including slaves would have been unthinkable. Including women would have gone way part sensibility. Establishing the Electoral College and leaving the determination of the qualifications to each state was, in reality, a deal which actually enabled the Constitution to be ratified.

According to Noah Webster
WOMAN, noun plural women. [a compound of womb and man.]

1. The female of the human race, grown to adult years. And the rib, which the Lord god had taken from the man, made him a woman Genesis 2:22. Women are soft, mild, pitiful, and flexible. We see every day women perish with infamy, by having been too willing to set their beauty to show. I have observed among all nations that the women ornament themselves more than the men; that wherever found, they are the same kind, civil, obliging, humane, tender beings, inclined to be gay and cheerful, timorous and modest.

In case you found the word pitiful alarming, this is Webster's definition:
PIT'IFUL, adjective [See Pity.] Full of pity; tender; compassionate; having a heart to feel sorrow and sympathy for the distressed. James 5:11. 1 Peter 3:8. [This is the proper sense of the word.]
Miserable; moving compassion; as a sight most pitiful; a pitiful condition.

2. To be pitied for its littleness or meanness; paltry; contemptible; despicable. That's villainous, and shows a most pitiful ambition in the fool that uses it.
3. Very small; insignificant.

It follows to investigate Webster's definition of MAN MAN, noun plural men. [Heb.species, kind, image, similitude.]
1. Mankind; the human race; the whole species of human beings; beings distinguished from all other animals by the powers of reason and speech, as well as by their shape and dignified aspect. 'Os homini sublime dedit.'.....Woman has, in general, much stronger propensity than man to the discharge of parental duties.

6. It sometimes bears the sense of a male adult of some uncommon qualifications; particularly, the sense of strength, vigor, bravery, virile powers, or magnanimity, as distinguished from the weakness, timidity or impotence of a boy, or from the narrow mindedness of low bred men. I dare do all that may become a man

9. One who is master of his mental powers, or who conducts himself with his usual judgment. When a person has lost his senses or acts without his usual judgment, we say, he is not his own man
11. In popular usage, a husband. Every wife ought to answer for her man

The point of being aware of definitions of this period is to provide context for many of the decisions made at that time. It appears that the well-educated were brilliant beyond our reality. They were enlightened as to knowledge and wisdom on many levels. However, their social norms would be considered stereotypes at an absurd degree.

It is also important to know our Constitution established a system of government. Personal and social factors were to be amendments as indicated by the Bill of Rights. Interestingly, arguments are debated in terms of subjects, rather than the organization after the ratification of the constitution.

The senior governmental problem we face in our times is enabling all qualified voters to participate. Thus, this book suggests Revamping the Constitution to change The Electoral College to a dedication to Voters and Voting Rights. This would be distinguished from All the People.

Our Constitution established the Electoral College process, wherein each state chooses the electors. Then, the electors meet and vote for the positions of President and Vice President, and the Congress counts the electoral votes. Each state establishes their own rules for choosing their electors.

From the ratification until the Twelfth Amendment, each elector cast two votes; the person who received the most electoral votes would become president. Each delegate had two votes. The president would have the most votes and the Vice-President, the second most. As you would imagine every delegate cast one of their votes for Washington, so he was unanimous. John Adams received the second most. In the first election only 10 states had ratified the constitution.

The method of determining electors was left to each state.

Some still required ownership of land to be eligible.

The Electoral College includes 538 electors. A majority of 270 electoral votes is required to elect the President. Each state's entitled allotment of electors equals the number of members in its Congressional delegation, one for each member in the House of Representatives plus two for the Senators.

Under the 23rd Amendment of the Constitution, the District of Columbia is allocated three electors and treated like a state for purposes of the Electoral College. For this reason, in the following discussion, the word "state" also refers to the District of Columbia.

The Framers established the Electoral College as a method wherein voters would elect the President, instead of the legislature, concerned that a large number of illiterate voters would be unduly influenced. The Electoral College numbers are based on the numbers of Congressional delegates in each state. Only two states divide the delegates according to the percentage of votes in that state. The other 48 states operate with a winner-take-all method. Therefore, a candidate who wins large states with a very narrow victory can win the election without winning the popular vote.

While advocates of the Electoral College claim this solves the problem of contested votes, another problem remains. In two of our last five elections, the candidate, who won the popular vote, nevertheless lost the election. In the case of Gore versus Bush, Gore would have won had the discrepancies in Florida been settled before the finalized count.

The fact that there have been more than 700 challenges to this system indicates that we need to rectify the system. To date, there has not been a challenge to the Framework itself.

What would happen if each state were required to have proportional electors rather than a winner-take-all process? What if the battleground states changed to proportional representation? It would not change the Framework itself. Would that remedy future elections in the short term? In a later chapter, I offer some alternatives toward a shift from the Electoral College to a Council for the Voters based on the Framework as an organizing system.

This example serves to demonstrate both the possibility and importance of only considering changes to the Constitution that do not violate the Framework itself. The power of our government springs from ALL THE PEOPLE, not citizens exclusively. That would have, at the time, only included male heads of families. The critical overwhelming matter was to limit the possibility of monarchy and the influence of religious institutions. Neither monarchies nor religious organizations would have power over individuals in America. That is the most fundamental aspect of our Constitution. The power does not come DOWN to the people. The people are the power. In other words, in America, the term "public servant" means that the power of elected officials is delegated by the voters. The people do not serve those in power.

This is the area that requires intelligent revamping, not reframing. The system is fine, but the nature of the Electoral College requires change. The purpose of including voters has not changed. We now need to address voters as a specific group within the whole. We need to expand and protect the most important element of our government. There are suggestions for the repurposing this sphere in "Chapter 15: Repurposing." The framework itself is the sacred foundation of our constitution. Our suggestion is that it be changed to Voters and Voter Issues.

We the People

The necessary clarification is that voting rights for slaves, women, and various nationalities could be expanded through the Constitution. We the People were the family groups headed most often by the male. However, the right of the people to choose leaders by their vote is sacrosanct. Abuse of power turns out to be the abuse of the most important quality of our republic.

This the foundation, the sphere of inclusion.

Chapter 21 |The Bill of Rights Preamble

The Conventions of a number of the States, having at the time of their adopting the Constitution, expressed a desire, in order to prevent misconstruction or abuse of its powers, that further declaratory and restrictive clauses should be added: And as extending the ground of public confidence in the Government, will best ensure the beneficent ends of its institution.

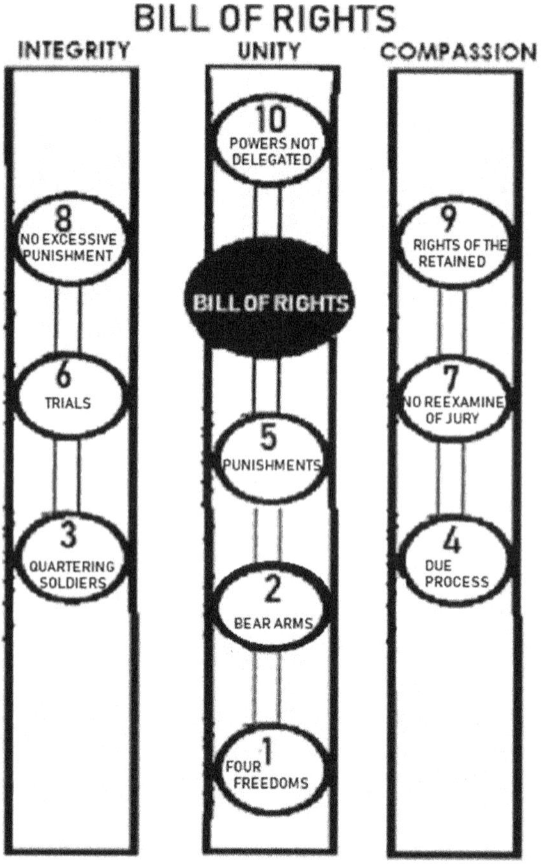

The Framework of our Constitution is the structure of our Republic. The Bill of Rights is the essence of the values we hold dear. They are the extra dimension of our Constitution. It is obvious that the Framers did not want the Constitution to be anything other than a perfectly balanced form. Including rights was just not possible for them. Who knows which of the major Framers thought of a Bill of Rights aligned in the same format or frame? It was an ingenious remedy. It obviously insured that amendments would be aligned properly.

This position on the Frame does not have a number and does not have direct pathways. It is on the center pillar but is clearly in a different dimension. Thus, it is the proper location for the Bill of Rights and the other amendments. One could explain the connected numbers and pathways as the foundation or "FREEDOM FROM." The Sphere for this component is connected to the Eye of Illumination. It embodies "FREEDOM TO." One could conceptualize this as the Soul of the Constitution.

In all other frames leading from the Constitutional frame, this is a flexible application related to the individual frames.

The Amendments

The Framers intended the amendments to enlarge and expand the values we hold dear. They designed them to make our Constitution a relevant foundation as we shift and change as a country and as a people.

It is critical to know that the Amendments will always shift and change. Their context is the rights of "We the People," individually and collectively.

The Constitution is the very structure of our government. The components are a stable system. The Framework itself must never be changed.

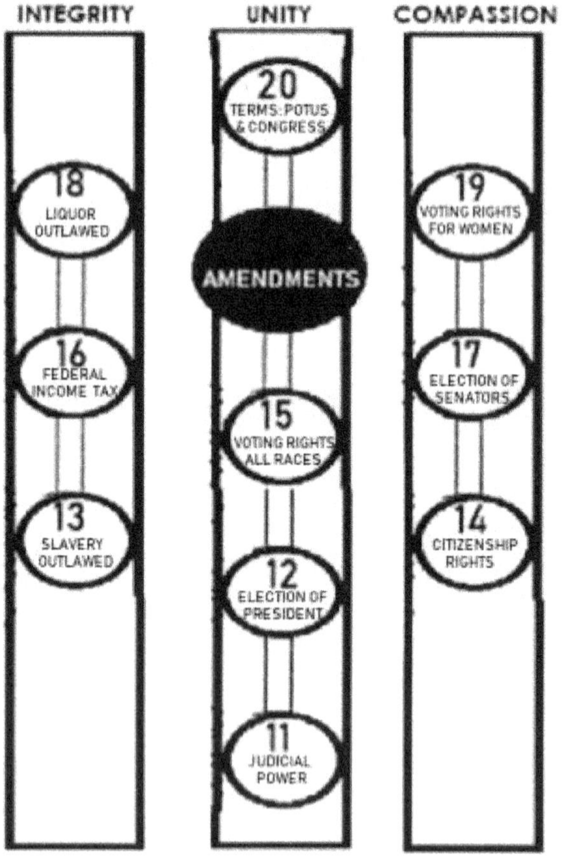
INTEGRITY
UNITY
COMPASSION
20
TERMS: POTUS & CONGRESS
18
LIQUOR OUTLAWED
AMENDMENTS
19
VOTING RIGHTS FOR WOMEN
16
FEDERAL INCOME TAX
17
ELECTION OF SENATORS
15
VOTING RIGHTS ALL RACES
13
SLAVERY OUTLAWED
14
CITIZENSHIP RIGHTS
12
ELECTION OF PRESIDENT
11
JUDICIAL POWER

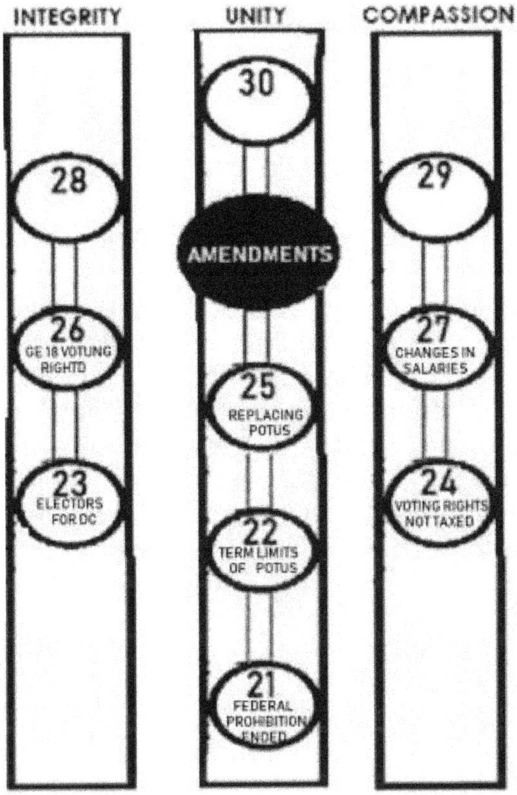
INTEGRITY
UNITY
COMPASSION
30
28
29
AMENDMENTS
26
GE 18 VOTUNG RIGHTD
27
CHANGES IN SALARIES
25
REPLACING POTUS
23
ELECTORS FOR DC
24
VOTING RIGHTS NOT TAXED
22
TERM LIMITS OF POTUS
21
FEDERAL PROHIBITION ENDED

Chapter 20 | Extending the Framework

The precepts of the Freemasons came from Pythagoras, Hermes, and other ancient teachers of the great wisdom through the Society of StoneMasons in Europe. The society evolved out of Scotland after stonemasons working on the country's public buildings in the 1500s banded together — in a similar way to modern trade unions — in a bid to protect the secrets and interests of their trade.

By 1599, William Schaw, who built castles and palaces for James VI of Scotland, had laid down rules for members to abide by, including: "They shall be true to one another and live charitably together as becometh sworn brethren and companions of the Craft." This was significant in the times when all strangers were suspect and masons had to move from one building site to another All of the magnificent cathedrals and castles used these ancient patterns.

Canterbury Cathedral

Norwich Cathedral Interior

Lincoln Cathedral Interior

Even a glance at the Hermetic Tree shows it is the basic pattern for all these magnificent Cathedrals. It is simply a matter of arranging this basic pattern in endless combinations. In their perceptions, God was the "Great

Architect in the Sky." The variable was the diameter. Each part had an identified spiritual component. It is, therefore, quite easy to understand the distinction between Freemasonry as an intelligent system totally separated from both church and state.

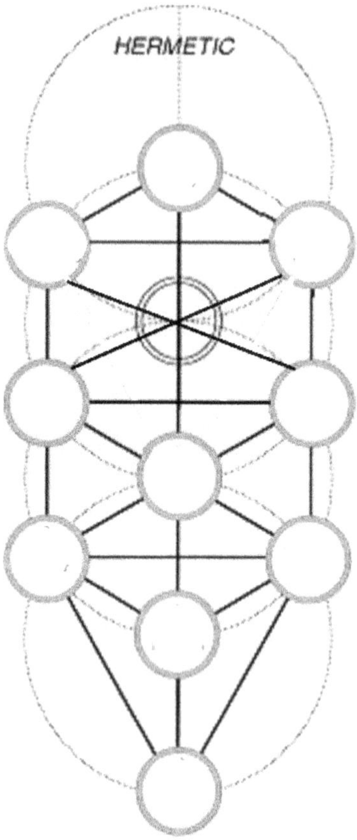

In 1641, soldier and diplomat, Sir Robert Moray, joined a stonemasons' lodge and subsequently formed The Society of FreeMasons. FreeMasons followed the same teachings and rituals, but were not doing the physical work of actual building.

As a system, the tree works in either direction. When we study the Tree of Knowledge and the Tree of Life, we understand that the Tree of Knowledge was created for all peoples to return to God according to individual choices. The Book of Genesis contains mathematics. In the application of the Framework for our government, the People represent that individual choice. Thus, the numerical components begin with each individual.

When the Jews were given the Tree of Life during the Age of Aries, they were mandated, as a nation, to follow the patterns as received from God throughout their generations. In the Tree of Life, the numerical order is from the top down.

In the configuration of the tree itself, there is no designation of movement. Each of the components or spheres in our government can be extended.

In conventional patterns in the Tree of Life and the Tree of Knowledge, the frames are joined in four segments. The segments are derived from the concept of four worlds ascending in the Return to God, as in the Book of Genesis. The Tree of Life manifests in the whole of the Torah. In this case, four worlds descended from God in an increasingly more dense reality.

The Constitutional Framework has only one Frame. Extensions for each aspect of government are appropriate and possible.

The most common extension, according to the Tree of Knowledge, is in a set of four frames. It is commonly called "The Four Worlds," formed by joining the number ten to the number one sphere in four frames. These two aspects are joined, but not combined. In operations, this format is sometimes appropriate, but never obligatory.

STRING OF FOUR

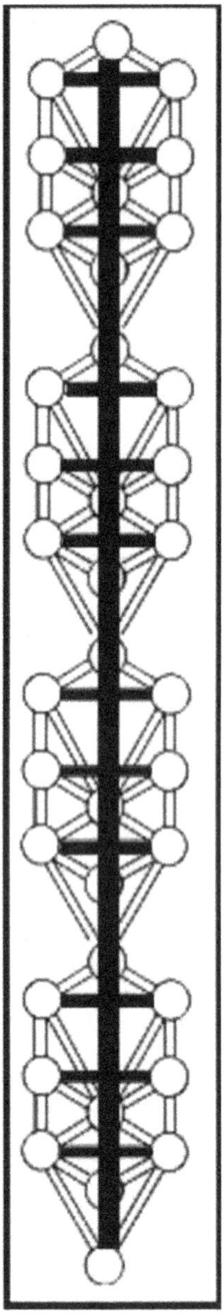

Configuration of our Bill of Rights & Amendments

In the Bill of Rights and the other Amendments, the list can be the same configuration of ten spheres or components. Our Framers deliberately configured the Bill of Rights in alignment with configurations in sets of ten, either in the standard frame or in the pillars. These are essentially stacked. As indicated in the String formation, they can connect with the frames numbered either from the top position down or beginning at the Number One position at the base of the frames. The first, eleventh and twenty-first positions can operate from the base or reverse. The tradition string has four frames, but it also works with numerous frames. The number ten position on each frame connects to the number one position on the next frame. The meaning of the conjoined frames is determined by the Framer.

SEQUENTIAL FRAMEWORK EXTENSION: The Caterpillar

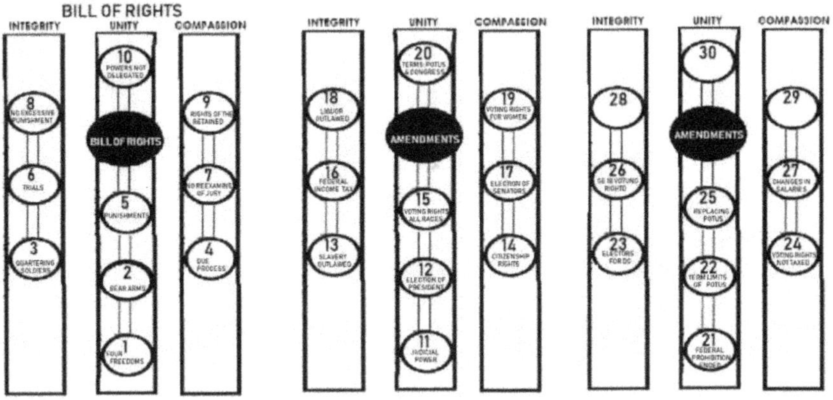

In our government, a different configuration is more appropriate. Rather than four distinct frames, we extend the frames in an elongated format with three pillars. We can call this grouping a ladder, or a string.

The Presidential frame delineates the specific areas under the direct leadership of the President.

In this case, the position of Vice-President is in the powerful position connected to the President, as differentiated from the Constitutional frame. In the Constitution itself, this position represents the significance of the document as the core foundation. Everything is subordinate to the Constitution. However, in the extensions and operations, this position may be used for configuring the specific extensions.

The connections from every sphere in the entire network begin in the reverse order in a new frame or extension. Thus, the leadership in every extension starts from the preceding sphere in the prior frame. The Constitutional Framework sources every position. The organization in the extensions are from the top down.

We the People, as expressed through the Voters, source the Framework. Thus, the Framework itself is from the lowest or bottom sphere as the Number 1 position.

It is an integrated network of organized frames. Information flows throughout the network in designated pathways. Authority flows from the initial Frame of the Government.

The Presidential Tree begins with the position of the President and descends in order of significance. Optionally, the order could be by the establishment of cabinet positions. The position of Attorney General was established after the government actually began.his is depicted in the Chapter called Extensions. The Vice-President is on the next lower position on the extended tree. He is not in the primary frame. Departments appear in order of establishment descending on the right and left pillars. Subsequent positions on the center pillar include the Chief of Staff, Bureaus, Committees, and other executive areas of responsibility. The First Lady or Spouse would also be on the Presidential Sphere. The executive responsibilities of the President are solely in this sphere. The President is not senior to the Legislative or Judicial Pillars. There are designated pathways to interact.

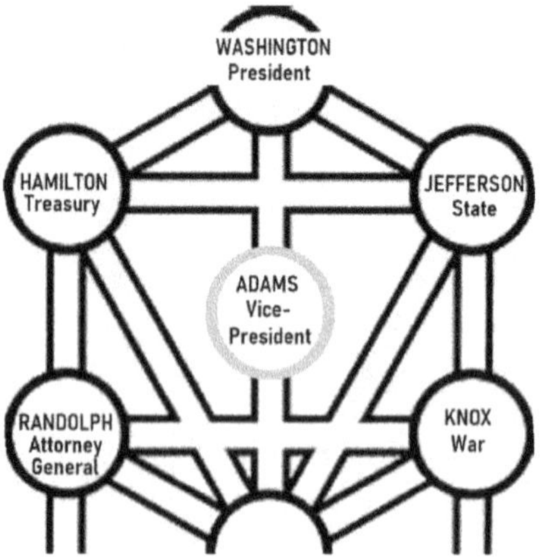

Since the applications of the extensions on the Framework are practical, I have chosen to use the 11th sphere as the position for the Vice-President. It makes best sense in that relationship, not as spirit, but rather a functioning specific active participant. As it has evolved, the responsibilities for each Vice-President are determined by each President. John Adams never attended a Cabinet Meeting. Some were instrumental in daily decisions. Others, obviously, became the next President. The determination to use this sphere was based on the concept that each Vice-President would his or her designated areas of authority. However, all other positions are connected to the President directly.

As the Office of the President has expanded over these years, the proper diagram to use is called the caterpillar. Unlike a traditional grouping of a string of four frames, this model extends directly and appropriately. This format is useful in the Legislature wherein each State would be represented by a sphere and related extensions.

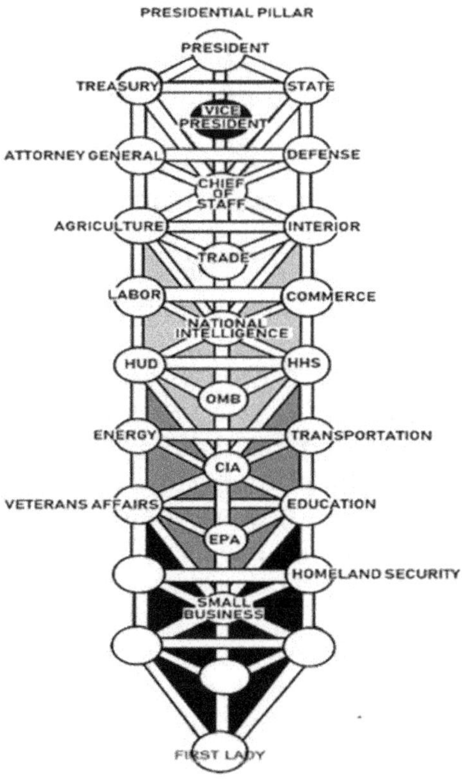

This model uses the center pillar for operations in the related extension.

The First Lady has evolved into a strategic position, again according to the Presidential operations. She (or He) would have her own tree of operations.

The Presidential Pillar does not interact with the Judicial and Legislative Pillars. Interactions occur primarily through the three leadership positions. They are co-equal in our Constitution.

In the cases of the House, the Senate, and the lower Federal Courts, this ladder is appropriate. In the legislative pillar, the right and left ladders contain the delegations from each state. The committees and designated functions are then located in the center pillar.

In the Federal Courts, the outer pillars are the districts.

In the leadership positions, the Speaker and the Chief Justice have a frame for their specific operations.

We can expand each sphere by either a ladder or a frame because each person acts as a team leader and unifier in their tree. This is the Constitutional Framework's form. The people source the government through their votes, and these people and areas are all team leaders or function leaders in their arena. In essence, each voter delegates power for others to combine and manage.

We can extend each sphere by connecting it to the number ten or the number one position in a frame or a ladder. Thus, the Framework becomes a composite of strings.

There is one distinction. The Constitutional Sphere, Sphere Zero, has only the straight linear progression with the Bill of Rights, and the other amendments, in order of passage. It contains the rules of our government as a whole. It is pure data, not relationships. However, in a string, this aspect designates a specific position or application.

Interactions between strings are not permanent or essential and are conditional on the Constitutional Frame. However, all are in conformity to the Constitutional frame and to the Constitutional sphere itself.

The zero space in the Constitutional frame is always the Constitution and the Amendments, including the Bill of Rights. No aspect of this differs from the Constitutional frame. It only grows in a linear formation of amendments. To be clear, the Constitutional Frame is the organizational system of our government. The Constitutional Sphere is the Constitution and Amendments. The Constitutional Sphere is in the same position in every frame of governance. There are no exceptions.

The other pattern contained in our Framework relates to lists, such as the Bill of Rights. This is a consecutive list that is not interactive. We comprehend the order as distinct sets of ten. The Framers wanted to make sure the amendments were not part of the interactive governance, but rather personal rights that are inherent in each individual. The Bill of Rights is a frame in and of itself. The amendments can be configured either as the worlds or in a ladder, as indicated earlier.

In a fundamental biblical perspective, recall that angels went up and down Jacob's ladder. That is a major aspect of the Tree of Knowledge, The Tree of Life, and the Framework of our Constitution.

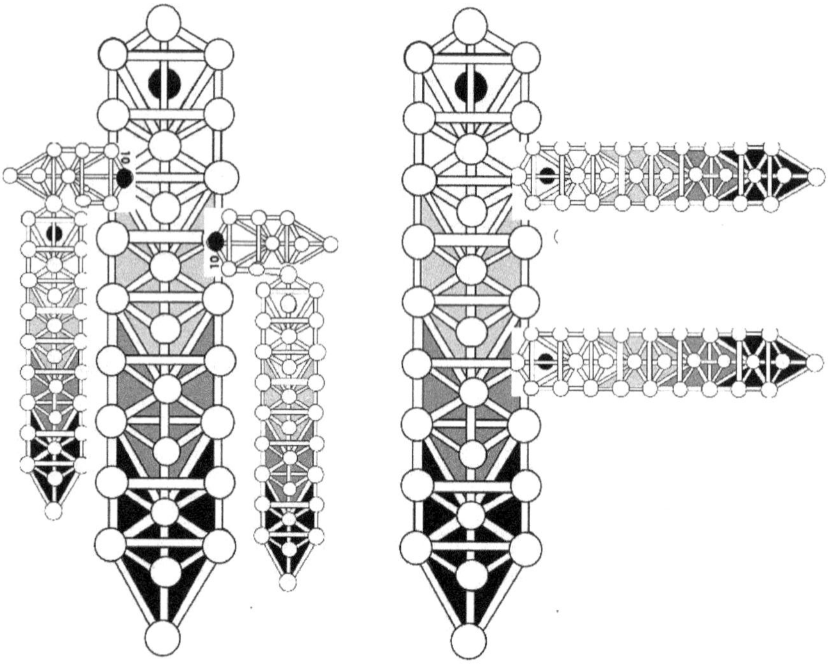

Each frame connects to the core frame. Therefore, the Constitutional Frame is the essential frame and all others follow. Any position on the Constitutional Frame has its own series of frames. Each sphere in the Framework becomes the senior position for the next frame or series of frames.

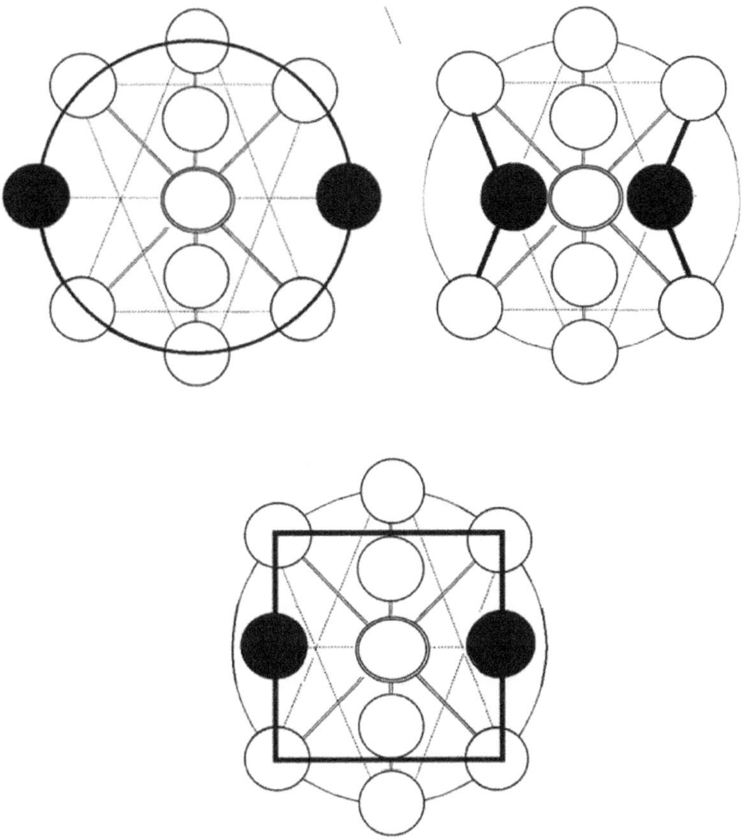

These are three variations of the tree formatted by shifting the midpoints.

1
3
2
4
6
5
7
9
8
10
12
11
13
15
14
15
17
16
18
20
19
21
23
22
24
26
25
27
29
28
30
32
31
33
35
34
36
38
37
39
41
40
42
44
43
45
47
46
48
50
49
DC
G
PR
NMI
VI
AS

To the left are two choices for configuration of the House and the Senate. They are listed numerically in this case. They can be listed according to all three pillars or secondly, on two pillars with committees in the center

The legislative configurations for both the House and Senate can use this format. Delineate them either by alphabetical order, or order of entry into the Union on the right and left pillars. The Speaker heads the House Pillar, and the Majority Leader heads the Senate Pillar. In the case of the house, each state would have a string enumerating the districts. Each district would have a string of its own for operations.

In the Senate, each state would the two Senators and each would have a frame or string of his or her own. The future States, Territories, and Washington DC would follow further in the basic pattern.

The number one position is the Speaker of the House or the Senate Majority leader.

In the Judiciary Pillar, there are three levels of Courts, which could be organized in three pillars. These could be organized in their strings as is the Legislative Branch

This circular frame possibly corresponds to the Law of the Iroquois, as well as the Tree.

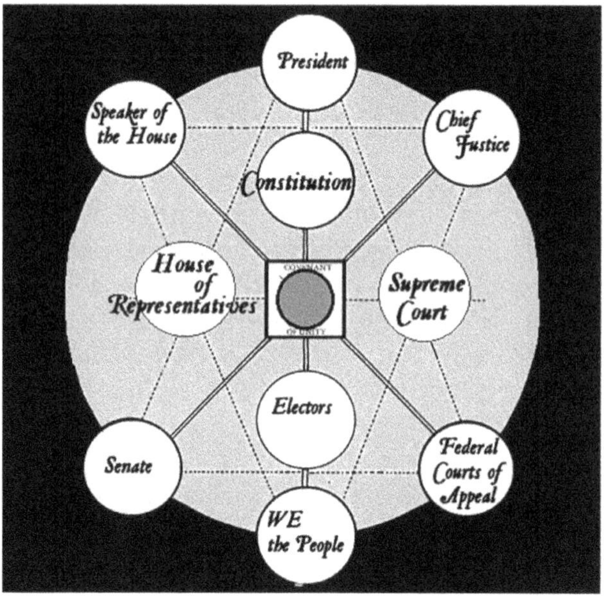
President
Speaker of the House
Chief Justice
Constitution
House of Representatives
Supreme Court
Electors
Senate
Federal Courts of Appeal
WE the People

Chapter 21 | Renewing the Basics

Changes to the Bill of Rights

In our time, there is a considerable challenge to the Second Amendment. At the time it was ratified, the right to bear arms was a significant issue for the Union. However, at no time did our Founding Fathers consider the possibility of assault rifles or high capacity ammunition magazines. In my heritage, John Irish of Vermont, a Quaker, was killed at his doorway by soldiers. The lead soldier later became a general. Such actions continue to challenge the rights of citizens today. Certainly, arms are a major concern for all Americans, and there must be a proper way to handle this sanely and constitutionally. My Facebook friends include many descendants of Peter Irish, the brother of John. Peter, a tax collector and a Quaker, was double taxed. In the end, he fled the Tories through the Vermont woods and on to safety in Canada. He served time after the Revolution before moving to Canada. It shows how deep we are in the ties that bind us as a nation and how points of view and commitment change.

One thing is apparent - Parkland students permanently changed the dialog on gun control. This change will happen through an amendment to the Constitution, rather than a change to the Framework of the government itself.

The Insurrection points to the mandate for clarification regarding weapons and their use. Using our American flag as a weapon was inconceivable before January 6, 2021.

If we consider original definitions, we note that individual families had, at most, a few muskets and rifles. They may have had a pistol and a tomahawk. Today, when visiting Colonial homes, which are museums, we often see one musket. No one then would have envisioned storage lockers filled with assault weapons, as is common today.

Consider that the killer in Dayton murdered nine people and wounded 27 others in 30 seconds. The week before, there were 22 people killed in El Paso, and 22 more wounded. All the victims were unarmed and unaware of the coming onslaught. No Framer, no person, could have conceived of those horrific events in our times.

Composition of the Senate

Term Limitations

There are advocates for term limitations. This would create our legislatures having people with the same age and experience. Having our legislative bodies without our elders would limit the breadth and depth of experience, knowledge and perspective.

It is quite remarkable at this time when we see the value of fresh new perspectives along with the elders. Incredible balance can result from the balance. Disaster can result from situations such as our 2010 elections, when the Republican Party purged themselves of all the moderate, experienced legislators. Those voices are gone. Now the Democrats are trying to keep the middle dominant and face the reverse problem of limiting Progressives, who are increasing in number.

Term limitations exacerbate these situations. They limit all the experience that comes with age. They eliminate knowledge within the system itself. These time constraints destroy the broad spectrum of outlook.

Mandating that experience be the guiding force can limit the voice that is coming forth. It is readily apparent by observing the 2010 elections that electing an entire group of people at once time served to remove an entire group of elder statesmen in the Republican party and they were the ones who would have made a constructive difference going forth.

Any manipulation that undermines the steady ongoing internal system should be avoided. Republicans have lost the voice of moderation. Democrats are mandating moderation.

Term limitations will serve to deepen the divide.

MOST OF ALL TERM LIMITATIONS WOULD DISTORT AND UNDERMINE THE CRITICAL ASPECT OF KNOWLEDGE WITHIN THE SYSTEM. THE SYSTEM WOULD BECOME THE VEHICLE OF THOSE WHO HAVE A TEMPORARY SHALLOW COGNIZANCE WITHOUT THE WISDOM OF EXPERIENCE WITHIN THE WHOLE.

ELECTORAL COLLEGE

Eliminating the Electoral College would be the first change to the Framework of our government. Rather than eliminating it, which would alter the Framework, it must be adjusted. However, if our Constitution is to survive going forward, voters and voting rights are the mandates we must face. Without active voter participation, we cannot address issues such as climate change and education. Voter participation is structured to be a vital component.

The proper foundation for this component is The Mayflower Compact

(We) do by these Presents, solemnly and mutually,

in the Presence of God and one another, covenant and combine ourselves together into a civil Body Politick,

for our better Ordering and Preservation, and

Furtherance of the Ends aforesaid:

And by Virtue hereof do enact, constitute, and <u>frame,</u>

such just and equal Laws, Ordinances, Acts, Constitutions, and Officers, from time to time,

as shall be thought most meet and convenient for the general Good of the Colony;

unto which we promise all due Submission and Obedience. [13]

Repeat: **do enact, constitute, and <u>frame,</u>**

In other words, WE FRAME A BODY POLITICK and, thus, the separation of church and state.

THE FRAMEWORK OF OUR CONSTITUTION

The Mayflower Compact was the first legal document in the colonies wherein every adult male was a signer without regard to rank, religion, or wealth. It was emphatically based on the separation of church and state. The compact was an enormous step forward in human rights.

Elias Boudinot, President of the Continental Congress at the close of the war, was another of the leaders dedicated to making blacks literate. His actions toward education in the first terms of Congress showed his dedication. Few understand this issue has substantively changed so that we need to review the purpose within the system for this position.

Eliminating the Electoral College would be the first change there has ever been to the Framework of our government. Rather than eliminating it, which would alter the Framework, it must be adjusted or revamped. However, if our Constitution is to survive going forward, voters and voting rights are the mandates we must face. Without active voter participation, we cannot address issues such as climate change and education. Voter participation is structured to be a vital component. Our Constitution was created without any reference point as to a federal democracy in action. They had the ancient system in the Framework, but not the experience in action. Changing the advanced design is a mistake. Revitalizing it in terms of experience within the system in action is, perhaps, a mandate in these disharmonious times.

"As Alexander Hamilton writes in "The Federalist Papers," the Constitution is designed to ensure "that the office of President will never fall to the lot of any man who is not in an eminent degree endowed with the requisite qualifications." The point of the Electoral College is to preserve "the sense of the people," while at the same time ensuring that a president is chosen "by men most capable of analyzing the qualities adapted to the station, and acting under circumstances favorable to deliberation, and to a judicious combination of all the reasons and inducements which were proper to govern their choice."

wanted to place a check on popular voting, which would include participation by uneducated and illiterate people. Hamilton, who had extremely high intellectual abilities, perhaps had the most reservations about giving too much voting power to "every man." (Miller, J)

It is important in our times to understand that our Founding Fathers were all highly educated men. They were considering the problem of including uneducated white men. It was a major feat that all men were included in signing the Mayflower Compact. Our constitution, however, increased the bar. The concern for this first constitutional democracy was including all white men regardless of status, money and education. It was an immense break-through. However, the greatest challenge was illiteracy. They were passionate to have every soldier take part in the right to vote. They also foresaw the potential problems. We face these today most seriously.

However, it was evident that white men could be educated. Educated slaves were few and far between. Educated women were an exception. No one could foresee blacks and women being educated. The three Master Framers did not get involved with issues regarding race and sex. Those aspects were debated in the convention as a whole. None of the members of the Committee of detail were part of or interested in those discussions. Their serious problem was white make voters without education.

In 1789 Franklin was taken to a school for black children. He was astounded. He, as with most people, had no idea blacks could be educated. He instantly had a profound shift in consciousness. He recognized not only that these children could be educated, but, more importantly, the reason for their dysfunction was that they were slaves. Obviously, they had no goals or opportunities outside of slavery. Franklin instantly got the entire picture and started a movement. At his age, however, he had only the time to initiate it.

Late in life, Franklin became an active leader of the Pennsylvania Abolition Society (PAS). He served as its president, in which capacity he is credited with the authorship of two documents that are the most significant writings of his final year. One was An Address to the Public, published by the PAS in October 1789 (Figure 4.9), which also took an environmental view of blacks, asserting that because of slavery the bondsman "too frequently sinks beneath the common standard of the human species. the galling chains, that bind his body, do also fetter his intellectual faculties, and impair the social affections of his heart."

The Address was accompanied by A Plan for Improving the Condition of the Free Blacks, which charged a committee of twenty-four PAS members with the responsibility for transacting "the business relative to free blacks." The committee was to do its work through four subcommittees, one of which was the Committee of Education, who shall superintend the school-instruction of the children, and youth of the Free Blacks; they may either influence them to attend regularly the schools already established in this city, or form others with this view; they shall in either case provide that, the pupils may receive such learning, as is necessary for their future situation in life; and especially a deep impression of the most important, and generally acknowledged moral and religious principles. The Plan and Address were followed early in 1790 by a petition to Congress, signed by Franklin as president, seeking to put slavery in America on the road to extinction." (Van Horne, John C.)

In all likelihood, Franklin being taken to a functioning school for blacks was the very beginning of our founders having any experience with educated blacks. It took seventy years until this reality came to the surface in the actuality of the Civil War. We can go back to see the dates of awareness, but we cannot impose the rocky road for self-determination without time and events.

There was not even a rudimentary thought that chants and dancing formed a direct interaction with a higher consciousness.

In this time there is no excuse for race and sex being a deterrent for civil rights including voting rights. Most assuredly, "our best minds" are not limited to white men. They are not the most educated as a group. Two hundred forty years ago, few people had experience of educated blacks. They would have been primarily in the north. Free blacks and slaves would have come from Northern Africa, where there was significant contact, albeit, much of it bad, but interaction with written language. In our time only severely uneducated and misguided people would question the capacity for any human being to vote and participate at every level.

To merely eliminate the Electoral College destroys the inherent Framework, balance, and interconnection of our Constitution. The challenge is to rethink and realign the

Second Sphere to Voters and voter rights. It is exceedingly important now to understand there is a huge void in our constitution. That void is protection of all voter rights. Voters are a separate category from "All the People."

REVAMPING THE FRAMEWORK

This chapter deals with making changes in the Constitutional Framework itself. Never forget that our Constitution was the first democracy. It was the very first government that was dedicated to the extraordinary inclusion of every soldier who fought for independence. Many did not read. Many more did not even speak English, but most spoke in the customary European languages. This government established the right to vote regardless of class, money, or distinguishing criteria of the time. All the porwancher actions on behalf of inclusion had their roots in the Framework. The concepts based on race and sex and national origin were established decades later but did not require a change in our Constitution.

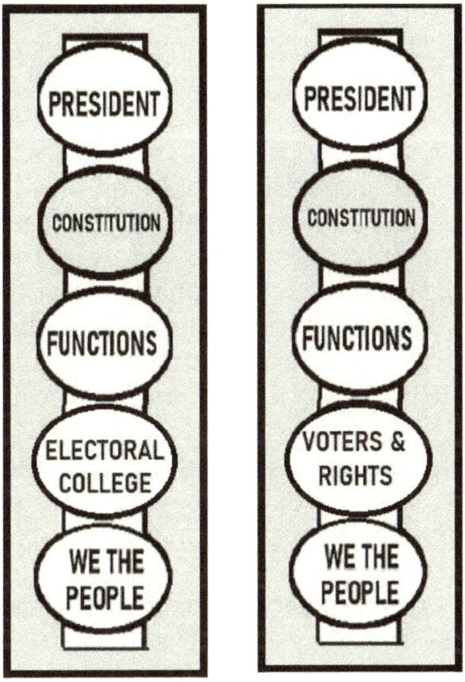

These are the number one and two positions on the Constitutional Frame. These are suggestions from the standpoint of the Framework itself and would require a change in the federal rules of our constitution.

These are concepts worth considering as changes far forthcoming. I assert voting for our President and Vice-President should be a dedicated constitutional concern that is consistent. There were signs of serious problems with our last election and there was no way to deal through the Electoral College. The very purpose of the Electoral College was violated.

Sphere 1 should be identified as "We the People." This would mean all people of all ages who are residents within the United States of America. Whether or not that designation means legal residents is to be determined, perhaps under the oversight of Sphere 2.

Sphere 2 contains the Electoral College. It can be altered, first of all, by changing "the winner takes all" concepts to representation according to a percentile of the voters.

Sphere 2 could be changed to "The Voters." This would be a radical change since this would eliminate the Electoral College as it was designed. All registered voters would be eligible, but only those who vote are participants. The purpose would be advocacy for all voter issues. Direct voting in a fair and responsible system would be the purpose. However, voting would be supported by a Voter Advocacy Committee with oversight from an Electoral Council.

Using the Framework as a guide, the Electoral Council would include past presidents and vice-presidents, the winners and the also-rans.

These people are an untapped resource. They have the sole direct expertise in the system, the election of the president and vice-president. They would assume their position upon completion of their term(s) in office. Appropriately, this group could also include the also-rans, those who ran for president, but were not elected. Throughout our history, many of these may have been the better choice. In any case, these people have the most expertise with our electoral process. Their purpose would be to oversee voter issues. I see them as a final authority.

I would call this group of experts, The Electoral Council."

As of today, this group would include Jimmy Carter, Michael Dukakis, Dan Quayle, Bill Clinton, Al Gore, Bob Dole, George W. Bush, Dick Cheney, John Kerry, Barack Obama, Joe Biden, Mitt Romney, and Hillary Clinton. This diverse group of people is the most prominent group alive, who have participated in the election process for President and Vice-President.

These are the experts on elections in America. Retired Supreme Court Justices would be appropriate members of such an august group. Perhaps retired long-term legislators could be invited to participate. One would hope this group could be responsible for a system to protect the voting by each and every American eligible to vote. Their purpose would be advisement. They could as a group decide if a President is not qualified to represent all of "The People" after their term of office.

Can you imagine that when a president took office, the losing candidate would become the leader of this aspect of government. They would join all those elected or not for our presidency, so there would be an automatic balance in party affiliation and, arguably, a stance for ALL THE PEOPLE, not party. In 2016 Hilary Clinton could have investigated election problems. In 2020, The president would have had a responsible avenue to proceed.

Certainly, they would have a staff of professionals for actual operations. This group does have the potential to be beyond political maneuvers and be concerned about All the People. They could be called the "Advocates."

The purpose of the committee would be to address voter issues. They would have the authority to address problems in all three branches of the Federal government as well as the governments of each state. The Legislative Branch would oversee implementation, signed into law by the President, and adjudicated by the Judicial Branch. Arguably, our voting system needs to be rectified. The cornerstone of our democracy is under attack, and participation is not a passionate mandate for far too many. Having these issues linked together would be a vast improvement over the helter-skelter manner that now exists. The problems are on-going, yet vital. We face serious gerrymandering this year in 2021. Having this aspect overseen or handled by the electoral council of past president, also-rans and vps would have the potential to establish boundaries that are not radical political divisions and manipulations.

This suggestion is aligned with the Framework itself.

The group would choose their designated leader and then deal with issues such as voter registration, voter suppression, gerrymandering, penalties, voting tallies, and security. In other words, the practices that directly affect the election of the leaders of this pillar of government, the President, and Vice-President.

These voter issues strike at the very foundation of our government. The situation is reprehensible, but also national in scope. All of the issues and aspects merit an on-going dedication, yet we have not had a single, focused system to rectify the problems and continue permanently. The problem is serious and unlikely to change without a significant on-going program that is not limited by the politics of the day.

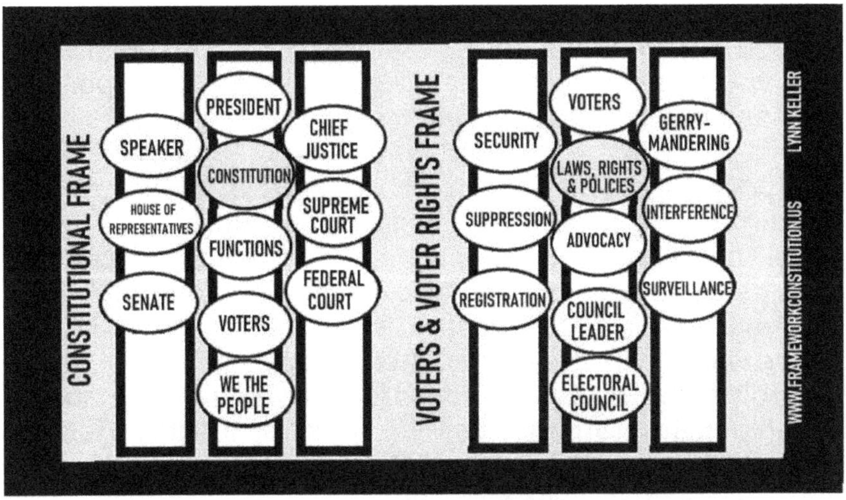

This recommendation for Revamping the Electoral College would bring together the voter issues. There is a strong case for unifying the procedures given the current problems.

This council would appoint a professional staff to establish and continue the operations. The National Democratic Redistricting Committee led by Eric Holder is a model in existence that could be the start of such a program. He has said "The biggest rigged system in America is Gerrymandering. Together we can fix that and restore fairness to our democracy. Join our fight because politicians should not be able to choose their voters - voters should choose their representatives."

"Getting to the Point with Eric H. Holder Jr" is an important talk at the Edward M. Kennedy Institute. He speaks with authority and involvement regarding this issue. (Getting to the Point with Eric H. Holder Jr)

The reality is that our Founding Fathers foresaw problems resulting from uneducated and illiterate voters. They foresaw problems from foreign intervention. They did not foresee the problems from a vast attack on our constitution and voters as a long term result of dedicated political passions and political parties.

The point is that we have an imperative to change our system at this point when it is broken and unfair. These initial thoughts include advisement by the Past Presidents, Past Vice-Presidents, and Also-Rans. The continual work for Advisement and Advocacy is mandatory now and the future was can foresee. There needs to be immediate action regarding these issues. The problems could be handled expeditiously, rather than through a lengthy judicial process. Many of these people have the potential to make non-partisan decisions with the whole nation in mind.

How would the structure itself work? Perhaps there could be a council of the entire group or one chosen by all members of this group and organized in alignment with the ten aspects of governance. It would seem advisable to have a leader, or a chairman and vice-chairman, for a three or four-year term. Bush, Clinton, and Obama have a fraternity of sorts, which would indicate a dedication to proper electoral determinations.

This is just a suggestion derived from the Framework itself. There are many options. The point is to make Voter Issues a co-equal sphere of the Framework. We can see that it must be revamped, given the alignment solely on party lines. That was not the intent of our Framers.

The Electoral College was created to address the problem of illiterate men being given the right to vote. The idea of blacks being literate was not in this time frame. The Electoral College addresses a concept that is unthinkable and absurd in our times. In our times the problem arises from those who are poorly educated and biased. The problem is still Voters and Voter issues. The reality has totally reversed. Our first black president and black first lady have led America in the very best alignment to our constitution in modern history. In fact, they are our new gentry and leading us to better and better application of our constitution and our democracy.

A mandatory problem in our government and in our society at this very time is to enable every single voter to have their vote represent them. Just eliminating the Electoral College does not address this deep and vital issue. It merely changes one aspect while destroying the very operating system of our Framework. This sphere of our constitution must be rethought and revamped intelligently, positively, and fairly.

WE THE PEOPLE

The other aspect needing clarification is "We the People," a matter for the Sphere 1. Once voters replace the Electoral College, the composition of the people in our nation becomes a challenge. This aspect demands clarification. We see the plight of DACA. There are numerous problems with identity. Not least, the frequent bias that this is a Christian Nation, decidedly not the intent of our founding fathers. They took serious steps for inclusion. We are mandated to include all marginalized people. No one should be excluded because of identity, whether chosen or not. It is a matter of status - being an American from birth to death.

This is just a suggestion derived from the Framework itself. There are many options. The point is to make Voter Issues a co-equal sphere of the Framework. We can see that it must be revamped, given the alignment solely on party lines. That was not the intent of our Framers.

Immediately after the 1940 elections, my mother, Anna Phifer, was contacted by the German American Alliance to join their cause. She was outraged and wrote the following letter:

Nov. 14, 1940

German-American National Alliance, Inc.
1606 N. Larrabee St.
Chicago, Ill.

Your voting recommendations were decidedly unwelcome in a household which is entirely American and totally without German antecedents. I view any recommendations from a notorious organization such as yours as doing only a great injustice to the candidates unfortunate enough to get your approval.

There is no place in the national picture of our great country for hyphenated Americans. Either you are Americans or you are Germans. There is no connection between the philosophies or way of life of the two. In times such as these, when the Nazi hordes are engaged in an attempt to destroy civilization, I would think that people in The United States of German origin would be busy living down that very fact.

Time Mag. Letters Col. Oct 28th

The enclosed quotation expresses precisely the feelings of all real citizens who owe no allegiance to a foreign country.

In the future, please do not send any more communications.

Sincerely,

Anna Smith Phifer

My family context taught me that we are not hyphenated Americans. To my family, "We the People" are not hyphenated. I hope we can attain that quality once again.

Could our non-contiguous Native Americans have a state of their own? Would Puerto Rico want to be the 51st State? What about Washington DC?

I wish every citizen knew that story of their ancestors who immigrated to America. My mother, who wrote this letter, descended from the Mayflower, as well as from Chief Canonicus. I have 235 recognized ancestral lines in America, the majority made an impact when they came as immigrants. It keeps America alive to our traditions.

I wish every person, whose ancestors came in slavery, knew the story of their ancestors, who were freed or born in freedom. We totally omit the stories of the many, who gave their lives and worked ceaselessly to free staves. Rather than repeating the stories of those who created our democracy as slave owners, we should recognize the wonders they did do in a far different time. Now it is paramount that we live and think as one people. Thurgood Marshall, whose ancestors immediately opened a grocery store, and Michelle Obama have extraordinary stories. Michelle's great-great-grandfather, James Robinson, had three jobs as a young man. One was delivering newspapers. This enabled him to make certain his children read the newspaper every day.

I have told these stories to many blacks. Not one is aware of personal stories of whites helping blacks to be freed or after freedom. Whites do not even know the stories of whites helping blacks. They do not know the stories of soldiers in the Civil War, who died or came back with what is no called PTSD. One of my American Revolution Ancestors had ten children. In the 2nd and 3rd generation, most of the men died or came back with what we would now call PTSD.

The women died spinsters. We are missing the personal stories. We are missing the stories of people helping people, people being kind. Call it "The Story Quilt of America."

Whites in general do not understand the cumulative effect of racism individually and collectively. The malpractices and issues are never resolved – over these centuries. Each horrifying act is part of a collective whole. It is not one event at a time. Some people and some acts are particularly significant, but they are representative and not isolated.

The point of this is that time is not flat. We cannot make judgments without a full range of data and experience. When a Black makes a great achievement, it is important to know their family history, to know the generation by generation steps that brought them to their moment in time. What are the family stories that led to destiny? What were the values along the way? This is the history we are missing.

There are so many great stories of inclusion. This would be the true story quilt of America. What is lacking are the stories of inclusion and dedication to the rights of all and the stories of those who broke through the barriers.

I would begin my story with William Phifer, who worked with the Underground Railroad. He was a 40-year-old bachelor during the civil war, often seen at night leading a riderless horse. As the blacks passed through Knox County, Ohio, on the way to freedom, William would take every couple to the Justice of Peace to get married, their first act in freedom. William's grandfather, Jacob Phifer, was a Mason. It appears that his sons were as well as his grandsons. Jacob Phifer, born in 1757, served in the Revolution and the War of 1812.

This story adds the other significant dimension to the blacks gaining self-determination after the Civil War. There are many good stories. Tell them. They got married. They got an education. Their values and actions were in the highest accord. We must not keep the sstories of kindness hidden.

My ancestor, Samuel Ogle, lived in Illinois before statehood. Samuel, a Quaker, purchased a slave in Delaware so that he could emancipate him immediately after bringing him to Illinois. That record enabled me to date Samuel being in Illinois before statehood.

Ideas that would result in changing the Framework, rather than eliminating the operation of the Electoral College, could have a sphere comprising the issues that significantly concern us in our times. But the Framework is the very cornerstone of our democracy. Serious problems have been manifested in the last two decades. Interference from outside groups and governments might come under this arena as well. All of this is presented here as an example of the Framework as an on-going component of our government.

We simply must present ourselves in order to become ONE PEOPLE. ONE DIVERSE PEOPLE. Inclusive, Open-minded, Compassionate, Aware and knowledgeable. What adjectives would you choose!

We, arguably, have entered the Aquarian Age. It has been cited as the "Brotherhood of Man." I assert a better term would be "The Age of Humankind." That would be an ideal purpose. All things considered, an imperative one.

It is the week after the murder of George Floyd. I consider my Mother's letter regarding "We are not hyphenated Americans. We are all Americans." I listen to responses. I find myself offended by people who identify this fine American as Black and decry Whites. George Floyd is an American Hero. He is an All American Hero. He was murdered by people who should not be called Americans. They are Trash. Uncapitalized "american." Americans are revolted. George Floyd is a Hero for Americans. Do not make him less. Do not make us less.

The punishment of anyone who commits a hate crime, such as this, should have their citizenship revoked.

PART THREE| THE FRAMEWORK IS IN PLACE

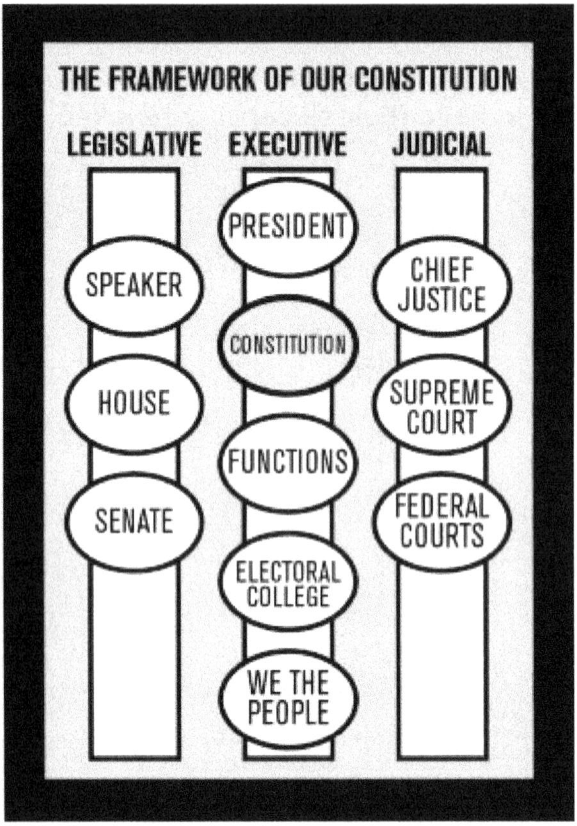

Chapter 18 | The Bonds of Our Fathers

We had four Preeminent Founding Fathers: Washington, Franklin, Jefferson, and Adams. Each of them had an imperishable bond with another statesman. Each was a colleague, confidante, and indelible connection that was totally trustworthy and competent. Each was a union. .Above all, they were chosen by John Hancock, President of the Second Continental Congress

John Hancock, President of the Founding Fathers

When John Hancock was seven in 1744 when his father died. John was then raised by his aunt and uncle in Boston. Thomas Hancock had a highly successful trading company. John grew into the business, including representing the Hancock Company at the highest levels of business and society in London. He inherited it in 1761 At age 24 he became of the richest and most powerful people in America. He had a degree from Harvard Law School. He was, therefore, in a strategic position with Great Britain in taxation issues from the beginning. During a trip to Quebec in 1762, Hancock was first made a Freemason in the Merchants Lodge No. 277. Upon his return to the colonies later that year, he became a devoted Brother to the Lodge of St. Andrew in Boston. He began the taxation problems believing in negotiating.

The strategy of the British was not good from the beginning. The first ship they entered to force taxation was "The Lydia," named for Hancock's daughter who died in infancy. They had no warrant, so nothing got out of hand. This led to the Townsend Acts, increasing the taxation outcries. Their next action was to enter "The Liberty," owned by Hancock. Unable to negotiate the return of his vessel, Hancock, defended by John Adams, was later cleared of smuggling charges. The evidence against him in the Liberty Affair was simply too flimsy. Then the Boston Massacre was waged in 1770. (Boston Massacre)

The Boston Tea Party happened in 1773. Boston Patriots who were members of the Sons of Liberty included Samuel Adams, his cousin, John Adams, John Hancock, James Otis, Josiah Quincy, Paul Revere, and Dr. Joseph Warren.

In 1775 Paul Revere made his famous ride. He warned Samuel Adams and John Hancock that they were the prime targets of the British.

John Hancock was President of the First Continental Congress and of the Second Continental Congress for a one year term.

Continental Congress

Peyton Randolph VA Sep. 5–Oct. 22, 1774 Master Mason and Uncle of Edmund Randolph

Henry Middleton SC Oct. 22–Oct. 26, 1774 (4 Days)
His son, Arthur, became delegate & Signer.

Second Continental Congress

Peyton Randolph	VA May 10–May 24, 1775
John Hancock	MA May 24, 1775–Oct. 31, 1777
Henry Laurens Freemason	SC Nov. 1, 1777–Dec. 9, 1778 See List of readings.Milestone. stance on Slavery
John Jay	NY Dec. 10, 1778–Sep. 27, 1778 1stChiefJustice Freemason, Signer
Samuel Huntington	CT Sep. 28, 1779–Mar. 1, 1781 Signer Grand Mason

Following the creation of the Articles of Confederation, **The Confederation Congress** convened on March 2, 1781.

Samuel Huntington CT Mar. 2–July 6, 1781 Signer, Mason

Thomas McKean DE July 10–Oct. 23, 1781 Signer, Chief Justice, Governor, Mason

John Hanson MD Nov. 5, 1781–Nov. 3, 1782 Hanson was chosen to be President under Articles of Confederation unanimously by Congress (which included George Washington). In fact, all the other potential candidates refused to run against him, as he was a major player in the revolution and an extremely influential member of Congress. He appointed 2nd Great Seal Committee

Elias Boudinot	NJ Nov. 4, 1782–Nov. 3, 1783 He Appointed 3rd Great Seal Committee
Thomas Mifflin	PA Nov. 3, 1783–Nov. 30, 1784 Convention delegate, PA first governor.

Richard Henry Lee VA Nov. 30, 1784–Nov. 4, 1785 Signer, Justice of Peace, Early leader for Revolution Author of The Independence Resolution: *"Resolved, That these United Colonies are, and of right ought to be, free and independent States, that they are absolved from all allegiance to the British Crown, and that all political connection between them and the State of Great Britain is, and ought to be, totally dissolved. That it is expedient forthwith to take the most effectual measures for forming foreign Alliances. That a plan of confederation be prepared and transmitted to the respective Colonies for their consideration and approbation."*

John Hancock	MANov. 23, 1785–June 5, 1786
Nathaniel Gorham MA	June 6, 1786–Feb. 2, 1787 Chairman of Committee of the Whole, Member of Committee of Detail
Nathaniel Gorham MA	June 6, 1786–Feb. 2, 1787
Arthur St. Clair	PAFeb. 2–Oct. 5, 1787 General, Mason, Governor, Northwest Territory
Cyrus Griffin	VA Jan. 22, 1788–Mar. 2, 1789 Mason, Judge

Washington's First Cabinet

His choices were Secretary of State Thomas Jefferson, Secretary of Treasury Alexander Hamilton, and Secretary of War Henry Knox. While the Department of Justice would not be created until 1870, Washington appointed and included Attorney General Edmund Randolph to serve in his first cabinet.

Thus, Adams as Vice-President was chosen by voters. Franklin was no longer in the picture. Jefferson was the other leader from the four preeminent Founders. They were the two subsequent Presidents.

Randolph, Hamilton, and Madison were in the above list of the most connected associates.

General Henry Knox continued in the fine military relationship he had with Washington.

With respect to the Committee of Detail, President Washington appointed Edmund Randolph to be his Attorney General. He appointed John Rutledge, James Wilson, and Oliver Ellsworth to be associate justices. He later appointed John Rutledge and Oliver Ellsworth to be Chief Justices. Nicholas Gorham was on the Committee of Detail as President of the Continental Congress at the time of the Convention. He was the sole person on the committee, who was not a lawyer. He, therefore, would not have been an appropriate choice for the Court. His bond was with Hancock.

Benjamin Franklin: John Rutledge

Franklin and Rutledge had been bonded because of their Freemason passions as well as their family loyalties being split. Both Franklin's son and Rutledge's father were on the path to return to England. Franklin had been active in The Albany Plan of Union of 1754.

Franklin's image against having the states split into individual units.

The plan was to have all the colonies in America be organized as a collective unit to deal with England. The path to the French and Indian Wars proceeded instead.

However, the concept government wherein the states would elect a Grand Council, while England would appoint a President General. It would resolve issues with the Native American Tribes and as well as those between the states. The plan also allowed the new government to levy taxes for its own support. The Plan failed but Franklin continued to work with the Indians. Rutledge joined him as his ally and confidante for three decades.

In 1789 when our new government was forming, Franklin had a new passion. He had been taken to a school in Philadelphia where black children were being taught to read. He quickly realized that illiteracy was the cause of all the attitude problems the slaves had was due to illiteracy and, thus, not having achievable goals. Black people finally had a passionate advocate, but he died the next year. His death altered history in America for this reason. Simultaneously, Rutledge lost his personal advocate. Washing appointed him to be the second Supreme Chief Judge of the Supreme Court, but he was not approved.

Franklin and Rutledge made their relationship low key in public. No one paid attention that he was the working partner of one of the greatest polymaths of all time in a time that had major significance.

"Never contradict anybody," Adams was advised by Franklin, whom he admired above all men, though it was advice he hardly needed."(McCullough) That principle was core to Franklin's life and consequently to Rutledge. Their pattern waa always to drop back from any confrontation. Find a different path. Was that key to the friction between Franklin and Adams, as well as the dismissal of Rutledge in Adams' mind?

George Washington: Edmund Randolph

Payton Randolph, Edmund Randolph's uncle, was President of the First Continental Congress before John Hancock. He died of a stroke in 1775. He was universally respected and it was assumed he would be the first President of our Country. He was extremely close friends with Washington and a cousin to Thomas Jefferson. Edmund became the protege of Washington during the Convention. He had a position akin to being heir apparent. He was on the Committee of Detail and was our first Secretary of State. He was responsible for negotiations of the Jay Treaty (though Alexander Hamilton wrote most of the instructions sent to John Jay).

Edmund had reservations regarding the Jay Treaty and voiced them to Washington. Washington was considering Randolph's suggestions when a letter from France was intercepted and given to the President. This letter implicated that Edmund had been discussing the turmoil in the Cabinet with the French Ambassador.

Washington must have crushed to the nth degree. He had held Edmund as a son. During a Cabinet meeting, in front of the other Secretaries, Washington handed Edmund the letter.

Randolph resigned immediately. He never had another Federal position.

This is a clear example of Washington in action. He never attacked another person without respect. Thus, he did not create enemies.

George Washington: Alexander Hamilton

Appointing Alexander Hamilton as the First Secretary of the Treasury has to be considered one of the best actions, if not the best, by any president. All that Hamilton did remains unchanged to a large degree.

There is an excellent new book about Hamilton as a Jew by Professor Andrew Porwancher.

There is a paragraph in The Jews and Freemasonry by Samuel Oppenheim that has an important perspective on Aaron Burr and the Duel.

"Samuel Simpson was also an officer for the Supreme Council of the Northern District in 1813 being the Inspector Lieutenant or Lieutenant Grand Commander. He was then 33 years old. He represented Clinton Lodge at Grand Lodge Meetings. And in 1812 and 1813 he was Grand Treasurer of the Grand Lodge of New York. Simson was the founder of Mount Sinai Hospital. An Account of him is given by the late Myer S. Isaacs. He studied law with Aaron Burr and is said to have been the first Jewish lawyer in New York." (Oppenheim)Simpson and Burr were both Freemasons. Hamilton was not.

That could have inadvertently been the source regarding Hamilton's mother being a Jew. Burr had abundant hatred against Hamilton. This might have the cruel fact that went over the top. Burr may well have announced to Hamilton that he knew his mother was a Jew. Being in a duel was totally out of character for Hamilton. His mother's honor was, perhaps, the only thing that Hamilton would not let pass.

Thomas Jefferson: James Madison

This is a very interesting pair. Jefferson was on diplomatic duty during the constitutional convention and Madison was the notetaker, who missed the main event, namely the Committee of Detail. Nor did they know the Framework. Certainly, Franklin and Washington, Rutledge and Randolph, knew that. However, both Jefferson and Madison were treated with such respect, they did not know what they did not know. In considering Jefferson and Madison were primarily involved after the Convention approved it, it is hard to assess them in terms of their partnership in terms of the Framework itself.

John Adams: John Quincy Adams

Certainly, John Adams was in sync with the other leaders during the Revolution. In his exhaustive book on John Adams, David McCollough has given us a plethora of wise and wonderful writings that embody our government and moral guidance. We have his letters to John Quincy and other family members. We lack their dialogue regarding JQA's clearly amoral degradation of Masons and their society. We start with John Adams quotes about our constitution and values

"Government is a plain, simple, intelligent thing, founded in nature and reason, quite comprehensible by common sense. . . . The true source of our suffering has been our timidity. We have been afraid to think. . . . Let us dare to read, think, speak, and write. . . . Let it be known that British liberties are not the grants of princes or parliaments, that many of our rights are inherent and essential, agreed on as maxims and established as preliminaries, even before Parliament existed. . . . Let us read and recollect and impress upon our souls the views and ends of our more immediate forefathers, in exchanging their native country for a dreary, inhospitable wilderness. Recollect their amazing fortitude, their bitter sufferings—the hunger, the nakedness, the cold, which they patiently endured—the severe labors of clearing their grounds, building their houses, raising their provisions, amidst dangers from wild beasts and savage men, before they had time or money or materials for commerce. Recollect the civil and religious principles and hopes and expectations which constantly supported and carried them through all hardships with patience and resignation. Let us recollect it was liberty, the hope of liberty, for themselves and us and ours, which conquered all discouragements, d angers, and trials. (McCullough)

"Improve your understanding for acquiring useful knowledge and virtue, such as will render you an ornament to society, an honor to your country, and a blessing to your parents . . . and remember you are accountable to your Maker for all your words and actions."(McCullough)

"Public business, my son, must always be done by somebody. It will be done by somebody or other. If wise men decline it, others will not; if honest men refuse it, others will not. A young man should weigh well his plans. Integrity should be preserved in all events, as essential to his happiness, through every stage of his existence. His first maxim then should be to place his honor out of reach of all men. In order to do this, he must make it a rule never to become dependent on public employments for subsistence. Let him have a trade, a profession, a farm, a shop, something where he can honestly live, and then he may engage in public affairs, if invited, upon independent principles. My advice to my children is to maintain an independent character. Oh!

"You are not singular in your suspicions that you know but little," he had told Caroline, in response to her quandary over the riddles of life. "The longer I live, the more I read, the more patiently I think, and the more anxiously I inquire, the less I seem to know. . . . Do justly. Love mercy. Walk humbly. This is enough. . . . So questions and so answers your affectionate grandfather." Adams"

That government is best which governs least.

"My Child Yours of March 20/31 I have received. I am well pleased with your learning German for many Reasons, and principally because I am told that Science and Literature flourish more at present in Germany than anywhere. A Variety of Languages will do no harm unless you should get a habit of attending more to Words than Things. But, my dear boy, above all Things, preserve your Innocence, and a pure Conscience. Your morals are of more importance, both to yourself and the World than all Languages and all Sciences. The least Stain upon your Character will do more harm to your Happiness than all Accomplishments will do it good. – I give you Joy of the safe Arrival of your Brother and the Acknowledgement of the Independence of your

Country in Holland. Adieu. John Adams to John Quincy Adams, 28 April 1782,

John Quincy Adams to his father

Sir,
you would give me some instructions, with regard to my time, and advise me how to proportion my Studies and my Play, in writing, and I will keep them by me, and endeavor to follow them. I am, dear Sir, with a present determination of growing better, yours.

To The Freemasons Of The State Of Maryland. ***July 1798***
Gentlemen,
I thank you for this generous and noble address.

The above letter was written by John Adams when President Adams. There were lodges in Boston before he was born. Masons led the Boston Tea Party in 1773. After the Battle of Bunker Hill in 1775, John Hancock became Grand Master of the Lodge and went on to be the first leader of the Continental Congress. Hancock appointed him to be on the committees to draft the Declaration of Independence and the Great Seal. He was involved with leading Masons in Massachusetts and in the formation of our government. Then in this letter, all his disdain comes forth. In the years of his diplomacy in the Monarchies of Europe followed by that of his son, it became apparent they both felt akin to the Monarchs.

John Dickenson: James Wilson

John Dickinson has been called "The Penman of the American Revolution. In reaction to the Townshend Acts regarding taxation in 1767, he wrote "Letters from a Farmer in Pennsylvania to the Inhabitants of the British Colonies." They are considered classics in our American cause. He wrote the final draft of the 1775 Declaration of the Causes and Necessity of Taking Up Arms. When Congress then decided to seek independence from Great Britain, Dickinson served on the committee that wrote the Model Treaty, and then wrote the first draft of the 1776- 1777 Articles of Confederation and Perpetual Union. Dickinson also composed The Liberty Song. "John Dickinson was a man trained by scholars. He used his knowledge to think for himself.".

The exceptional aspect of the relationship began very simply. Wilson studied law under Dickenson. Both had exceptionally high intelligence. However, both were independent and self-contained. Each took his own independent stance as their modus operandi. Dickenson was not a Federalist, which meant he had no place going forward

Oliver Ellsworth

Along with William Paterson and Luther Martin (both of whom served with him at the Constitutional Convention in 1787) and Aaron Burr, Ellsworth founded the "Well-Meaning Club." Founded in 1765, it became the Cliosophic Society. It was a literary, political, and debating society, which was organized as a secret society. I derived this list from the biographies of these men.

William Paterson studied at the College of New Jersey (later Princeton), where he received a B.A. in 1763 and an M.A. 3 years later. At the same time Paterson had studied law under Richard Stockton, who later was to sign the Declaration of Independence. In addition, he was one of the founders of the American Whig Society, a debating society.

When the War for Independence broke out, Paterson took a leadership role in many activities. In 1786, he was chosen to represent New Jersey at the Constitutional Convention. He authored the Paterson Plan, which asserted the rights of the small states against the large. He signed the Constitution, supported its ratification in New Jersey and went on to participate in our new Government. He was elected to the first U.S. Senate, where he played a pivotal role in drafting the Judiciary Act of 1789. His next position was governor of his state (1790-93). During this time, he began work on the volume later published as Laws of the State of New Jersey (1800) and began to revise the rules and practices of chancery and common law. He then was appointed to be Associate Justice of the Supreme Court under the Chief Justice, Oliver Ellsworth. Full Circle

Luther Martin became an anti-Federalist and The Constitutional Convention. Thus, he never held national office. He spent 28 years as Attorney General in Maryland. The first years of the 1800s saw Martin as defense counsel in two controversial national cases. In the first Martin won an acquittal for his close friend, Supreme Court Justice Samuel Chase, in his impeachment trial in 1805. Two years later Martin was one of Aaron Burr's defense lawyers when Burr stood trial for treason in 1807.

Aaron Burr. Mason. Founding member of the Society. Revolutionary War veteran, New York Senator, third Vice-President of the United States

Soon thereafter, an opposing club, The American Whig Society, was founded by James Madison, William Bradford, and others.

John Hancock: Nicholas Gorham

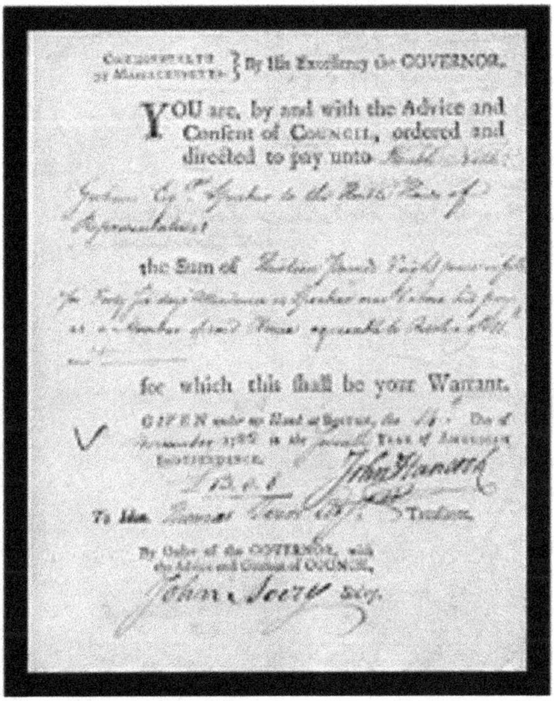
By His Excellency the GOVERNOR.

YOU are, by and with the Advice and Consent of COUNCIL, ordered and directed to pay unto

the Sum of

for which this shall be your Warrant.

John Hancock

Treasurer.

Gorham was a delegate to the Congress of the Confederation from 1782 until 1783, and also from 1785 until 1787, serving as its president for five months from June 6 to November 5, 1786, after the resignation of John Hancock. In the Constitutional Convention, he served as President of the Committee of the Whole when the entire convention was not open and led by Washington.

They were both highly successful businessmen, who were leaders in the Revolution as well as leaders in the Confederation. They had knowledge and experience in areas that the lawyers did not have. Obviously, when Washington and Franklin selected the Committee of Detail, they deemed Hancock's experience and attributes as essential.

Charles Thomson

When it came to the presidency, George Washington harbored both desire and doubt. In this illustartion, Charles Thomson, the secretary of Congress, formally notifies him that he has been elected. (Granger Collection, New York)

Secretary of the Continental Congress for all 15 years, who administered the Oath of Office to Washington

Charles Thomson was working with Benjamin Franklin and the Iroquois as the same time as did Rutledge. A schism developed. Thomson worked on his own with the Delaware Indians serving as their Secretary and Representative. He did this well. However, there is no further connection between Thomson and Franklin or Rutledge. He remained active in the Patriot cause and was strategically important as the Secretary of the Continental Congress. In essence, he was the Administrator for the Continental Congress under all 15 Presidents. Thus, his relationship with Hancock was noteworthy. His actions in designing our Great Seal were significant and lasting. Franklin did not challenge those with opposing views, so Rutledge was sent to deal with the serious problems with incorporating the pyramid, broken pyramid at that. The only thing he was able to do is submit Franklin's design to Heraldist, William Barton. Thomson made the proposal with two images: The Obverse with his own design of the eagle and the Reverse of Franklin's "13 Steps" without comment or identification.. Thomson's descriptions in words for both sides were included.

They did it without focus on themselves or their plan.]There was no overt opposition and the designs passed.

Meanwhile, Franklin, Washington, and Rutledge enacted their own plan for a strong Federal Government based on ancient wisdom.

Thomson administered the Oath of Office to Washington on March 4, 1789. His term began on April 30. Four months later Thomson wrote to Washington that he was going to retire.

Washington immediately responded. New York] July 24th, 1789 "The present age does so much justice to the unsullied reputation with which you have always conducted yourself in the execution of the duties of your Office, and Posterity will find your Name so honorably connected with the verification of such a multitude of astonishing facts, that my single suffrage would add little to the illustration of your merits. Yet I cannot withhold any just testimonial, in favor of so old, so faithful and so able a public officer, which might tend to sooth his mind in the shade of retirement. Accept, then, this serious Declaration, that your Services have been important, as your patriotism was distinguished; and enjoy that best of all rewards, the consciousness of having done your duty well."

Obviously, Thomson realized he was not going to have a position. But why?

In New York, they had punitive laws against Americans, who had been Loyalists. Alexander Hamilton represented these Loyalists and won. It seems the action was started by Sons of Liberty, who had led the Revolution. Not one had a position in the new Federal Government. Washington wanted an open government without partisanship. He did not include anyone who had strong biases. The list included Masons. Meanwhile, Hamilton became the First Secretary of the Treasury.

This is a shortlist of Sons of Liberty members. Boston: Samuel Adams, Benjamin Church, John Hancock, Paul Revere, Joseph Warren, Joseph Allicocke, Hyam Solomon, Benedict Arnold, Patrick Henry, Charles Willson Peale, Benjamin Rush, Charles Thomson, William Paca, Samuel Chase,

One wonders how many overzealous men received glowing affirmations, which led them to local issues and local opportunities. Rather than the practice of "damning with faint praise," Washington left those he was dismissing with outstanding praise. Who would complain?

We should consider the initial appointments made by Washington as his first act as President. He was putting our constitution in action. He included divergent points of view. He allowed no partisans. Their performance in the Revolution was not a factor. He rejected anyone, who badly treated those, who had been Loyalists during the war. He was against classes This was, in actuality, the first step toward Emancipation.

A little mentioned fact is that at Washington's Inauguration the governors of all thirteen states were Freemasons. (Dryfoos)

Elias Boudinot

Elias Boudinot was the third generation of a Huguenot family in America. He, notably, was President of the Continental Congress when the Great Seal was passed. He apparently took no direct interest in the passage. He had no Masonic interests whatsoever. He was a devout reader of the Bible as his reference for all things and years later became the First President of the American Bible Society.

As the first Congress began on September 24, 1789, Congressman Boudinot proposed that the House and Senate jointly request that President Washington "proclaim a day of thanksgiving for "the many signal favors of Almighty God." This was to be the first action of the newly drafted Constitution'

> " I cannot think of letting the session pass over without offering an opportunity to all the citizens of the United States of joining, with one voice, in returning

> to Almighty God their sincere thanks for the many blessings he had poured down upon them."

From Washington's Papers is this account: "On 25 September 1789, Elias Boudinot of Burlington, New Jersey, introduced in the United States House of Representatives a resolution "That a joint committee of both Houses be directed to wait upon the President of the United States, to request that he would recommend to the people of the United States a day of public thanksgiving and prayer to be observed by acknowledging, with grateful hearts, the many signal favors of Almighty God, especially by affording them an opportunity peaceably to establish a Constitution of government for their safety and happiness."

In Congress and for years after, he was the passionate advocate for the rights of Blacks and Native Americans, beginning with the Delawares as citizens. He was particularly involved with the Delaware Indians and teaching them to read. No doubt that meant the Bible.

He had been charged by Washington during Revolutionary War to deal with prisoners. His passion for reading the bible as the best basis for a moral life led to his focus on reading as a necessity. He was not phased with the concept that blacks could not be educated. (EliasBoudinot) In particular, He taught three young Cherokee boys to read, one of whom took his name. He wrote "An Attempt to Discover the Long-lost Tribes of Israel" (1816), in which he concurs with James Adair in the opinion that the Indians are the lost tribes.

The point Boudinet's story is that he was a trail blazer for Native Americans. His efforts were unique at the founding of our country. He was at the beginning of awareness as our government began. (Virtual American Biographies)

Chapter 19 | Statements by President George Washington

"Nothing can illustrate these observations more forcibly, than a recollection of the happy conjuncture of times and circumstances, under which our Republic assumed its rank among the Nations; The foundation of our Empire was not laid in the gloomy age of Ignorance and Superstition, but at an Epoch when the rights of mankind were better understood and more clearly defined, than at any former period, the researches of the human mind, after social happiness, have been carried to a great extent, the Treasures of knowledge, acquired by the labours of Philosophers, Sages and Legislatures, through a long succession of years, are laid open for our use, and their collected wisdom may be happily applied in the Establishment of our forms of Government; the free cultivation of Letters, the unbounded extension of

Commerce, the progressive refinement of Manners, the growing liberality of sentiment... have had a meliorating influence on mankind and increased the blessings of Society. At this auspicious period, the United States came into existence as a Nation, and if their Citizens should not be completely free and happy, the fault will be entirely their own. (Washington, G.)

The government of the United States of America began with these steps

April 1, 1789: House of Representatives first achieved a quorum and elected its officers. April 6, 1789: Senate first achieved a quorum and elected its officers April 6, 1789: The House and Senate, meeting in joint session, counted the Electoral College ballots, then certified that George Washington had been elected President of the United States and John Adams was elected as Vice president April

21, 1789: John Adams was inaugurated as the nation's first Vice president. April 30, 1789: George Washington was inaugurated as the nation's first president at Federal Hall in New York City

President George Washington began our governmental operation with an open and inclusive leadership. The steps of the American Revolution, the Declaration of Independence, the Continental Congress with the Great Seal, the Constitutional Convention, and the Ratification and the Election were now settled history. He chose all the officials based on merit and appropriateness. Affiliations and prior work toward our Nation were not considered. In many cases, prior stances were, in fact, assets. He was deliberate in appointing only a few Freemasons. America was to be a republic of all the people. His exception was not to include anyone who had a significant stance for a confederation of states and states rights. He was clear America is a democratic republic.

Chapter 20 | Franklin's Final Speech in the Constitutional Convention

This address is from the notes of James Madison

The Constitution of United States – "the Signing" by Howard Chandler Christy

Mr. President:

I confess that I do not entirely approve of this Constitution at present, but Sir, I am not sure I shall never approve it: For having lived long, I have experienced many Instances of being oblig'd, by better important Subjects, which I once thought right, but found to be otherwise. It is therefore that the older I grow the more apt I am to doubt my own Judgment and to pay more Respect to the Judgment of others. Most Men indeed as well as most Sects in Religion, think themselves in Possession of all Truth, and that wherever others differ from them it is so far Error. Steele, a Protestant in a Dedication tells the Pope, that the only

Difference between our two Churches in their Opinions of the Certainty of their Doctrine, is, the Romish Church is infallible, and the Church of England is never in the Wrong. But tho' many private Persons think almost as highly of their own Infallibility, as of that of their Sect, few express it so naturally, as a certain French Lady, who in a little Dispute with her Sister, said, I don't know how it happens, Sister, but I meet with nobody but myself that's always in the right. Il n'y a que moi qui a toujours raison.

In these Sentiments, Sir, I agree to this Constitution, with all its Faults, if they are such; because I think a General Government necessary for us, and there is no Form of Government but what may be a Blessing to the People if well administered; and I believe farther that this is likely to be well administered for a Course of Years, and can only end in Despotism as other Forms have done before it, when the People shall become so corrupted as to need Despotic Government, being incapable of any other.

I doubt too whether any other Convention we can obtain, may be able to make a better Constitution: For when you assemble a Number of Men to have the Advantage of their joint Wisdom, you inevitably assemble with those Men all their Prejudices, their Passions, their Errors of Opinion, their local Interests, and their selfish Views. From such an Assembly can a perfect Production be expected? It, therefore, astonishes me, Sir, to find this System approaching so near to Perfection as it does; and I think it will astonish our Enemies, who are waiting with Confidence to hear that our Councils are confounded, like those of the Builders of Babel, and that our States are on the Point of Separation, only to meet hereafter for the purpose of cutting one another's throats. Thus I consent, Sir, to this Constitution because I expect no better, and because I am not sure that it is not the best.

The Opinions I have had of its Errors, I sacrifice to the Public Good. I have never whispered a syllable of them abroad. Within these walls, they were born, and here they shall die. If every one of us in returning to our Constituents were to report the Objections he has had to it, and use his Influence to gain Partisan in support of them, we might prevent its being generally received, and thereby lose all the salutary Effects and great Advantages resulting naturally in our favour among foreign Nations, as well as among ourselves, from our real or apparent Unanimity. Much of the Strength and Efficiency of any Government, in procuring and securing Happiness to the People depends on

Opinion, on the general Opinion of the Goodness of that Government as well as of the Wisdom and Integrity of its Governors. I hope therefore that for our own Sakes, as a Part of the People, and for the sake of our Posterity, we shall act heartily and unanimously in recommending this Constitution, wherever our Influence may extend, and turn our future Thoughts and Endeavours to the Means of having it well administered.

On the whole, Sir, I cannot help expressing a Wish, that every Member of the Convention, who may still have Objections to it, would with me on this occasion doubt a little of his own Infallibility, and to make manifest our Unanimity put his Name to this instrument.

Benjamin Franklin is the only person directly involved with the Three Fundamental documents of The United States of America

Declaration of Independence
The Great Seal
Constitution of The United States of America

In addition, he installed the Framework Washington put it into action. Our Framework is the sacred foundation of our Constitution. All solutions respecting our Framework have the optimum potential for success and well-being of us all.

Chapter 21 | WASHINGTON'S INAUGURAL ADDRESS OF 1789

A

Transcription

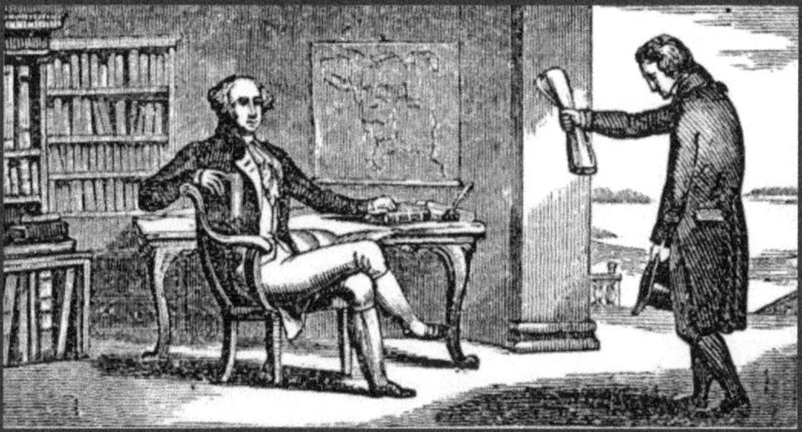

When it came to the presidency, George Washington harbored both desire and doubt. In this illustartion, Charles Thomson, the secretary of Congress, formally notifies him that he has been elected. (Granger Collection, New York)

Thomson delivered this message and at the Inauguration gave Washington is oath of office. He then disappeared into history.

[April 30, 1789]

Fellow Citizens of the Senate and the House of Representatives.

Among the vicissitudes incident to life, no event could have filled me with greater anxieties than that of which the notification was transmitted by your order, and received on the fourteenth day of the present month. On the one hand,

I was summoned by my Country, whose voice I can never hear but with veneration and love, from a retreat which I had chosen with the fondest predilection, and, in my flattering hopes, with an immutable decision, as the asylum of my declining years: a retreat which was rendered every day more necessary as well as more dear to me, by the addition of habit to inclination, and of frequent interruptions in my health to the gradual waste committed on it by time. On the other hand, the magnitude and difficulty of the trust to which the voice of my Country called me, being sufficient to awaken in the wisest and most experienced of her citizens, a distrustful scrutiny into his qualifications, could not but overwhelm with despondence, one, who, inheriting inferior endowments from nature and unpracticed in the duties of civil administration, ought to be peculiarly conscious of his own deficiencies. In this conflict of emotions, all I dare aver, is, that it has been my faithful study to collect my duty from a just appreciation of eve ry circumstance, by which it might be affected. All I dare hope, is, that, if in executing this task I have been too much swayed by a grateful remembrance of former instances, or by an affectionate sensibility to this transcendent proof, of the confidence of my fellow-citizens; and have thence too little consulted my incapacity as well as disinclination for the weighty and untried cares before me; my error will be palliated by the motives which misled me, and its consequences be judged by my Country, with some share of the partiality in which they originated.

Such being the impressions under which I have, in obedience to the public summons, repaired to the present station; it would be peculiarly improper to omit in this first official Act, my fervent supplications to that Almighty Being who rules over the Universe, who presides in the Councils of Nations, and whose providential aids can supply every human defect, that his benediction may consecrate to the liberties and happiness of the People of the United States, a Government instituted by themselves for these essential purposes: and may enable every instrument employed in its administration to execute with success, the functions allotted to his charge. In tendering this homage to the Great Author of every public and private good I assure myself that it expresses your sentiments not less than my own; nor those of my fellow-citizens at large, less than either. No People can be bound to acknowledge and adore the invisible hand, which conducts the Affairs of men more than the People of the United States. Every step, by which they have advanced to the character of an independent nation, seems to have been distinguished by some token of providential agency. And in the important revolution just accomplished in the system of their United Government, the tranquil deliberations and voluntary consent of so many distinct communities, from which the event has resulted, cannot be compared with the means by which most Governments have been established, without some return of pious gratitude along with an humble anticipation of the future blessings which the past seem to presage. These reflections, arising out of the present crisis, have forced themselves too strongly on my mind to be suppressed. You will join with me I trust in thinking, that there are none under the influence of which, the proceedings of a new and free Government can more auspiciously commence.

By the article establishing the Executive Department, it is made the duty of the President "to recommend to your consideration, such measures as he shall judge necessary and expedient." The circumstances under which I now meet you, will acquit me from entering into that subject, farther than to refer to the Great Constitutional Charter under which you are assembled; and which, in defining your powers, designates the objects to which your attention is to be given. It will be more consistent with those circumstances, and far more congenial with the feelings which actuate me, to substitute, in place of a recommendation of particular measures, the tribute that is due to the talents, the rectitude, and the patriotism which adorn the characters selected to devise and adopt them.

In these honorable qualifications, I behold the surest pledges, that as on one side, no local prejudices, or attachments; no separate views, nor party animosities, will misdirect the comprehensive and equal eye which ought to watch over this great assemblage of communities and interests: so, on another, that the foundations of our National policy will be laid in the pure and immutable principles of private morality; and the pre-eminence of a free Government, be exemplified by all the attributes which can win the affections of its Citizens, and command the respect of the world.

I dwell on this prospect with every satisfaction which an ardent love for my Country can inspire: since there is no truth more thoroughly established, than that there exists in the economy and course of nature, an indissoluble union between virtue and happiness, between duty and advantage, between the genuine maxims of an honest and magnanimous policy, and the solid rewards of public prosperity and felicity: Since we ought to be no less persuaded that the propitious smiles of Heaven, can never be expected on a nation that disregards the eternal rules of order and right, which Heaven itself has ordained: And since the preservation of the sacred fire of liberty, and the destiny of the Republican model of Government, are justly considered as deeply, perhaps as finally staked, on the experiment entrusted to the hands of the American people.

Besides the ordinary objects submitted to your care, it will remain with your judgment to decide, how far an exercise of the occasional power delegated by the Fifth article of the Constitution is rendered expedient at the present juncture by the nature of objections which have been urged against the System, or by the degree of inquietude which has given birth to them. Instead of undertaking particular recommendations on this subject, in which I could be guided by no lights derived from official opportunities, I shall again give way to my entire confidence in your discernment and pursuit of the public good: For I assure myself that whilst you carefully avoid every alteration which might endanger the benefits of an United and effective Government, or which ought to await the future lessons of experience; a reverence for the characteristic rights of freemen, and a regard for the public harmony, will sufficiently influence your deliberations on the question how far the former can be more impregnably fortified, or the latter be safely and advantageously promoted.

To the preceding observations I have one to add, which will be most properly addressed to the House of Representatives. It concerns myself, and will therefore be as brief as possible. When I was first honoured with a call into the Service of my Country, then on the eve of an arduous struggle for its liberties, the light in which I contemplated my duty required that I should renounce every pecuniary compensation. From this resolution I have in no instance departed. And being still under the impressions which produced it, I must decline as inapplicable to myself, any share in the personal emoluments, which may be indispensably included in a permanent provision for the Executive Department; and must accordingly pray that the pecuniary estimates for the Station in which I am placed, may, during my continuance in it, be limited to such actual expenditures as the public good may be thought to require.

Having thus imparted to you my sentiments, as they have been awakened by the occasion which brings us together, I shall take my present leave; but not without resorting once more to the benign parent of the human race, in humble supplication that since he has been pleased to favour the American people, with opportunities for deliberating in perfect tranquility, and dispositions for deciding with unparellelled unanimity on a form of Government, for the security of their Union, and the advancement of their happiness; so his divine blessing may be equally *conspicuous* in the enlarged views, the temperate consultations, and the wise measures on which the success of this Government must depend.

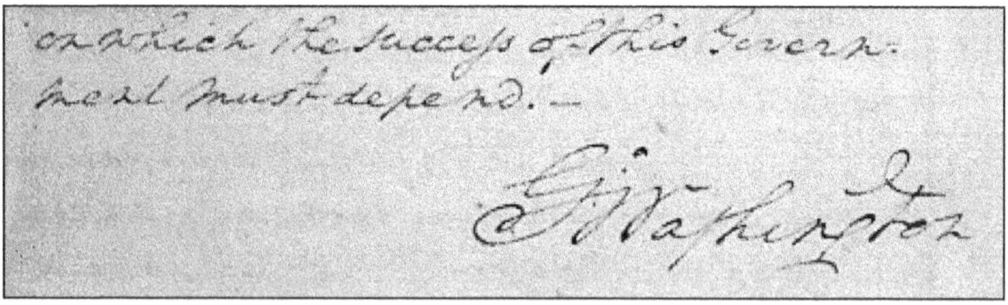
on which the success of this Govern-
ment must depend.—

G° Washington

Washington's distinctive signature

This transcription was taken from the original document in the Records of the U.S. Senate, Record Group 46, in the National Archives.

His very first official act as President was the appointment of his Cabinet and the Supreme Court. He appointed these officials with utmost concern. No one went forward into governance, who had advocated punishment of citizens, who were Loyalists. They were not leaders in our Federal Democracy. They did receive glowing letters of acknowledgement. We began with a Master.

The government of the United States of America began with these steps April 1, 1789: House of Representatives first achieved a quorum and elected its officers. April 6, 1789: Senate first achieved a quorum and elected its officers April 6, 1789: The House and Senate, meeting in joint session, counted the Electoral College ballots, then certified that George Washington had been elected President of the United States and John Adams was elected as Vice president

April 21, 1789: John Adams was inaugurated as the nation's first Vice president. April 30, 1789: George Washington was inaugurated as the nation's first president at Federal Hall in New York City

President George Washington began our governmental operation with an open and inclusive leadership. The steps of the American Revolution, the Declaration of Independence, the Continental Congress with the Great Seal, the Constitutional Convention, and the Ratification and the Election were now settled history. He chose all the officials based on merit and appropriateness. Affiliations and prior work toward our Nation were not considered. In many cases, prior stances were, in fact, assets.

There was never a discussion or a debate regarding the Framework itself. Franklin, Washington and Rutledge considered the Framework to be their sacred trust. There would be no debate. President Washington chose his first appointments based on competence and diversity. He specifically omitted all those he considered to be partisan and challengers to the Constitution.

The eighty-six words that form the context of the Mayflower Compact include the word "FRAME." Think about it.

Those who wrote the Compact did not explain it. It was used by the Committee of Detail, which no doubt Washington and Franklin knew. They did not explain it.

The Frame can assert the is an inner core, an organized, meaningful system. It can be construed as the structure or the foundation or even the unifying dynamical force. The Framework may well be the very soul of our constitution.

GOING FORTH IN THE CONTEXT OF OUR FRAMEWORK

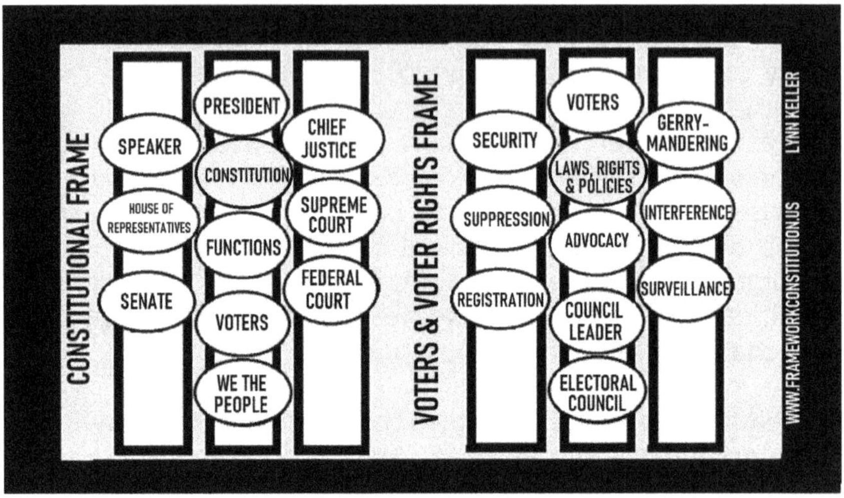

Appendix I

THE IROQUOIS AND THE ORIGINS OF AMERICAN DEMOCRACY

Speech by Dr. Donald A. Grinde, Jr., Distinguished Professor of Interdisciplinary Studies, Gettysburg College, and Crawford Research Fellow, 1987-1988. Delivered at Cornell University September 11, 1987.

First of all, I would like to thank the Iroquois people that I worked with some fifteen or more years ago. They gave me encouragement in this project since I did not receive much encouragement outside of the Iroquois people. I want to also thank the Indian Historian Press whose stated purpose, then as well as now, is to publish works by American Indian scholars and others that contribute to new viewpoints on American Indian history. Finally, I would like to thank Americans for Indian Opportunity and the Meredith Fund for research funds that made my present research possible. Today, I would like to share with you some of the new data that I have found in the last year or so that supplements my earlier findings. I will focus on four items:

1. The Treaty Congress at Albany in August of 1775

2. Benjamin Franklin and his ideas about the Covenant Chain of the Iroquois.

3. Thomas Paine and some of the things that he wrote that have not been attributed to him.

4. John Rutledge of South Carolina and how he learned of the Great Law of the Iroquois, and how he helped to write the first draft of the U. S. Constitution. As Eugene

Crawford Memorial Fellow for 1987-1988, my purpose will be to analyze, from a historian's viewpoint, the extent and impact of the Iroquois ideas on American democracy. This analysis will include, of course, the U. S. Constitu- tion. I want to make this study an integral part of the analysis of the Constitution. In the future, I want to make sure that when people talk about the roots of the Constitution, they include the ideas of the Iroquois. Ancient Greece and Rome, John Locke and Jean Jacques Rousseau, no doubt, influenced the thinking of the Founding Fathers, but Iroquois concepts had a profound influence upon the formation of our government as well. The ideas of the Iroquois influenced the thinking of the English and the French theorists of the eighteenth century also. I will also attempt to approach the Founding Fathers as human beings, and this is extremely important since I have found that it is the best way to look at them. When one looks for Iroquois ideas in the Founding Fathers, I have to always remember that these men were politicians.. Many of them, of course, had a good education for the times and were wealthy.

However, most of them had a fairly long history of political activity in one way or another.

The noted Cherokee humorist, Will Rogers, said that politicians are like fog- horns; they call attention to the problems but they don't do a damned thing about them. When I read the Records of the Constitutional Convention and other materials leading up to the first draft of the Constitution, I see a lot of foghorn stuff. What about the problem of money and debts? What about the executive and legislative powers? How can we secure a stronger union? For brevity's sake, I will not go back to the Albany Plan of Union because I think that it will be discussed later, but Albany is an important place to begin the discussion of the Iroquois' influence on American democracy.

In August of 1775, before the Declaration of Independence, the Continental Congress sent a group of treaty commissioners to speak with the Six Nations of the Iroquois Confederacy at Albany, New York. The Congress and the American people were contemplating independence and a long war. Already, there was much tension and the Congress did not want to fight a two front war against the British in the East and the Indians in the West. In the spring of 1775, Congress began to formulate a speech that was to be sent to the Iroquois in the summer of 1775. Signed by John Hancock, this speech recalls the history of the relations between the Iroquois and the American colonists since the 1740s. The speech quotes the Iroquois chief, Cannassatego, at the Treaty of Lancaster in 1744. In that speech, Cannassatego admonishes the Americans to unite and become strong as the forefathers of the Iroquois had done under the Great Law. The speech from the Continental Congress said that the American people are united and have taken the advice of the Iroquois. The U. S. treaty commissioners added: "...the advice was good, it was kind. They said to one another, the Six Nations are a wise people, let us hearken to their Council and teach our children to follow it. Our old men have done so. They have frequently taken a single arrow and said, children, see how easy it is broken, then they have tied twelve together with strong cords–And our strongest men could not break them–See said they–this is what the Six Nations mean. Divided a single man may destroy you–United, you are a match for the whole world."

Unity is a major concept in this speech by the Congress, and it is one of the foremost concepts of the Iroquois Great Law.Unity is not a novel concept, but the way in which the Iroquois did it, fascinated Europeans and particularly, American colonists. Hence, the treaty commissioners at Albany, in 1775, were not just engaging in the rhetoric of Iroquois diplomacy, they were demonstrating that they had a knowledge of and were using parts of the Great Law in their deliberations even before independence was declared. The speech goes on to point out that the American people have delegated leaders to go to Philadelphia and kindle a great fire and plant a Great Tree to become strong like the Iroquois. At the conclusion of the analogy, the treaty commissioners invited the Iroquois to come to Philadelphia to their "Grand Council".

A few days after this speech, the treaty commissioners tell the Iroquois that: "We live upon the same ground with you–the same island is our common birthplace. We desire to sit down under the same Tree of Peace with you; let us water its roots and cherish its growth, till the large leaves and flourishing branches shall extend to the setting sun and reach the skies."

In some more references to Iroquois cosmology, the Americans say when this "island began to shake and tremble along the Eastern Shore, and the Sun darkened by a Black cloud which arose from beyond the great water, we kindled up a Great Council Fire at Philadelphia...so...that we are now twelve colonies united as one man...And...As God has put it into our hearts to love the Six Nations...we now make the chain of friendship so that nothing but an evil spirit can or will attempt to break it." Through these words, we can see the extent of the Continental Congress' knowledge of the Great Law of the Iroquois and its cosmology a year before the Declaration of Independence. In an analysis of this cultural and intellectual exchange, it is significant (since it often goes unnoticed) that the Iroquois people delegated leaders or had self-appointed people to educate the colonists to the wisdom of unity. A generation before the conference at Albany in 1775, the Mohawk Chief, Hendrick, had admonished the colonists to unify. In August of 1775, when the Iroquois chiefs had asked the Americans who should speak for the Iroquois at the conference, the Americans immediately asked that Abraham be appointed the main speaker. Abraham was the adopted brother of Hendrick, and the Americans remembered his words urging unity at the Albany conference in 1754. It should be noted that the treaty commissioners recognized that Abraham and Hendrick were part of an Iroquois tradition to teach the American people strength through unity. After he is made speaker, Abraham rose and stated that he was glad that "...your grandfathers had inculcated the doctrine into their children...". He noted that an invitation had been extended to go to Philadelphia where the Great Tree was planted and "...sit under it and water its roots, till the branches should flourish and reach to heaven...". Abraham said, "This the Six Nations say shall be done." In May of 1776, the Iroquois chiefs would go to Philadel- phia as the Continental Congress was readying itself for independence (the Iroquois camped outside of Independence Hall in the square). After John Hancock welcomed the Iroquois chiefs to the Congress as "brothers", an Onondaga chief named the President of the Continental Congress, (John Hancock), "Karanduawn, or the Great Tree", on June 11, 1776.

In effect, the Iroquois were present during the debates on independence and when a draft of the Articles of Confederation was introduced (this draft was a revision of Franklin's Albany Plan and it has been demonstrated that it was borrowed from the Iroquois Great Law). With the Iroquois in the halls of government on the eve of independence, it is no longer a question of whether the Iroquois had an impact on the nature of American government but rather it now becomes a question of degree. We can now see that both the Americans and the Iroquois were aware of the interchange of ideas for over a generation. Essen- tially, the Iroquois had a tradition of instructing, cajoling and admonishing the colonies to unity, and the Americans were cognizant of this process in some very profound ways.

Now, I would like to discuss Benjamin Franklin and his knowledge of Iroquois imagery and ideas. Franklin, of course, was the author of the Albany Plan of Union. However, an examination of the oral traditions about Franklin has yielded some interesting insights into Franklin's use of Iroquois ideas. By looking at the record of the people that knew Franklin in England before the Revolution and in France during the Revolution, it is apparent that Franklin talked a great deal about the Iroquois. In England, Franklin's circle of friends gave him a silver tea service that was engraved "keep bright the chain" because it was one of his favorite phrases. His friends remarked that he used it often and that they sought Franklin's ideas about American Indians.

When Franklin goes to France in late 1776 as the Congress' Minister to France, he was welcomed as a hero. There was a rumor that he was coming with 100 American Indian warriors. Once in France, Franklin "...loved to cite and to practice faithfully the proverb of his friends, the American Indians, "Keep the chain of friendship bright and shining", when discussing the concept of liberty among distinguished French philosophers like Turgot, Helvetius, La Rochefoucault and Condorcet. French observers in the salons stated that Franklin would discuss the politics of the Indians with great exactness and interest. Furthermore, Franklin thought the ways of American Indians more conducive to the good life than the ways of "...Civilized Nations". Frequently, Franklin used the French curiosity about Native Americans and particularly the Iroquois to his personal and diplomatic advantage.

When Franklin came back to America after the Revolution, he became a member in the Constitutional Sons of Saint Tammany in Philadelphia. This was a society of non-Indians that dressed up as Indians, entertained Indian delegations to Philadelphia, stood for a unicameral legislature like Franklin, and freely used Iroquois ideas and imagery in its rhetoric. In 1785, George Washington attended a St. Tammany society meeting in Richmond, Virginia. Washington was called our "Great Grand Sachem" and our "brother" by the society. Franklin was often toasted as "brother" also. During the Constitutional Convention, Franklin wrote several letters to American Indians like "the old chief", "the...Beloved Indian Woman", and the "Cornstalk". These terms and names were used by the Constitutional Sons of Saint Tammany. Since they were written on June 30, 1787 after the bitter controversy over the Virginia and New Jersey Plans were resolved, they may well be "coded" letters to the Constitutional Sons of Saint Tammany.

The Saint Tammany Society was intensely interested in the outcome of the Constitutional Convention and the structure of the new government. At any rate, Franklin stated in one of these letters that: "I am sorry that the Great Council fire of our nation is not now burning, so that you cannot do business there. In a few months, the coals will be rak'd out of the ashes and will again be rekindled."

Franklin also had designed currency using the Iroquois Covenant Chain at the beginning of the Revolution that was reissued in 1787. The currency depicted a Covenant Chain of thirteen links with an admonition to unite. Hence, there is plenty of evidence that Franklin continued and cultivated his interest in the Iroquois after he used their ideas of unity to forge the Albany Plan of Union in 1754.

Thomas Paine was also influenced by the Iroquois. Although it is generally not acknowledged, Thomas Paine was a secretary to an Iroquois Treaty at Easton, Pennsylvania in early 1777. It appears that Paine heard an Iroquois prophecy about struggling beasts that would shake the very foundation of the League of the Iroquois. In the end, lesser beast (the Americans) would win and take up the ideas of the Iroquois. A pamphlet published by the Continental Congress recounts a similar prophecy. It is printed in France in 1777 before the French publicly began to support the American cause. Thomas Paine was appointed to the Committee for Foreign Affairs of the Continental Congress in April of 1777. He may have sent over to Franklin an account of the prophecy since Franklin and the other American ministers to France were constantly asking for good news (the good news would come late in 1777 with the victory at Saratoga). Again, it is important to note that the Continental Congress is writing propaganda using the imagery and prophecies of the Iroquois since they knew that the French were fascinated by Iroquois ideas. After Paine leaves America for France, he was reputed to have talked a great deal about the Iroquois.

Finally, there is John Rutledge of South Carolina, chairman of the Committee of Detail that writes the first draft of the U.S. Constitution. According to his biographer, Rutledge learned of the Great Law while attending the Stamp Act Congress in New York City as a young man. During the Stamp Act Congress, Rutledge rented a cab and rode out to see Sir William Johnson and some Mohawks camped on the edge of Greenwich Village. Sir William Johnson was upset about the Stamp Act because it was cutting into his Indian trade. Sir William Johnson had come down in the fall from Albany to get supplies for the Indian trade. Johnson greeted Rutledge by saying: "I see you've come to comb the King's hair", and Rutledge was puzzled by this phrase (an obvious allusion to the evil Onondaga wizard, Tadodaho, that Hiawatha tamed to pave the way for the creation of the Great Law of the Iroquois). In this way, Johnson characterized the Stamp Act Congress as attempting to pacify the King's mind about taxation and other things. With this opening remark, John Rutledge sits down and has a few glasses of rum with Johnson and the Mohawks and gets his first lesson about the Great Law of the Iroquois.

In late July, 1787, twenty years after the Stamp Act Congress, John Rutledge found himself chairing the Committee of Detail at the Constitutional Convention. The Committee was charged with taking all of the resolutions that had been passed in Convention and drafting a document that could be polished and refined through debate on the floor of the convention.

Rutledge's biographer states that he opened the meeting with some passages from the Great Law of the Iroquois. The main passages relate to the sovereignty of the people, peace and unity. Rutledge had asserted earlier that a great empire was being created so it must be firmly rooted in American soil.

With this said, Rutledge bent over and began the task of drafting the Constitution.

Pressure in the printed media was already being brought to bear upon the Framers of the U. S. Constitution. In the August, 1787 issue of The American Museum (a Philadelphia magazine), "A Fable

- Addressed to the Federal Convention" was printed that used the bundle of arrows imagery of the Iroquois Constitution (Section 57) and styled the Iroquois as "fathers" urging unity to their "sons". No doubt, the Constitutional Sons of Saint Tammany were, in part responsible for this reference. Alexander Hamilton, in Federalist No. 69, felt compelled to address an editorial written by 'Tamony' that expressed reservations about the executive powers in the proposed constitution. Appearing in Virginia and Pennsylvania newspapers, the editorial clearly represented the fears of the St. Tammany Society of a strong executive in peacetime. These examples are but a few of the references to the Iroquois roots of American government.

The major thing to remember is that if you know the code words like "combing the King's hair" or "keep the chain bright" the Iroquois influence can be easily seen.

Indeed, there seems to be a kind of ignoring of these references in the records. This ignoring of important references glosses over the fact that Iroquois images were used frequently in eighteenth century America.

But to modern scholars such references probably appear as anomalies since many people are unfamiliar with the rhetoric and imagery of the Iroquois. In short, the attitude might be: "What's this, Thomas Paine writing an Indian treaty?" What does this have to do with political theory or his ideas?

In conclusion, I think that the concept of unity was an important transference that went on for generations between the colonists and the Iroquois. Rutledge recalled that exchange as he began to write the first draft of the Constitution (the press of Philadelphia and the Saint Tammany society were also bound to remind him and the other delegates to the convention of the American roots of our unity and freedom). Federalism is another important concept here. The Iroquois had a working federalism that gave maximum internal freedom while providing for a strong defense.

I think it is time to take away the veil that has deprived Americans from realizing the Iroquois roots of American democracy. The new evidence that we have all brought to bear here is extremely exciting. I hope that it will convince people that when they look at the origins of American democracy that one can no longer look only to the ancient Greeks and John Locke for sources but you must also look to the Great Law of the Iroquois as a valid source of ideas for the formation of our nation. With evidence at hand, the question is not whether the Iroquois had an influence on formation of the American govern- ment but to what degree.

The next job. after this conference, is to increase cross-cultural kinds of studies. I think that research funds in the institutions that study Indians should be allocated in ways that reflect more the interests and questions that are important to Indian people.

Certainly, American Indian people and American Indian scholars should have a greater say over research priorities and the allocation of funds in places like the Smithsonian Institution. In the final analysis, it was the Iroquois people that came to me and said "we're interested in this, are you interested in the Iroquois roots of American democracy?" In the future, questions that American Indian people deem important should have a great deal of validity in institutions of culture and learning, i.e. the National Endowment for the Humanities and the Smithsonian.

Let us hope that the call is heeded. Why can't people recognize that Native Americans have priorities about their history? American Indian people should not be ignored in their pursuit of a new Native American history.

Thank you.

BILL OF RIGHTS

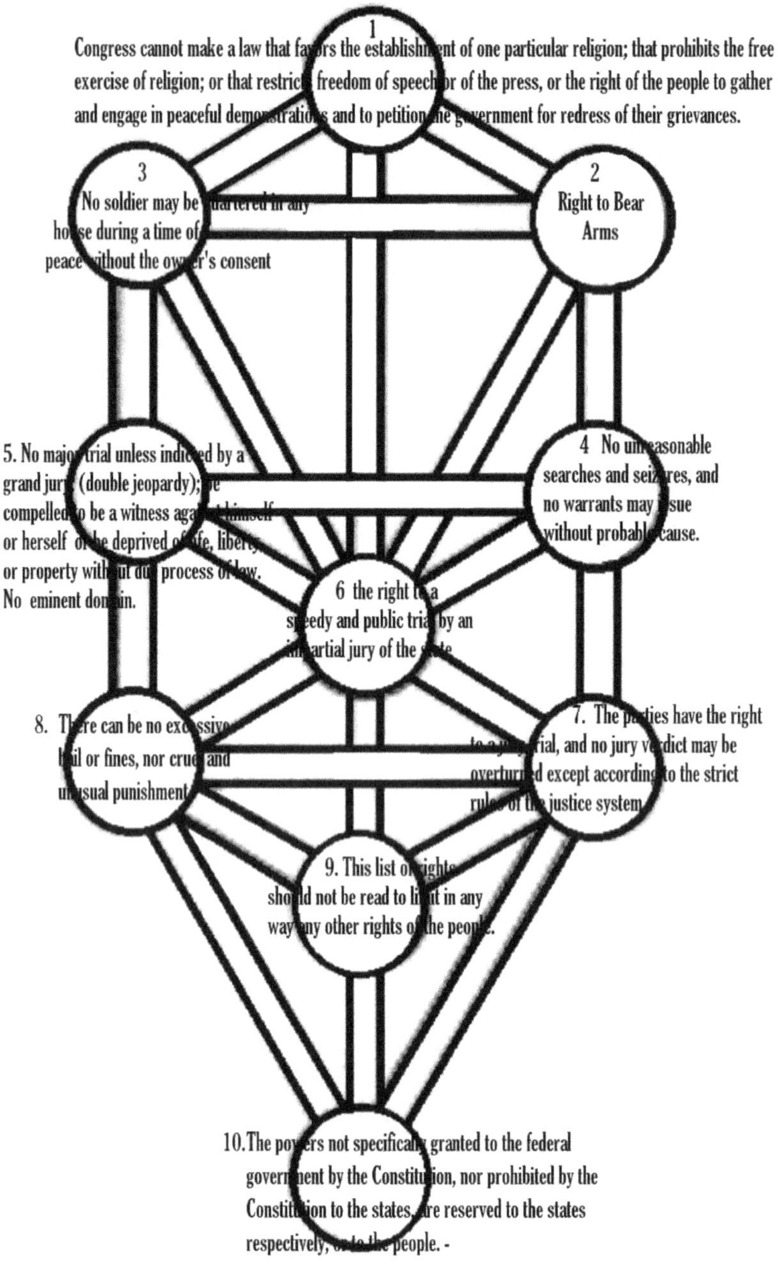
1
Congress cannot make a law that fa rs the establishm nt of one particular religion; that prohibits the free
exercise of religion; or that restric freedom of speech or of the press, or the right of the people to gather
and engage in peaceful dem s and to petition government for redress of their grievances.
3
No soldier may be
ho se during a time of
peace without the ow r's consent
2
Right to Bear
Arms
5. No majo trial unless indi ed by a
grand jur (double jeopardy);
compelled o be a witness aga
or herself deprived f life, liber
or property with process law.
No eminent do in.
4 No un asonable
searches and sei res, and
no warrants may sue
without probab cause.
6 the right a
s eedy and public tria by an
artial jury of the
8. T re can be no ex
il or fines, nor cru and
u sual punishment
7. The ies have the right
rial, and no jury v dict may be
d except according to the strict
justice system
9. This list o
sho ld not be read to li it in any
way ny other rights o he peo .
10.The po rs not specifica granted to the federal
gover ent by the Constitu ion, nor prohibited by the
Constit ion to the states, re reserved to the states
respectively, eople. -

www.ingramcontent.com/pod-product-compliance
Lightning Source LLC
Chambersburg PA
CBHW032049020426
42335CB00011B/259
9798895182185